Praise for *The Financial Times Guide to Data-Driven Transformation*

'This book stands out for its clarity about key analytics and AI concepts, the many real examples it provides, and the very helpful guidelines and methods for becoming data-driven. And, yes, it includes AI too.'

Thomas H. Davenport, Distinguished Professor, Babson College; Fellow, MIT Initiative on the Digital Economy; author of *Competing on Analytics and All In on AI*

'A complete and very actionable overview for any company to become more data driven, from creating the foundations to sustainable value creation.'

-Erwin Logt, Group CIO, Danone

'On weekly basis, people from large and small companies from around the world ask me: "How do I start my journey towards leveraging data efficiently and effectively?". Now I can simply send them a link to this book - *The Financial Times Guide to Data-Driven Transformation* by Andrea De Mauro and Michele Pacifico. A must-read for all who are interested in building an effective data and analytics environment.'

-John K. Thompson, Global Head, Artificial Intelligence, Ernst & Young; author of *Building Analytics Teams*

'Complete, easy-to-understand and immediately applicable. A great support for any business leader to navigate through the digital transformation.'

Antonio Fazzari, General Manager and Chief Operating Officer, Fater

'*The Financial Times Guide to Data-Driven Transformation* by Andrea De Mauro and Michele Pacifico is an essential guide for anyone looking to navigate the complexities of data transformation (and there are plenty of complexities to navigate!). The authors offer a clear, step-by-step approach, complemented by practical tools and real-world examples, making the integration of data analytics into business operations both accessible and achievable. I particularly appreciate the inclusion of various diagrams throughout the book, like the RACI Diagram for key Data Governance activities, which visually enhance the understanding of complex concepts.'

Kate Strachnyi, Founder, DATAcated

'A comprehensive guide for every data leader striving to drive impactful initiatives by bridging the gap between technical and business language. This book is an essential resource for transforming data strategies into real-world successes.'

Ermanna Maiuri, Head of Analytics, Refurbed

'In an era where data is the king and at least that is what everyone around keeps telling us and data leaders like us keep propagating the same, this book by Andrea De Mauro and Michele Pacifico empowers leaders and practitioners alike to demystify this topic beyond the theoretical allure to practical implementation. With its structured guidance, practical tools and frameworks, addressing intricacies of complex subjects such as AI algorithms and data governance it is a must-read for those ready to harness the full potential of their data and carve out a legacy of innovation, value and growth.'

Vikrant Bhan, Group Head Analytics, Data and Integration, Nestlé

THE FINANCIAL TIMES GUIDE TO DATA-DRIVEN TRANSFORMATION

THE FINANCIAL TIMES GUIDE TO DATA-DRIVEN TRANSFORMATION

MAXIMISE BUSINESS VALUE WITH DATA ANALYTICS

ANDREA DE MAURO AND
MICHELE PACIFICO

Pearson

Harlow, England • London • New York • Boston • San Francisco • Toronto • Sydney
Dubai • Singapore • Hong Kong • Tokyo • Seoul • Taipei • New Delhi
Cape Town • São Paulo • Mexico City • Madrid • Amsterdam • Munich • Paris • Milan

PEARSON EDUCATION LIMITED
KAO Two
KAO Park
Harlow CM17 9NA
United Kingdom
Tel: +44 (0)1279 623623
Web: www.pearson.com

First edition published 2024 (print and electronic)

ISBN: 978-1-292-46214-1 (print)
978-1-292-73031-8 (ePub)

British Library Cataloguing-in-Publication Data
A catalogue record for the print edition is available from the British Library

Library of Congress Cataloging-in-Publication Data
Names: De Mauro, Andrea, author. | Pacifico, Michele, author.
Title: The financial times guide to data-driven transformation : maximise business value with data analytics / Andrea de Mauro and Michele Pacifico.
Description: First edition. | Harlow, England ; New York : Pearson, 2024. | Includes bibliographical references and index.
Identifiers: LCCN 2024023680 | ISBN 9781292462141 (paperback) | ISBN 9781292730318 (epub)
Subjects: LCSH: Finance--Technological innovations. | Organizational change. | Electronic data processing.
Classification: LCC HG173 .D387 2024 | DDC 332--dc23/eng/20240605
LC record available at https://lccn.loc.gov/2024023680

10 9 8 7 6 5 4 3 2 1
28 27 26 25 24

Cover design by Michelle Morgan
Cover image Brain light / Alamy Stock Photo

Print edition typeset in 9.5/14pt Stone Serif ITC Pro by Straive
Printed and bound by CPI UK

NOTE THAT ANY PAGE CROSS REFERENCES REFER TO THE PRINT EDITION

CONTENTS

Acknowledgements ix
About the authors xi
Preface by Francesco Marzoni xiii
Introduction xv

1 Unleashing the value of data 1

Three types of data analytics 2
Amplifying value with a digital operating model 12
Navigating an industrial revolution 18
The Flywheel Effect: driving momentum with data analytics 21
The golden checklist on data value 26

2 Mastering the Data Transformation process 27

Crafting a winning data strategy 27
False Starts and how to avoid them 31
The Data Transformation process 35
The golden checklist on Data Transformation process 50

3 Designing your data blueprint 53

The Data Activation Canvas model 54
Turning big bets into enablers 77
The golden checklist on the data blueprint 78

4 Leveraging machine learning for value creation 81

A gentle introduction to AI and other trendy terms 82
Algorithms in action: the ML-Way of doing business 84
When the ML-Way wins 88
Selecting the algorithm that works for you 89
Getting it right: evaluating ML algorithms 102
The golden checklist on AI 107

5 Building a strong technology foundation 109

Laying the groundwork: digital technologies and cloud systems 110
Organising data for maximum impact 116
Essential tools for data analytics and AI 124
The golden checklist on the technology foundation 134

6 Nurturing a data-driven culture and organisation 137

Nurturing the right talent 139
Designing the right organisation 146
Building the right culture 157
The golden checklist on the human journey 163

7 Data governance done right 165

Governing data as an asset 166
Enabling data governance: the unmissable elements 168
Who does what? Introducing the data governance actors 176
Setting up data governance 182
The golden checklist on data governance 187

8 Leading the Data Transformation change 189

The Data Maturity Model: where do you stand? 190
Managing the transformation journey 199
Driving the Data Transformation: who and how 206
The golden checklist on the Data Transformation journey 209

Ready to make it happen? 211

Guided notes 214
Glossary 221
Index 227

ACKNOWLEDGEMENTS

As we wrote this book, we realised how fortunate we were.

Fortunate to have access to inspiring leaders and data practitioners to exchange our thoughts with. Fortunate to be supported by caring families throughout the demanding and time-consuming process of transforming ideas into helpful content. Fortunate to have found companies, universities, and informal groups that provided the best platforms for putting our thoughts into practice. In the end, being fortunate in so many ways has left us with a heartfelt sense of deep gratitude to numerous people.

Writing a book that tries to conjugate the theory and practice of such a vast field has been possible only thanks to the eye-opening inputs, the rigorous feedback, and the heartfelt encouragement of so many wonderful people, including Adam Graham, Giuseppe Papaianni, Roberto Bellotti, Marcello Lando, Fabio Pistilli, Francesco Marzoni, Nicola Lopez, Antonio Fazzari, Luca Merlo, Nicolas Kerling, Daniele Abbate, Barbara Del Neri, Jamilya Baimukhambetova, Davide D'Andrea Ricchi, Osman Peermamode, Barbara Cavaleri, Alessandro Patruno, Greta Carini, Alain Pascal, Daniela Meo, Giovanni Battisti, Vikrant Bhan, Zeman Bhunnoo, Gautam Dullu, Kriti Rai, Isa Martins, Mariana Shabanova, Valentina Dashinamzhilova, Gabriel Menezes, Martin Lucan, Prashanth Reddy, Ravi Arja Kiran, Rodolfo Vollet, Slava Tyunyaev, and all the other amazing friends, colleagues, and leaders with whom we have passionately worked alongside to run (with success!) the data-driven transformation at P&G, Nestlé, Fater, Vodafone, and all other companies we have worked with.

It would have been impossible for us to address this subject without having the opportunity to investigate it systematically together with our many precious partners in academic research and university teaching: Valentina Poggioni, Mohamed Almgerbi, Adham Kahlawi, Cristiano Ciappei, Luca Petruzzellis, Pasquale Del Vecchio, Giusy Secundo, Andrea Bacconi, Gaetano Cascini, Francesca Montagna, Nikos Tsourakis, Dogan Duven, Alberto Pezzi, Andrea Sestino, Paola Demartini, Simone Malacaria, Marco Greco, Michele Grimaldi, Andrea's fellow faculty members at LUISS and the other universities he teaches at, Michele's partners at the Observatories of the School of Management of Polytechnic

University of Milan, the University of Lausanne Corporate Data Quality Competence Center's research team, and all the industry peers who participate with their experience and ideas.

We are also very grateful to our inspiring publisher, Eloise Cook, whose quality content on publishing myth-busting has been such a motivation for non-fiction writers (check out her social profiles!). Thanks to Yashmeena Bisht, Sudhakar Murugan, Lou Attwood, and the rest of the amazing team at Pearson and the Financial Times for their professional support; they made a real book out of our manuscript and showed us immense patience over the last few months.

Without our families, we wouldn't have gone any far, really. Michele is thankful to Maria, Ester, Eva, and his entire family for their endless support and genuine interest along the way. Andrea is grateful to Sławka (the "real writer" in the family and a continuous source of inspiration for pretty much anything) and his family for their enthusiasm and constant backing.

Thank you all for being part of this journey.

Andrea and Michele

ABOUT THE AUTHORS

Photo by Domenico Gargarella

Andrea De Mauro has over 15 years of international experience managing data analytics and data science organisations. He is a data and AI executive advisor, a fractional CDO and a popular science author of several books on data analytics. He appeared in the 2022 global 'Forty Under 40' list by *CDO Magazine*. He served as Head of Data & Analytics at Vodafone Italy and as Director of Business Analytics at Procter & Gamble, looking after the continuous elevation of data analytics in the business and developing digital fluency across global organisations. He holds a PhD in management engineering from Rome Tor Vergata University, a Master of Science in electrical and computer engineering from the University of Illinois at Chicago, a Master's degree in ICT engineering from the Polytechnic of Turin and a diploma in Innovation from Alta Scuola Politecnica at Milan. He is a professor of Marketing Analytics and Applied AI at Luiss Guido Carli University in Rome, Italy, and has previously taught at the International University in Geneva, Switzerland, and the Universities of Bari and Florence, Italy. In his academic research, he investigates the essential components of big data as a phenomenon and the impact of AI and data analytics on companies and people. He is the author of popular science books on data analytics (his latest book in English is *Data Analytics Made Easy*, 2021) and research papers in international journals, with more than 3000 citations to date. He regularly speaks about data and AI at conferences and corporate events and can be reached at his website at www.ademauro.com.

Photo by Domenico Gargarella

Michele Pacifico has spent the last 15 years in various business intelligence and data analytics roles in fast-moving consumer goods and software industries, mostly focusing on business-facing responsibilities across countries and organisations. From building valuable analytics use cases to helping develop analytics roadmaps and data strategies in different organisations, data analytics has been a key passion accompanying him throughout his whole career. He is currently senior product manager for commercial analytics in the global analytics team of Nestlé. Previously, he had various roles at Procter & Gamble, including business intelligence leader for several regional businesses. He holds a Master's degree in micro and nano technologies for ICT from the Polytechnic of Turin, Institute National Polytechnique of Grenoble and Ecole Polytechnique Fédérale de Lausanne. Along with his business engagements, he is involved in various university testimonial events related to data analytics practice in the industry, and he is a member of the Advisory Board of the Big Data & Business Analytics Observatory Research of Milan Polytechnic.

PREFACE

Data is no longer just a resource; it is reshaping industries, redefining competitiveness, and reinventing business models altogether.

In an era marked by the exponential evolution of AI and the fear of missing out (FOMO) driven by generative AI, businesses face unprecedented challenges and opportunities. One of the most significant risks for companies today is to remain stuck with shiny proof of concepts and neglect real chances to create systematic value.

As we navigate through this transformative phase, executives across every functional area play a crucial role in steering their organizations toward sustainable value creation rather than succumbing to the allure of FOMO. It is their responsibility to ensure that their companies are not just chasing trends but are strategically positioned to leverage AI in meaningful and impactful ways.

The landscape of AI (and the Human-AI interface itself) will continue to evolve rapidly, and we are merely at the beginning of this journey. However, one constant will remain: there is no AI without data. A robust data strategy is a prerequisite for creating value, regardless of the future states of AI we will encounter.

In these pages, you will find the tools and knowledge needed to develop a comprehensive data strategy and integrate AI into your business processes effectively. This guide will help you transform your organization into a data-driven powerhouse, capable of thriving in the ever-changing AI landscape.

As you embark on this journey, remember that the key to success lies not just in adopting new technologies, but in understanding and leveraging the data that powers them and that allows for effective problem-solving. With the guidance provided in this book, you will be well-equipped to lead your organization through the challenges and opportunities of the AI revolution.

And it isn't solely about your organization. As an organization matures in its capacity to manage, exchange, and create value from data reliably and responsibly, it becomes increasingly capable of participating in future digital ecosystems. In these ecosystems, organizations (and individuals) can partner up, leveraging agile data flows, to address some of the most significant challenges that we face as a society, ranging from human well-being to environmental preservation.

Supporting both individuals and organizations in improving their data literacy and maturity has become a critical contribution to society, today and in the years to come. As a reader of this book, you certainly have the opportunity to lead by example, for the benefit of us all.

Francesco Marzoni, Chief Data & AI Officer, Ingka Group | IKEA

INTRODUCTION

A mix of conflicting emotions often accompanies the arrival of data analytics in a company. On the one hand, we feel optimistic and energised: big data, AI and the automation of decision-making processes arrive together with a fair amount of euphoria and positivity, propelled by the many anecdotes and success stories that are now ubiquitous in our readings.

On the other hand, the same topics come along with a generalised sense of inadequacy and also a certain suspicion, often unspoken, that sounds like this: 'Is this data really as important as they say, or is it yet another bubble that does nothing but divert attention from our core business?' In any case, the moment we decide to invest in it properly or to accelerate the journey we already have begun, we may get stuck on the most straightforward question, 'And now? Where do we get started?'

Business leaders, analytics managers and practitioners are currently struggling to move from theory to practice, and this book is all about solving this problem for them. According to the 2024 Data and AI Leadership Executive Survey conducted by Wavestone, companies are aggressively investing in data analytics, with 88 per cent of the organisations describing them as a top priority in the current year despite the macro-economic uncertainty. Although the need is clear, managers are still far from reaching their objectives when it comes to data. In fact, only 48 per cent of companies report that they have created a data-driven organisation and 43 per cent state they have established a data culture.

This book will support you by offering a path and a set of practical tools to get started and accelerate analytics programmes. The path is designed to guide you step-by-step through the process of *Data-Driven Transformation* (or, simply, *Data Transformation*), which is the systematic integration of data analytics into your business's operating model. Along the way, we will encounter new operational tools and conceptual models to help you finally put anecdotes in perspective. We will master a new language of managerial and technical terms (all explained from scratch, without making any assumptions on prior knowledge).

As authors, our promise to you is not to answer all your doubts but to help you focus on the right questions and offer proven tools to address them. Those already familiar with artificial intelligence and big data management will find some known content structured within a framework that will let them put technical aspects into a managerial and operational perspective. For those lacking this background, each page is meant to help them build it step by step.

The book's learning journey is ambitious: we will approach it gradually through eight stages, one for each chapter.

In **Chapter 1**, we will explore how data and algorithms can bring concrete business value through real-life examples. This chapter will also introduce important terminology to help you navigate the field confidently, such as the *three types of analytics*. You'll see how companies, both large and small, can transform their operating model by using data and leveraging the *Data Analytics Flywheel Effect*. Furthermore, we'll provide an overview of the *four enablers*, the essential components for getting consistent value from data utilisation.

Chapter 2 is the strategic heart of the book and has the important task of guiding you in setting up a *Data Transformation process* for your company. You will discover the possible mistakes we can make at the beginning of such a challenging enterprise – we call them the *False Starts* – and acquire proven tools and methods for building an effective plan for Data Transformation, starting from the definition of a *data strategy*.

In **Chapter 3**, you will learn a structured methodology for defining data capabilities that clearly outlines how data can be utilised in specific business processes. This chapter will take you through all the fields of the *Data Activation Canvas*: this model lets you frame 'what needs to be true' for data analytics to solve your company's pain points or tap into your high-potential value-creation opportunities.

In **Chapter 4**, you will learn about the fundamental concepts of artificial intelligence, machine learning and generative AI. You will have the chance to meet vis-à-vis various AI algorithms and get an easy-to-understand explanation of how they work. You will identify the four *ML-Way scenarios* that demonstrate how to use a catalogue of algorithms to solve real-world business problems. Furthermore, you will be introduced to the *key evaluation metrics* that can help you assess if an AI model suits your business needs, anticipating the potential trade-offs you must consider while integrating machine learning into a company's operating model.

Chapter 5 will explain the enabling factors related to the technology infrastructure for storing and processing data, starting from the need to build an effective *modern data stack* architecture. Regardless of your technical background, this chapter will provide you with the necessary knowledge to understand the required technology tools and the challenges that must be addressed. We will discover critical concepts such as *cloud, data lakes* and *data warehouses,* placing them in a managerial perspective.

Chapter 6 covers the three *human drivers* of Data Transformation and will unveil the fundamental cultural and organisational challenges we have to deal with. We will define the *role and skillset mapping* of data professionals such as data analysts, data scientists and data engineers. We will also examine a few proven *organisational design models* for incorporating these roles into our organisational chart. Additionally, we will address the cultural barriers that can prevent a company from becoming data-friendly and learn strategies for overcoming them.

In **Chapter 7**, you will find everything you need to establish and manage an effective data governance framework for your business. You will learn about creating a *data catalogue*, setting up *data quality* tools, and designing *governance roles* and processes. This chapter also includes a reusable template to create or review a *data governance policy*, and it explains a three-phase *governance roadmap* to establish a fully functional data stewardship framework, covering risks and opportunities related to privacy.

Chapter 8 pivots on what you will have already seen to drive Data Transformation in a company's ongoing operations. It addresses the prioritisation choices required to develop the level of maturity in the use of data (*Data Analytics Maturity*), as well as techniques to measure progress and identify bottlenecks. This chapter offers operational tools for managing an enterprise-wide Data Transformation programme, using the right trade-off between agility, flexibility, structure and focus.

We have written this book focusing on the practical needs of three groups of people and hope you will see yourself in one of them.

1 **Top managers** who may not seek expertise in data analytics but need to pose the right questions, grasp a common language, understand frameworks for data strategy design and recognise organisational and cultural complexities to drive appropriate change. This book is crafted for you! It is a handbook guide outlining the essentials for successful Data Transformation and business impact.

2 **Data leaders** struggling to convey technical complexities in terms that resonate with business relevance. This book acts as a bridge, providing you with a translator's guide to ensure your voice is heard and your influence felt among your peers and top management. It offers proven methodologies and science-backed frameworks to link data to value, facilitating successful Data Transformation effectively.

3 **Data practitioners** in search of a broader managerial perspective, practical tools, and tips to enhance the business value of their work. Here, you will learn how to effectively communicate your contributions, navigate organisational complexities, embrace your role as a catalyst for cultural change and make a significant impact. This book addresses common frustrations data talents face in complex organisations – these are normal, so don't feel alone! – and provides strategies for overcoming them effectively.

We have incorporated several features throughout the book to ensure your journey is both straightforward and enjoyable.

- Graphical templates and schematics throughout the book simplify learning and subsequent application within your organisation. These templates, detailed with practical examples, are also available for download from the book's website, where applicable.
- At the end of each chapter, a comprehensive checklist helps you review key concepts and apply them to your company's unique situation. We aim to enable a seamless transition from theoretical models to practical applications.
- Information boxes scattered throughout the chapters offer definitions, deep dives and intriguing facts to enrich your learning experience and make your journey more engaging and memorable.

We strongly believe that brevity is the mother of clarity. Thus, we have always opted for conciseness over exhaustiveness, leaving the task of compiling the 800-page 'Ultimate body of knowledge of data analytics' to another time. This book is succinct by design, providing precisely what you need – no more, no less – to implement your knowledge and drive your organisation's Data-Driven Transformation.

We understand that reading takes time and that, despite its allure and excitement, the topic of data analytics can be complex and daunting. We know that you are busy. Hence, we did our best to keep the book accessible, aiming to save you precious time and effort.

That's our proposition for you: go through the eight chapters, take some practical ideas away and put them into practice – we promise you will see the outcome. We will provide our contact details in the conclusion so you can reach out if we fail to fulfil our end of the deal.

It's time to embark on our journey towards Data Transformation, finally. In the first chapter, we will cover all the essential elements of our quest, leaving you with a clear understanding of what this book is all about – creating tangible business value from data. So fasten your seatbelt and enjoy the ride!

CHAPTER 1 UNLEASHING THE VALUE OF DATA

In this chapter

- What are the three types of analytics, and how do they differ in terms of complexity, required maturity, and potential value generation?
- How can organisations shift from traditional operating models to digital ones that maximise the value amplification of data analytics?
- What is really 'revolutionary' in how data analytics brings value to entire industries, and how can we benefit from this?
- How does the Flywheel Effect of data analytics create a virtuous cycle of value creation in organisations?

Data is nothing if you can't turn it into value. Although data abounds around us, unlocking its potential business value remains such a rare commodity. This is why our journey must start here: from the awareness and contemplation of what *value* truly means when it comes to data and algorithms.

Navigating the vast land of the many potential value opportunities of data analytics is no easy task. There are many reasons one can easily get lost. The hype around the latest hyped trends everyone talks about, like the many 'myths' surrounding the almighty power of artificial intelligence (AI) algorithms, can lead us to a dead end. The nomenclature, far from being universally recognised, can misguide us to the wrong path. Lacking a clear description of the destination can cause us to wander in circles, losing precious time to competitors.

This chapter is all about shedding light on the business value of data and giving you practical tools to keep the light on throughout the journey. We will visualise value through several reusable frameworks, illustrate it with practical examples from different industries and learn what it takes to enable it in a scalable and repeatable manner. This foundational knowledge will empower you to identify opportunities for leveraging data in your company, make informed decisions about extracting business value and engage in effective and productive discussions with your stakeholders about your Data Transformation ambitions.

We will see the concept of value from data at different levels. We will start from the practical, specific capabilities we encounter daily (like dashboards, chatbots and statistical models) and then zoom out to the industry-level macro transformations that impact many lives and jobs. Let's dive in and begin visualising the three types of data analytics you can use at work.

Defining 'data analytics'

Let's get some nomenclature straight at the start of our journey. The term 'data analytics' refers generically to methods, processes and tools used to extract value from data. If value extraction from data is the 'what', data analytics will be your 'how'. Some of you will remember the closest predecessor to this term, used until the early 2010s – data mining: this referred more specifically to extracting insights from vast databases using statistical methods. Modern data analytics covers a broader concept: it includes exploring and analysing data, plus deploying artificial intelligence solutions to augment and automate human capabilities.

Three types of data analytics

Data can unveil its potential in so many ways. In the following pages, we will introduce a few schematic models of the 'ways' such potential can come to life. The reason to do so is pragmatic rather than theoretical: every time we think of a proposition to use data at work – be it a dashboard, an AI recommendation system or a chatbot – we can locate it in its precise spot in a framework. By doing so, we will be more confident in assessing the proposition, comparing it with others and anticipating its strategic role in the transformation path. This is what frameworks are all about: they offer us the coordinates system to navigate complexity at best.

The first framework we will acquire splits data analytics into three main types: descriptive, predictive and prescriptive. Each type has its own unique features and benefits. Let's explore the three types of data analytics, their essential features, typical questions and examples of products.

1 **Descriptive analytics** is the simplest way of making use of data. It answers fundamental questions regarding the past or the present status of your business, such as 'What happened?' or 'What is happening?' Typical outputs of descriptive analytics include data tables and charts. Both types of output share the same intent: to summarise what is going on with your key performance indicators (KPIs). Examples of descriptive analytics products range from file-based **static reports** (yes – the typical Excel or PDF reports shared via email, however rudimentary, fall within this category) to the fancier web-based **interactive dashboards** with filters, drop-downs, navigation buttons and so on. From a management perspective, descriptive analytics is useful for identifying trends and patterns that can inform decision making and for enabling quick benchmarking versus some relevant references (such as targets, previous periods, competitors and so on). For example, a company may use descriptive analytics to identify which products are selling well and which are not and use this information to adjust their marketing strategies.
2 **Predictive analytics** is a more advanced way of leveraging data and answering questions such as 'What is likely to happen?' and 'Why has this happened?' The key addition to descriptive analytics in predictive analytics is that the data is not just summarised but gets processed using statistical modelling. A statistical model can intercept interesting patterns in data (some of which might repeat in the future) and can unveil the drivers of what has happened in the past. Examples of products driven by predictive analytics include **forecasts** of metrics over time (they are technically called time series), **simulations** of alternate outcomes, data-based **segmentation** of entities (such as customers or stores) and **diagnostics** of interesting previous patterns, including the recognition of abnormal events (**anomaly detection**). From the perspective of decision makers, predictive analytics is useful for figuring out potential business opportunities and current threats. For example, a company may use predictive analytics to forecast sales for the upcoming quarter and adjust their production and inventory levels accordingly.
3 **Prescriptive analytics** is the most advanced way of doing data analytics, and it involves the use of algorithms to identify the best course of action

based on data insights and constraints. Prescriptive analytics is used to answer questions such as 'What should we do?', 'How should we do it?' The algorithms used in prescriptive analytics do not stop at understanding and modelling what's happening but go to the next level and figure out the best course of action, prescribing the specific activities to run. This can happen both at a granular level, such as when simulating products to recommend to a specific user on an online shop, and at a more aggregated level when advising managers on what strategic decisions to make. Prescriptive analytics products include **scoring** models, which anticipate the propensity in the behaviour of individual customers; **optimisation** systems able to recommend the best course of action; and **generative agents**, like chatbots, capable of providing human-like interaction and guiding through the best course of action. From a management perspective, prescriptive analytics act as co-pilots in steering the direction of the business, leveraging data insights and acknowledging constraints. For example, a company may use prescriptive analytics to optimise their pricing strategy based on market demand and customer preferences.

Reality is always more complex than any framework attempts to explain. Indeed, even our descriptive–predictive–prescriptive analytics model is a simplified representation of real-world applications: data capabilities often fall within the interstices of these three blocks or embody multiple aspects within themselves. The demarcation line between the various types is subtle. For instance, in interactive dashboards (descriptive), we often find diagnostic elements that arise from implementing statistical models (predictive). Generative agents like chatbots (prescriptive) can be used to describe some important trends and synthesise their true meaning (descriptive and predictive). Therefore, the advice is to keep this framework in mind as a general compass and be ready to accept that the various 'souls' of descriptive, predictive and prescriptive analytics intermingle. This is not only natural but also desirable in a company as we would like data capabilities to integrate with each other to simplify their usage.

However intertwined they can be, the descriptive, predictive and prescriptive types of data analytics products display unique value propositions and necessitate varying levels of maturity in both their methodologies and the readiness of decision makers, as Figure 1.1 suggests.

In terms of output, descriptive analytics provides **hindsight**, enabling a clear and holistic comprehension of past events. Conversely, predictive and

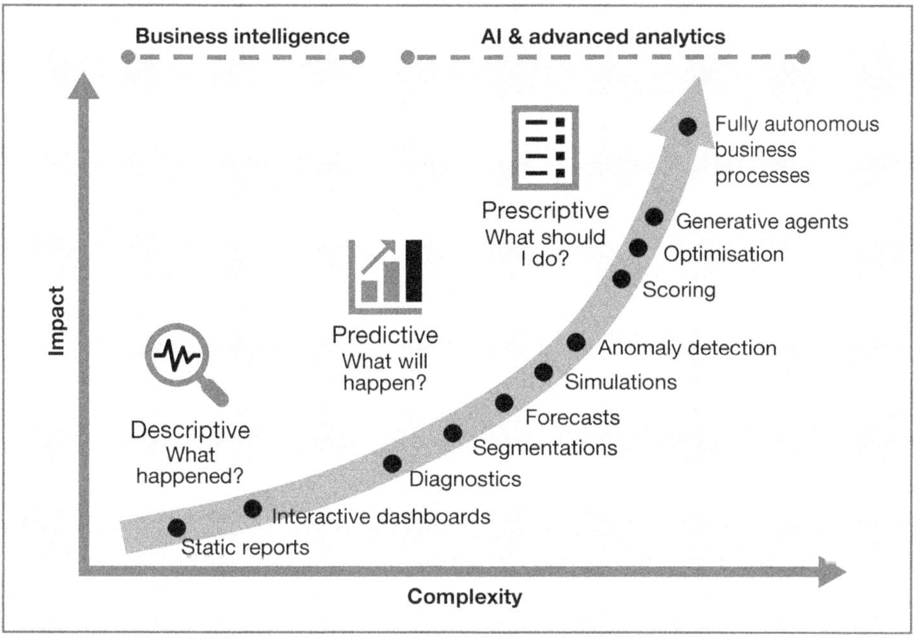

Figure 1.1 The descriptive, predictive and prescriptive analytics framework: higher potential value comes with bigger complexity to manage

prescriptive analytics offer both **insight**, resulting in a deep understanding of some critical aspects of the present, and **foresight**, the capacity to foresee future outcomes based on current trends and data patterns. Although each form of output – hindsight, insight and foresight – can be a major help in managing a business, there is an ascending value trajectory from descriptive to prescriptive analytics, enriching the decision-making process with increasingly profound layers of understanding and potential.

The methodologies required for each type of analytics also vary drastically. Descriptive analytics leans on **summarisation** and **visualisation**, which are fundamental skills for data professionals and are implemented in any business intelligence tool. Predictive analytics requires mastery of **statistical modelling**, whereas prescriptive analytics demands the command of **optimisation** methods, often involving more sophisticated algorithms, and the utilisation of AI and advanced analytics platforms.

Decision makers' readiness is also specific to each type of data analytics. For descriptive analytics, the decision maker's role is limited to reading and exploring data, so they just need to have some **curiosity for data**. As they progress to predictive analytics, something more is required: they need an **open-minded approach** to accept the insights deriving from statistical models, especially when they diverge from their gut feel and previous experience. Finally, the acceptance of data-driven prescriptions requires an even higher level of **trust in data and algorithms** and a broad cultural readiness towards AI and analytics. As we will see in Chapter 6, such cultural openness cannot be taken for granted in a complex organisation and needs to be carefully nurtured.

Finally, the support each type of analytics provides for decision making and human intelligence also varies. Descriptive analytics **enables** decisions by providing data, predictive analytics **enhances** decisions by offering insights and prescriptive analytics **recommends** decisions based on its optimisation processes. Similarly, descriptive analytics **feeds** human intelligence with data, predictive analytics **augments** it with insights and prescriptive analytics can ultimately **automate** it by coming up with decisions.

It's crucial for you at this point to appreciate that the journey from descriptive to predictive to prescriptive analytics isn't a matter of substitution but of addition and expansion. These analytics types are not alternatives to each other: they coexist in a company, each serving its unique purpose. You won't have to choose one over the other; rather, the journey involves the gradual incorporation of each, beginning with descriptive and progressively integrating more predictive and prescriptive elements.

In practice, any single business case will likely require all three levels of analytics, whose features are summarised in Table 1.1. This understanding can help us visualise a roadmap for each business case, showcasing the increasing maturity levels achieved through the application of data analytics (we will provide examples of such roadmaps in the next few pages).

As such, the transformation process we're describing in this book is designed to accommodate this evolutionary approach, fostering an integration of more advanced analytics as companies mature. It's not about pushing for the most sophisticated prescriptive modelling from day one but about gradually introducing and increasing the presence of predictive and prescriptive elements into the existing descriptive analytics foundation.

Table 1.1 The three types of analytics: every type has its role and comes with its requirements

	Descriptive	Predictive	Prescriptive
What questions are answered?	What happened? What's happening?	Why has it happened? What will happen?	What should I do? How should I do it?
What's the output?	Hindsight	Insight and foresight	
What methodologies are needed?	Summarisation and visualisation	Statistical modelling	Optimisation
What's required by decision makers?	Curiosity for data	Open-mindedness	Trust in data & algorithms
How is decision making supported?	Enable decisions	Enhance decisions	Recommend decisions
How is human intelligence supported?	Feed intelligence (with data)	Augment intelligence (with insights)	Automate intelligence (with decisions)

Let's now explore real-world examples of how companies across various industries and sizes utilise all three types of analytics to meet the same business needs.

Data analytics for customer churn

Katia is the chief data and analytics officer of a large telco company offering mobile and broadband connectivity in France. She explains that one of their biggest business opportunities has been the bleeding of customers leaving the company to pursue better rates and services elsewhere – a well-known phenomenon known as customer churn. Katia decided to pull together a programme called 'churn analytics' with the vision of supporting this business priority by employing data and algorithms. Let's go through some of the data capabilities Katia and her team have delivered as part of the programme:

- At first, the churn phenomenon was tracked using an Excel-based report updated every week through a series of manual steps. These included collecting data points from multiple systems and aggregating them into a single view. The report included the number of customers who left over different time periods and, in its simplicity, enabled the marketing team to keep track of the phenomenon.

- One of the first innovations brought by Katia's team as part of the churn analytics programme has been to automate the process of pulling together all the data points related to churn. Thanks to this new automated feed, the team built an interactive dashboard that would refresh every morning and offer more details than its Excel predecessor. For instance, the dashboard includes the split by competitor the lost customers migrated to, the detail by sales region, a deeper time granularity and more history. The marketing team was delighted by this advancement, as they were equipped with a fresher and deeper view of churn and, more importantly, were able to explore the data freely and find answers autonomously without having to wait for someone else to collect the needed data.
- By applying statistical modelling to the churn events dataset, Katia's analysts managed to equip the dashboard with some valuable diagnostics: if the churn rates over to a specific competitor in a given geographical region experienced an abnormal surge, an automated email and smartphone alert would reach the marketing managers responsible for that scope, with a link to a dashboard page displaying more details of the event. Additionally, utilising a simple time-series model, the dashboard displayed an estimate of what the churn rates would have been at the end of the month. By comparing such forecasts with the month-end target, the marketing team can now identify shortcomings and act on them proactively by adjusting their plans.
- The next challenge for the churn analytics programme has been to model the behaviour of individual customers. To do so, data scientists within Katia's team pulled together a more granular dataset where every customer was described through features such as tariff, tenure, average data and call usage, age, place of residence, and so on. Thanks to the application of some machine learning algorithms, this data has been translated into useful insight and capabilities. For instance, data scientists have built a decision tree model for churning customers, which explains the most typical combinations of features that characterise leavers. Thanks to such an 'identikit' of churners, business functions could identify the pain points that caused the systematic bleeding of customers, such as unclear bundles, faulty equipment models, aggressive local competition and so on.
- Data scientists didn't stop here. Using more sophisticated machine learning algorithms, they could assign a churn propensity score to every customer. The lists of customers with the highest probability of churn are targeted with laser-focused prevention activities (such as extra-bundle allowance,

discount on the monthly fee or a free upgrade of the smartphone), which sensibly reduced the churn levels. The team plans to implement fully automated retention activities: prescriptive algorithms will soon be able to infer the specific retention actions to be implemented on a customer and trigger their application, without any human intervention, through autonomous AI-powered agents.

What Katia has just proudly described is a typical representation of the journey companies undertake with the application of data analytics to one specific business need – customer churn in this case – as Figure 1.2 illustrates.

The example illustrates well how the descriptive–predictive–prescriptive framework applies in the real world. Descriptive analytics and reporting are naturally the first things that need to be fulfilled. Reports and dashboards will never 'disappear', but will be progressively enriched with predictive features, such as diagnostics alerts, anomaly detection and forecasts. Data feeds become automated, and this is the basis of the industrialisation of data capabilities, which, over time, tend to become more sophisticated and based on more detailed and granular datasets.

Notice the evolution of the role of data in this example. At first, human intelligence is simply aided by making data available to decision makers. Afterwards,

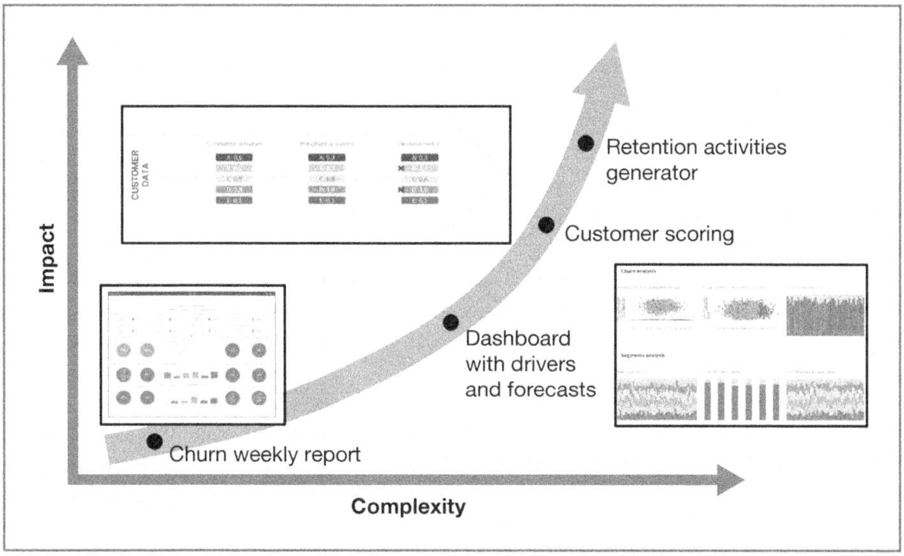

Figure 1.2 Analytics framework applied to the churn case: how can data help you retain your customers?

algorithms start offering deeper insights and prescriptions that can even substitute human thinking, as algorithms are delegated in executing optimised actions.

Let's now move to another example of a different industry and company size.

Data analytics for retail optimisation

Eric is a passionate, self-taught data analytics enthusiast who wants to apply the power of data to his family-run local corner shop chain in Newcastle upon Tyne, in the North-East of England. Eric's family has been operating their corner shop business for the past 30 years, offering a variety of food items, newspapers, tobacco and general household items to the local community. Although their small business had been stable over the years, Eric understood the potential benefits of implementing data analytics to optimise their inventory, increasing profitability while also better serving their customer base. As Eric explains his journey, we can see that – similar to what Katia did – everything started from the 'basics'.

- Eric started by integrating all disparate data sources, including the ones based on paper, into a single, comprehensive spreadsheet. This document tracked weekly and monthly sales, costs, cash flow and inventory levels. It was a simple but significant step, allowing the family to view their operations holistically.
- The turning point in Eric's data analytics journey was the integration of the data collected by the chain's cash registers. Previously, the various point of sales (POS) systems functioned separately, with data dispersed across multiple registers in different stores. Eric addressed this by collating the data from all cash registers into a single, unified dataset. This integration automated the previously laborious process of data collection. Eric no longer needed to input data into his spreadsheet manually. The POS system automatically recorded and transmitted data, freeing up Eric's time to focus on extracting and applying insights from the data.
- One of Eric's breakthroughs was the forecast of inventory levels. Through the analysis of sales data, he could anticipate the future stock inventory and determine the ideal stock levels for each product, considering both its sales velocity and lead time. This innovation led to significant improvements

in cash flow, as capital was not tied up unnecessarily in overstocked items. Additionally, it also reduced the occurrence of out-of-stock situations, leading to a better experience for his customers.

- Further exploring the data, Eric turned his attention to fresh products with limited shelf lives. By logging the expiry dates in a dataset, he was able to identify items close to their sell-by date and initiate promotional offers to expedite their sale. This reduced food waste and related losses and gave customers a chance to benefit from spontaneous discounts, enhancing their shopping experience.
- Eric also installed a footfall counter at the store's entrance. This device tracked the flow of customers in and out of the stores, providing visibility about customer traffic patterns. By analysing this data, Eric was able to schedule staff more effectively to match busy periods and plan promotional events during slower days to increase traffic. For instance, he introduced a 'Senior Citizens Day' every Wednesday, offering extra discounts to pensioners, which improved the shop's performance on a traditionally slow day.
- Currently, Eric is exploring the realm of prescriptive analytics. He is working on an algorithm that will use predictive models to recommend actions in real time – like when to reorder specific items that will soon go out of stock. Although this is still a work in progress, the potential is there to create a self-optimising system that can make autonomous decisions to maximise sales and customer satisfaction.

The journey Eric undertook, shown in Figure 1.3, is another clear example of the gradual, iterative process of data analytics adoption. It started with basic reports enhancing the visibility of where the business is going and proceeded to more sophisticated capabilities able to optimise his retail operations. His story shows that no matter the size of a business, data analytics can provide significant benefits when implemented carefully.

Both Katia's and Eric's stories, although grounded in their specific circumstances – a large telecom company and a family-run corner shop chain – echo broad patterns, challenges and opportunities that are universally applicable. Many of you will likely see parallels in your own experiences, regardless of industry or company size. The descriptive, predictive and prescriptive framework provides a valuable lens through which to view and understand these experiences.

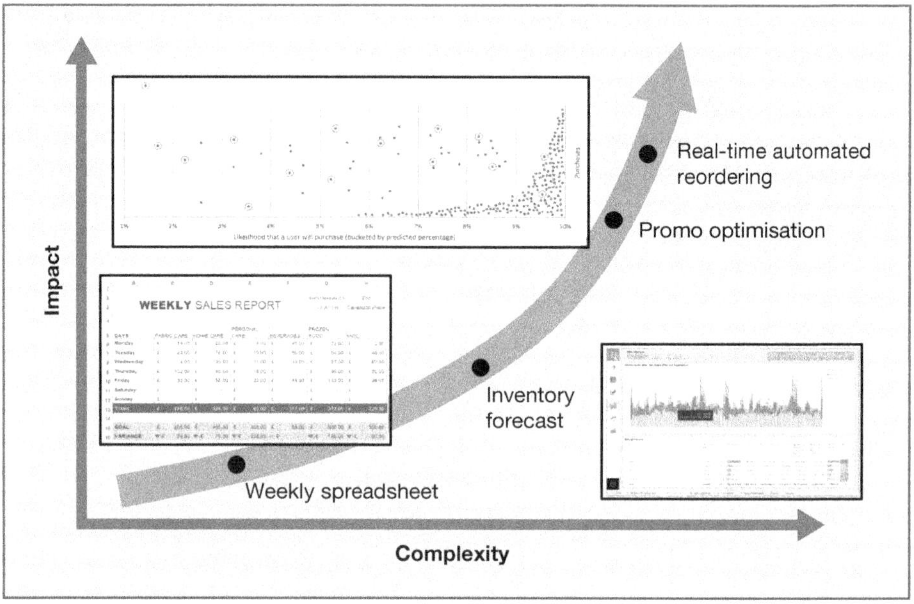

Figure 1.3 Analytics framework applied to the retail case: from Excel spreadsheets to real-time stock management

Amplifying value with a digital operating model

The exciting realisation research has unveiled in the last few years is that as companies progressively deployed data analytics capabilities, the value didn't just sum up incrementally but started to multiply. When data and algorithms begin to automate the way a company thinks and operates, value tends to be amplified. This amplification factor is our ultimate ambition in the data analytics transformation journey: putting data at the very core of how a company operates feels like a quantum leap forward.

Let's think for a second about what the defining constituents of a company are: the business model and the operating model.

(a) The **business model** explains the fundamental economic purpose of any enterprise. It includes two elements: the value proposition, which describes the unique products or services that will improve customers' lives, and the value capture, which shows how the company plans to monetise the value it promises. Businesses try to differentiate themselves from others through a distinctive value proposition and an advantageous value capture model. The business model is linked with the ultimate reason why the company exists: if you are a maker of laundry detergents, your business model is – as simple as that – to produce detergents with the highest and 'most unique' washing benefits and to be able to sell them in large quantities, at the right price, and in the most appropriate retail channels, in a way that is profitable and sustainable for everyone in the value chain.

(b) The **operating model** defines the way a company works. If the business model is the 'what', the operating model is the 'how'. You can think of it as the blueprint of the core business processes of a company, including the organisational choices that make the whole thing run. Although all laundry detergent manufacturers have a similar business model, it's their operating model that defines who wins and who loses in the marketplace. Those who manage to build and maintain a robust yet lean and cost-effective operating model will accrue a competitive advantage over others and have a higher chance to thrive.

The value amplification factor of data analytics kicks in when a company transforms its operating model by allowing data and algorithms to have a more central role in its core business processes. To visualise where this value amplification comes from, let's consider the two extremes: a full data analytics-driven operating model and a traditional operating model. We will focus on how the marginal value changes as the company grows.

In a traditional operating model, increasing the scale of the company (more customers, bigger production volumes and so on) will, at some point, result in a lower level of marginal value. As the size of the business increases, the problems inherent in its management will grow with it. Indeed, marginal operating costs tend to increase (more people are required and the need to coordinate them also grows). In contrast, the level of service tends to decrease, squeezed by the difficulty of managing so many users.

Supermarkets that grow fast will get long lines at the tills until they rethink their shop layout. Factories hit by high demand will struggle even if the number of workers in the production line increases since the floor size stays limited and machinery reaches its maximum capacity.

These diseconomies of scale are also driven by a typical feature of all human endeavours: people naturally tend to 'bureaucratise' the activities they handle regularly and become rigid in the status quo. As a result, the organisation tends to get slower as it grows in size, thus increasing the complexity of the whole system and lowering the marginal value of any further development.

To manage this uncomfortable 'giant with feet of clay' situation, when companies have grown too much (and are poorly digitised), they feel the urge to simplify themselves: they declare the need to go 'back to basics', drive efficiencies and reset expansion expectations. They might, for example, execute painful mass layoffs or 'break up' their structure into smaller and manageable parts and divest some lines of business. This is why many companies' scaling desire gets trapped into a dead-end loop of alternating cycles: a 'pendulum' oscillating between growth and decline, expansion and deflation, innovation and stagnation, driven by the constant tension between ambitions of scale and the realities of operational inefficiencies.

The law of diminishing returns

The economic principle known as the 'law of diminishing returns' neatly encapsulates the idea of decreasing value as scale increases. This rule suggests that, in any production process, if you incrementally increase one production factor while keeping others constant, the output per additional unit of input will eventually start to decrease. So, as you ramp up, you might not always get the increased productivity you're hoping for. This principle was initially articulated by French physiocrat Anne Robert Jacques Turgot in the 18th century and then further developed by British economists David Ricardo and Thomas Malthus. It was first applied in the context of agricultural production – specifically, the declining productivity of additional labour on a fixed amount of land.

In a full data analytics-driven operating model, the story is different. First, consider the nature of data: unlike physical assets, data is intangible, infinitely replicable and can be transmitted almost without cost. Then, think about the 'people' involved: algorithms are indefatigable operators and can potentially enhance their performance autonomously and in real time. When data and algorithms come together to execute a business process, they create an unbeatable duo capable of scaling up with almost zero marginal cost.

On top of this, AI brings in an additional amplification factor: when machines have more data to learn from, they become more effective at what they do. In other words, the more material they have to study, the better they get at executing their jobs. Take Facebook Ads, for example. The platform uses an algorithm to anticipate what ads should be served thanks to the complex patterns of interests, behaviours and friends' networks that users expressing interest in similar ads have displayed. If a million users get added to Facebook, the algorithm benefits from this additional data and recognises more interesting and articulated patterns. The greater the number of users and, hence, the more the data fed to the algorithm increases, the higher the efficiency of ads and the potential profit Meta can get from a single display. It's a paradoxical situation: the harder these machine learning algorithms work, the less they struggle to provide value.

You might notice that also human operators get better at their jobs over time since they progressively learn through practice and mistakes as they work through more cases. However, there's a key distinction: while both can improve efficiency, human operators eventually reach their cognitive limitations. There is a cap to the amount of work they can handle, and their capacity for information storage and learning cannot grow indefinitely. For AI, these limitations nearly don't exist. Machines are also more effective at transferring know-how seamlessly, while human operators are required to codify their implicit knowledge – a costly and demanding activity – to pass it better on.

Hence, digital operating models, because of the unique characteristics of data and algorithms, show continuous growth in the value generated as the 'scale' of the business served increases. Thanks to the paradox outlined above, they even tend to follow an exponential progression once AI comes into play.

Such a model flips the conventional 'giant with feet of clay' scenario on its head. Rather than resorting to painful downsizing or divestments, companies can now grow efficiently, unrestricted by the usual bureaucracies and complexities that come with size. We can visually follow the destiny of the two extreme cases in Figure 1.4: the plot shows the marginal value generated by any additional user (vertical axis) as the scale of the company grows (horizontal axis).

In a fully traditional operating model, the value grows steadily until the diseconomies of scale we mentioned earlier kick in. The curve starts to flatten and then ends up in a precarious situation where the benefits of growth are offset by the increasing costs and complexities. At this tipping point, the operational inefficiencies become so crippling that the company's survival is put at risk, leaving the only option to pull back and reduce the scale, entering the vicious loop you see on the right end.

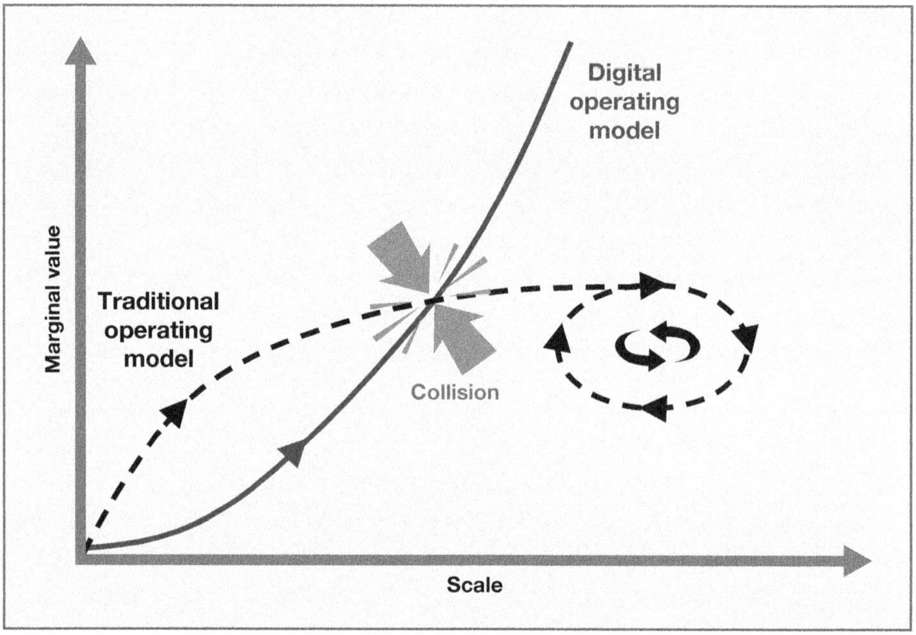

Figure 1.4 Traditional vs digital operating model: which one would you like your company to have?

In the case of a fully digital operating model, where data and algorithms are deeply integrated within the company's clockwork, the curve has a very different shape. It starts below that of the traditional model. At a smaller scale, the extreme flexibility of human operators in handling individual cases and exceptions gives them an edge over algorithms, which initially have limited data to learn from. Additionally, the cognitive power of human beings can still cope with the limited scope and complexity of this early level of scale. There is no need for modern descriptive analytics to help understand what is going on in the company and make decisions.

However, as the scale expands, the situation shifts dramatically. The digital operating model soon catches up and overtakes its traditional counterpart. Serving more customers results in more data, leading to increasingly smarter decisions, whereas the traditional model grapples with overhead costs owing to the amplified complexity. Realistically, the digital operating model will also encounter diminishing returns at some point and, indeed, fully digital companies are never exempt from crises, reorganisations and the need for simplification. When this moment arrives, however, lagging traditional companies will be too far down to pose a serious competitive risk.

If two companies in the same industry, one with a fully digital and the other with a traditional operating model, were to expand, they would inevitably clash during their growth trajectory. This point of collision, as described by Harvard professors Marco Iansiti and Karim R. Lakhani, represents a new level of industry disruption and forces companies to reconfigure their operating models to remain competitive.

We have seen many of those collisions happening already and reframing the way entire industries work. Some of them require little introduction.

- Monzo and other fully digital banks are colliding with traditional banking institutions. Monzo operates on a digital first model, with machine learning algorithms automating banking operations, including credit decisions and fraud detection. According to a Bain study, an attacker bank like Monzo, founded on a modern, cloud-native technology platform, can have a cost base 60–70 per cent lower than a mid-tier legacy bank. Monzo's model allows it to serve two to three times as many customers per employee compared to major incumbents.
- Uber is colliding with traditional taxi companies. They use prescriptive analytics in their dispatch system to efficiently allocate rides. The system deviates from the human-reliant traditional approach, optimising the matching of drivers with riders, reducing waiting times and augmenting customer satisfaction.
- Amazon is colliding with traditional brick-and-mortar retailers such as Walmart and Tesco. Its dynamic pricing and product recommendation systems rely nearly solely on algorithms. This data-centric approach enhances customer experience, making shopping more personalised and efficient, thus driving sales up.

This is what happens when we integrate data into the heart of a business: traditional and digital operating models collide, and companies propelled by data analytics gain the upper hand, leveraging the amplification factor of data coupled with algorithms.

The good news is that you don't need to be Amazon or Uber to benefit from such an amplification factor. Remember what we said earlier regarding the digital and traditional operating models: they represent the two extremes of a continuum. Most of our companies lie somewhere in between. The closer we are to the full digital case, the more we benefit from the value amplification factor that data analytics brings. It's all about making choices to raise the bar progressively and give data and algorithms the role they deserve in any modern economic enterprise.

Navigating an industrial revolution

Technology evolution has always shaped human history. The advent of impactful innovations has provided the rhythm of large transformations in how people live and organise themselves in society. Over the past two and a half centuries, the emergence of certain pervasive technical advances, known as **general-purpose technologies** (GPTs), dramatically transformed entire economies, inducing what we know as industrial revolutions.

The first of such revolutions was sparked in the late 18th century by a Scottish engineer who took a potential but inadequate technology and managed to make it 'good enough' for mass adoption. The engineer was James Watt, and his invention was the steam engine.

Steam engines fundamentally changed the world. Harnessing the power of steam to drive machinery, these engines propelled society into a new era marked by significant growth in wealth and productivity. This didn't come without its drawbacks, though, such as increased economic inequality, air pollution (visibly attested by the dark skies of London, blanketed in the black fumes of coal combustion) and the terrible condition of the novel work environment.

Factories powered by steam engines were, indeed, a cacophony of noise, a chaos of motion and a landscape of hazards. Steam engines powered a single massive drive shaft, which ran through the entire factory, driving all the machinery. If just one machine needed to run, the engine had to be fired up, consuming coal and labour. These factories were dark and dense, packed around the shafts. The steam engine set the pace, and workers had to keep up, often at great personal risk. Thousands of drip oilers lubricated machines, and there was always the danger that a worker might snag a sleeve or bootlace and be dragged into the relentless machine.

When electricity became viable for industrial use, factory owners saw a chance for improvement. The first alternating current (AC) induction motors were invented by Galileo Ferraris and Nikola Tesla in 1885 and 1887, respectively. Despite the attractive promise of substituting steam engines, by 1900, only 5 per cent of mechanical drive power in US factories was provided by electric motors. The age of steam still lingered, while the electrification of factories suffered a slow start.

It took approximately two decades to reverse the situation. It wasn't until 1929 that electric AC motors accounted for around 78 per cent of the total capacity for powering machinery in US factories. The explanation behind this seemingly inexplicable lag is simple: merely possessing the new technology wasn't sufficient for value to emerge. Companies required two more ingredients to benefit from electricity fully: the reliable supply of cheap electric energy and the adaption of the operating model to the new technology.

Electric power wasn't affordable or high quality enough to replace steam engines for a while. Modern electric power plants were crucial to this transformation. One such notable example is the Edward Dean Adams Power Plant at Niagara Falls, built in 1895. It was the first large-scale, alternating current electric generating plant in the world, marking an important milestone in electricity history. However, constructing more advanced facilities like the Niagara Falls plant took several years, and it wasn't until the following decades that such plants became common.

The availability of electric energy wasn't enough for the new GPT to shine: companies realised they needed to rethink the way they worked.

The first factories going electric were, in fact, only slightly better than the old ones. The chaos and mess on the production floor were still there. Factory owners replaced steam engines with electric motors but kept everything else the same. The central steel drive shaft that ran along the factory's length remained, with the only difference being that it was now powered by the single, massive, electric AC motor that had replaced the good old steam engine. Drip oilers were still there, together with the noise and the hazard of massive moving parts, as you can see in Figure 1.5.

Everything changed with the introduction of a novel design concept for the factory layout called unit drive. Engineers realised that powering each machine with its own individual electric motor worked much better than having a massive drive shaft powered by a single motor. In other words, many small motors were much better than a single big one.

Heritage Images/Hulton Archive/Getty

Figure 1.5 The Birmingham Small Arms factory shop in 1917. Although powered by electricity, the rotating line shafts on the ceiling were driving every piece of machinery

With unit drive, each machine operated independently, allowing for turning off machines that were not needed, saving energy and labour. The system also resulted in significant energy and cost savings, almost doubling the overall full-load efficiency of power production, transmission and distribution. Factories became safer and brighter, improving the working environment for workers.

The transition to unit drive was not immediate since it wasn't a mere replacement of old machinery with new. It required a fundamental rethinking of business processes and the physical layout of factories.

For instance, in a car assembly plant, the old system might require all welding to be done in one area, all painting in another and so on. The advent of portable power tools made it possible to move 'machines to the work' rather than transporting the 'work to the machines'.

In summary, it took approximately 20 years for companies to benefit from the game-changing potential of electric engines. The arrival of the new cool gadget (the AC power engine) wasn't enough: a steady feed of cheap electric power supply and the rethinking of the operating model was what made the actual trick.

We are living now those '20 years' of data analytics and AI. The technology is there, but most companies are struggling with two crucial enablers: first, securing a steady feed of good-quality and usable data and, second, rethinking their operating models to allow for data and algorithms to get the protagonist part they deserve.

One final consideration on this: the real advantage of the electric motor was not in simply replacing the steam engine – it was in the transformative ability of electricity to redefine (and improve) the *entire* factory system. Data can have the same effect on our companies today if we allow it to happen. Data-Driven Transformation forces us to challenge the status quo and rethink our operating model. Bright managers are taking advantage of the transformative ability of data analytics to modernise operating models entirely. They know that the benefit of leveraging data and AI can go well beyond the direct impact of adopting analytics applications.

The revolution of computers at work

Much like the transition from steam to electricity in factories, the introduction of computing technology in businesses needed more than just adopting the technology itself. Erik Brynjolfsson and Lorin M. Hitt noted that the impact of computers on economic growth in the 1990s wasn't achieved by simply introducing computers in the workplace. Businesses had to undergo significant changes in their processes, skills, organisational structures and industry structures to utilise the potential of the technology entirely. The same needs to happen today with data and AI.

The Flywheel Effect: driving momentum with data analytics

We must confront a challenging reality: even the least sophisticated data analytics product within the descriptive–predictive–prescriptive framework requires certain prior steps and enablers to be in place. And they don't come for free. For example, even the simplest static reports, like those mentioned by Eric and Katia, demand a meticulous process of sourcing the right data in the right format, which is hard to achieve in real-world companies.

Consider the multiple steps required to put together a simple report.

1 First, there is the crucial task of **data discovery**, identifying and understanding what data is available and where it is located. Data assets are often buried

in Excel files stored on an employee's drive or hidden in a legacy system that not even the IT department knew about. An organisation's data landscape can be unexpectedly complex and shadowy.

2. Once the appropriate data has been discovered and you find that it lies in different places, the next step to make it usable is **systems integration**. This involves connecting various systems and platforms where the data resides, ensuring all necessary datasets can be aggregated and cross-referenced as needed.
3. The third step is the creation of a **common data model**. The data must be organised and structured to allow for a unified view across various data sources. A common data model ensures that different data points can be combined effectively to be presented within the same analytics application.
4. To ensure the consistent interpretation of data, there's a need for a well-governed **data catalogue**. This document defines data assets and explains how calculations are done, supplying the required business rationale. For example, converging on an accepted version of KPI's definition (with all the alignments required across organisations) is necessary to obtain a single version of the truth.

Connected to these specific steps, certain broader **enablers** or foundational conditions must be in place for successful data analytics.

- A robust **technology stack** is the necessary infrastructure for data collection, processing and analysis.
- Equally important is **data governance**, the process by which an organisation manages its data assets to ensure data integrity, accessibility and reliability.
- Moreover, having the right **data skills** within the teams is pivotal. Qualified personnel are required to transform data into actionable insights.
- Finally, fostering a **data culture** is essential for creating an environment where data-driven decision making is embraced by everyone and encouraged by top management.

As you can see in Figure 1.6, the entrance ticket to any data analytics ambition entails some fundamental enablers and preparatory steps that cannot be neglected, even if they lie below the spotlight of management attention. They are our only way in. The fancy descriptive–predictive–prescriptive applications

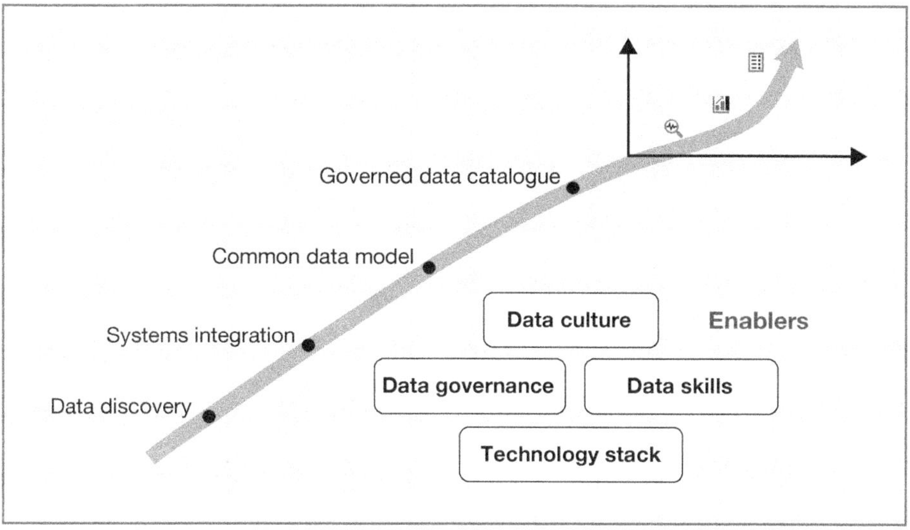

Figure 1.6 The hard reality behind the descriptive-predictive-prescriptive framework: even for the simplest applications, some hard work must happen in the back shop

cannot become a sustained reality if we don't get these – less glamorous, we must admit – enabling conditions in place. And many analytics programmes fail because these conditions are either fully neglected or considered a deferrable, secondary priority.

In fact, when one or more of these enablers are not in place, a vicious cycle can swallow us in and jeopardise our Data Transformation journey. If you feel you are in this situation, you are not alone. Many organisations feel trapped in this condition. For example, teams without the necessary skills, resources and budget are ill-equipped to create value from data. They might stay in this status indefinitely, failing to become convincing enough to attract more funds. The lack of a well-established and effective data team causes individual business units to build their own data capabilities and assets. The proliferation of 'shadow' analytics organisations endangers the attempt to create synergies in data utilisation and enables the creation of data silos. The lack of proper data governance leads to inconsistencies and inaccuracies in data interpretation. Without accepted ways to measure the value generated by data and with an unsatisfactory return on investment (ROI) management becomes disengaged and less inclined to invest further in data analytics, making it more challenging to improve the intricate situation.

As agents of the Data-Driven Transformation endeavour, we can't let this happen. Our job is to mix the right strategic and tactical elements to spark an initial momentum that can self-sustain – we call this the **Data Analytics Flywheel Effect.** Inspired by Amazon's customer-centric strategy, our Flywheel Effect is about creating a virtuous cycle of growth and value creation in the realm of data analytics.

Amazon's flywheel

In 2001, amid the dot-com bubble's aftermath, Amazon's future was uncertain. However, Jeff Bezos sketched what he termed the 'Flywheel Effect' on a napkin, encapsulating an innovative model of sustainable business growth. This is how the cycle unfolds: everything initiates with customer obsession, which leads to an increase in sales volume, thereby attracting more third-party sellers to their marketplace. Having more sellers broadens the selection of products, enhancing customer experience and lowering cost structures. Lower costs enable lower prices, drawing in more customers and creating a cycle of continuous growth that perpetuates itself. The key lies in triggering the cycle and maintaining momentum, resulting in an ongoing, self-sustaining loop of value creation and business expansion.

The idea is to focus punctual actions on specific enablers that will make the flywheel win the initial inertia and start a slow but sure spin. There are a few places where we can apply the initial pressure required for the flywheel to start: people, tools, organisational choices, data governance, minimal data assets, business sponsorship and value tracking. Don't worry at this stage about the seemingly broad range of areas to look after. The remainder of this book is all about working on these aspects and will equip you with practical tools to get them right. At this stage, the important point is to notice the encouraging reality that making even small improvements in these areas is enough to make the flywheel start.

At the heart of the Flywheel Effect is an effective analytics team equipped with a modern tech stack which includes a toolbox of accessible instruments to manage data and algorithms and a foundational layer of usable critical data assets.

When aligned to serve the broader company strategy, their initial achievements demonstrate the value of leveraging data as an asset, making the need to

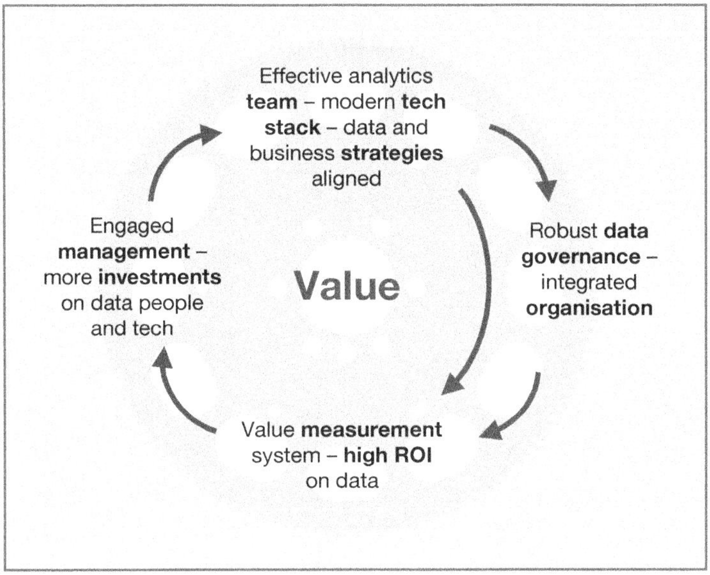

Figure 1.7 The Data Analytics Flywheel Effect: by applying the right pressure on what matters most, you can get the virtuous cycle to start

establish a robust data governance discipline apparent and desirable. A trusted data analytics team, well integrated with the rest of the organisation, eliminates the need for shadow analytics organisations, redirecting the resources coming their way onto the central analytics programme.

As the flywheel gains momentum, a simple but convincing value measurement system can provide evidence of the material return of investing in data analytics. This visible initial success secures management engagement and triggers more investments in data people and tech.

This investment, in turn, fuels the continuous improvement of the analytics team and technology stack, leading to even better data governance and greater value generation. Once the Flywheel Effect is set in motion, it could potentially continue indefinitely, creating a sustainable and self-perpetuating system for substantial value creation in data analytics, as Figure 1.7 portrays.

The existence of the Flywheel Effect is a message of hope: organisations can escape the vicious cycle of insufficient resources and misalignment and instead foster a culture of sustainable, data-driven growth.

The golden checklist on data value

In the end, what matters in business is sustainable value creation. This is why our journey in Data Transformation began with envisioning and framing value at various levels (capability, competitive, industry and strategic), pre-empting both the promises and risks that lie before us.

As for every chapter of the book, let's review a checklist of key items to consider.

- Reflect on how your current (or desired) data capabilities align with the descriptive, predictive and prescriptive analytics framework. Now, ponder over your critical business operations or existing challenges: can you map out a continuum of data capabilities for each, spanning all three analytics levels?
- In the context of your industry and competitive landscape, identify the ongoing or imminent 'collisions' between traditional and digital operating models. What transformations are unfolding, and which do you anticipate might occur shortly?
- We're living through the '20 years' when data and AI progressively enter our companies, similar to what happened during the electrification of plants. Are you ready to change the operating model of your company? Or do you feel that you are just applying new data technologies on the 'old' operating model, without reconsidering the way things are done?
- Considering the data flywheel model, which specific components of the wheel are 'rusty' today in your company and might be stopping the flywheel from kicking in?

During this first stage of our journey, we have explored how data and algorithms can be utilised in a company to create genuine business value. In the upcoming chapter, we will delve into the Data Transformation process, which will show us how to achieve this goal.

CHAPTER 2
MASTERING THE DATA TRANSFORMATION PROCESS

> **In this chapter**
>
> - What is a data (and analytics) strategy? How can you design one?
> - What are the most common pitfalls when approaching a Data Transformation journey?
> - How can we approach a Data Transformation process in a simple, effective and robust way?

'Data-driven', 'Powered by AI', 'Data-centric', 'AI-driven': these buzzwords adorn mission statements and press releases of companies eager to showcase their commitment to leveraging data to create business value.

The journey ahead of us requires us to move beyond mere corporate declarations. Our goal is to 'transform' the very way a company operates, with data serving as the driver of this transformation. A **Data-Driven Transformation** is more than just implementing new technologies; it means rethinking how a company operates, with data and algorithms taking a central role in driving change.

Such a transformation is not a tactical move but a strategic shift and necessitates deliberate planning and execution. This is why we will start this chapter by establishing a solid foundation for a successful data strategy. Then, we will delve into actionable steps to translate such a strategy into a practical, executable plan.

Crafting a winning data strategy

Data, analytics and AI strategy topics have attracted much interest recently. As you can see in Figure 2.1, especially as of 2022, companies are enquiring

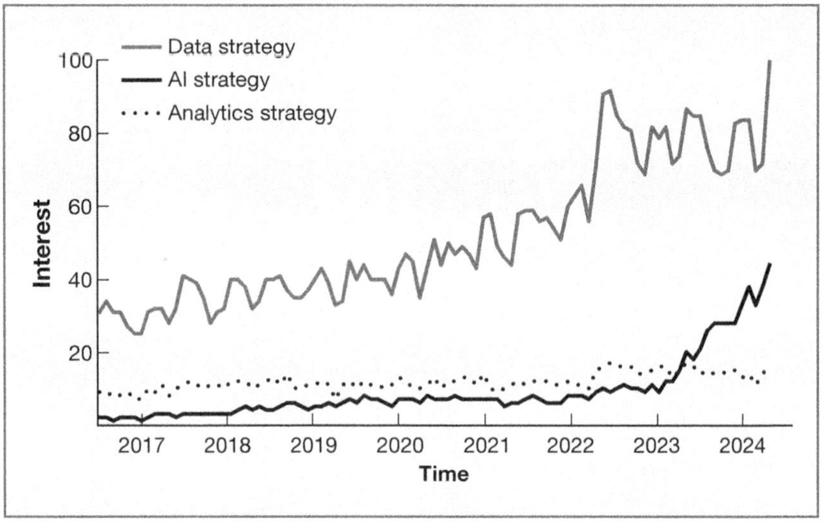

Figure 2.1 Google Search worldwide interest over time for the terms 'data strategy', 'analytics strategy' and 'AI strategy'. The interest index represents a relative measure of the number of searches of specified keywords

about ways to build a data strategy and, more recently, they are crafting AI strategies as well.

A fictional, but realistic, example will help us grasp such needs better.

Paulina leads uTrip, a burgeoning start-up with the compelling mission of offering 'unforgettable experiences that turn travellers into locals'. Through a sophisticated digital ecosystem encompassing mobile app, website and APIs, her team connects travellers with authentic local events and hidden gems advertised by local groups.

The start-up revenue streams are multiple: the local sellers can buy targeted advertising, leverage on-platform secure payment options, and host catalogues of cross-selling products or services, while travellers can opt-in for advanced services like exclusive events access, priority bookings and subscription programme perks.

Despite the platform's success in terms of expanding user base and positive customer feedback, Paulina is concerned about the sustainability of their growth in the face of potential competition from larger digital companies. This concern prompts her to call an urgent strategy meeting with her leadership team: Tim, the technology and operations chief; Annette, the finance chief; and Hong, the marketing chief. The team has previously celebrated their holistic success, pleasing customers and investors alike and envisioning optimistic growth scenarios. Yet, they share Paulina's concerns and are eager to explore new strategies to maintain their competitive edge.

The discussion quickly turns to how uTrip can further differentiate itself. Recognising that mere technology and financial resources are no longer definitive advantages, the team considers leveraging their rich data on travel patterns, local events and user demographics to offer even more personalised and unique experiences. They brainstorm ways to use this data to suggest tailored travel experiences, to improve the quality and success of local events and to introduce new services that could also serve as additional revenue streams.

The meeting ends on an optimistic note, realising that their data has significant untapped potential. However, as Paulina ponders the day's conversations, she asks herself: why is the company strategy not encompassing data and its usage as one of the core pillars already? Do they have the right technology, skills and people in place? Do they have the right mindset? Or do they need a new strategy? She clearly sees a new priority: it is time to talk about uTrip data strategy.

Before diving into the data and analytics specifics, it is worth discussing and aligning on what sits at the top of the data strategy, which typically is the business strategy.

Defining strategy

Exploring the precise definition of a business strategy proves to be a complex endeavour, as it encompasses many facets and frameworks that have evolved and been extensively debated since the dawn of the 20th century.

For many, the cornerstone of the definition of business strategy has been set by Alfred Chandler in his 1962 book *Strategy and Structure*. In this book, he defined strategy as 'the determination of the basic long-term goals and objectives of an enterprise, and the adoption of courses of action and the allocation of resources for carrying out these goals'. By embracing this definition, we can see the business strategy as a set of choices to help us achieve our business goals. Also, Michael E. Porter, author of the 1979 seminal management book *Competitive Strategy: Techniques for Analysing Industries and Competitors*, says that a company creates sustainable competitive advantage by 'deliberately choosing a different set of activities to deliver unique value'.

Interestingly, by tying business strategy to making choices, we also tightly link it to making decisions (in this case, strategic decisions). And enhancing decision making is typically one of the data and analytics goals and objectives.

To better explore what business strategy is and how it is set, we will rely on a framework that perfectly combines simplicity and effectiveness, developed in one of the largest and oldest corporations in the consumer goods industry, Procter & Gamble (P&G). The P&G business strategy framework is represented as an integrated cascade of choices articulated around five interrelated questions:

1 **What is your winning aspiration?** These are the long-term goals you have captured in your vision and mission statements.
2 **Where will you play?** This means identifying the right playing field, i.e., what the product or service categories, the consumer segments, the geographies and the channels you want to focus and compete in are.
3 **How will you win?** This refers to the right way you would like to win, including your value proposition and competitive advantage.
4 **What capabilities must be in place?** This helps establish the set and configuration of the capabilities we need to implement to win in the decided way.
5 **What management systems are required?** This is the ensemble of necessary systems, structures and measures to support our choices.

To complete our strategic definition, we must go across all of them and verify that the choices made in each step support the ones above. This way of defining a business strategy can be seen as a cascaded set of choices, in which we will define what we want to do and what we don't, that comes to life with an iterative process: as you uncover insights at one stage in the cascade, you may need to revisit choices made elsewhere in the cascade.

Moreover, this approach can be replicated in complex organisations at multiple hierarchical levels (business units, functions, markets) in a nested process, where interdependencies are considered and exploited to reach a shared set of goals. As an example, the company level of where to play choices will influence the sector and, therefore, the category level and brand level choices.

Now that the concept of business strategy is more concrete, we can discuss what a data strategy entails while keeping in mind what we have learned thus far from a business perspective. Once again, we are embedding the framework within the realm of data analytics and aiming to identify long-term objectives, determine where to play, how to win and establish the necessary capabilities and management systems in a crucial area that not only enables the company's business strategy but also provides a competitive edge.

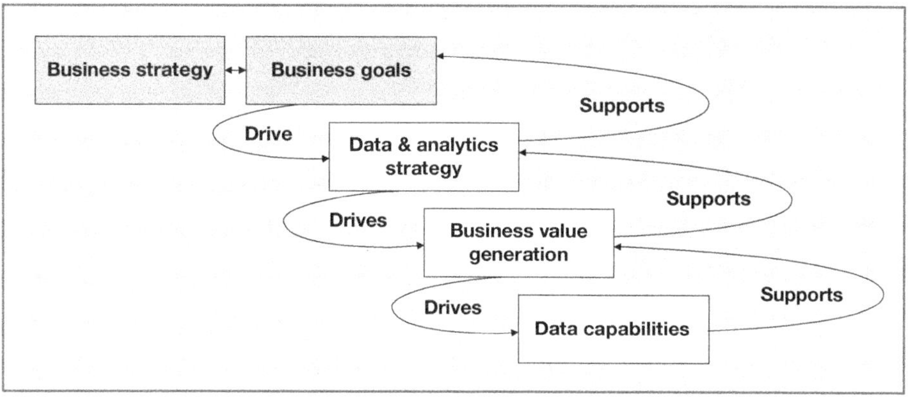

Figure 2.2 Interdependencies between business strategy and data & analytics strategy

As represented in Figure 2.2, the role of a data, analytics and AI strategy is to serve and support the business goals that the business strategy has set. To achieve this, it must generate business value via data capabilities (that we will better define later). Similarly, we can look at the diagram from bottom to top. Every data capability will have to generate value that supports the **data and analytics strategy** in helping to meet the business goals defined in the business strategy. It should be straightforward now that we cannot even start talking about the data strategy if we are not clear about our overall business strategy or the part of it we would like to support. Starting the journey without a clear business strategy would be like sailing the open sea with no compass.

In the following paragraphs, we will discover how to build a Data Transformation plan that feeds a data and analytics strategy.

Before getting into the process, it is essential to understand that if we do not move with a strategy in mind, we risk getting off on the wrong foot.

False Starts and how to avoid them

When it comes to data, analytics and AI, companies often consider themselves to be 'late to the party' in terms of adoption and maturity. This is a perception that the hype around these words has created.

Our impatience may become unhealthy when the risk level of our choices gets compromised by the search for immediate returns, moving away from the long-term focus. When we add to this context the general euphoria that today accompanies the emergence of AI in the business world, it is easy to imagine that the odds of this scenario have further increased.

Therefore, the prerequisite to our journey is to avoid any **False Starts** carefully, i.e. those initial choices made hastily and superficially that can undermine the company's Data Transformation journey. Luckily, the common mistakes that managers typically make at the beginning of their journey and the lessons they have painfully learned have been well captured in business literature. In the following paragraphs, we will recap a few of the most important ones.

Beware of starting with data acquisition

Beginning a Data Transformation journey with data acquisition is a common but misguided initial step. In an era of abundant data generation, the focus often shifts to collecting more or better data assuming that more data means better insights. However, this approach overlooks the crucial need for a strategic foundation outlining how data will create value.

How can we decide what data we need when we have not yet determined its use? Before embarking on acquisition, it's essential to define the objectives and applications of data in the business strategy. This ensures that data serves a purpose, aligning with specific business goals and avoiding the trap of becoming data-rich but value-poor.

The DIKW pyramid

'Where is the wisdom we have lost in knowledge? Where is the knowledge we have lost in information?' These lines from the poem 'Choruses' by T.S. Eliot are sometimes considered the origin of the DIKW pyramid, a well-known framework used to represent the relationships between data, information, knowledge and wisdom. Sitting at the bottom of the pyramid, raw *data* is useless per se. When we embed it within a relevant context, it morphs into *information*, gaining clarity and purpose. Further analysis and application within specific processes transforms this information into *knowledge* that lets us understand patterns, principles and trends. Knowledge, enriched by experience and applied judiciously, culminates in *wisdom*, the pinnacle of the pyramid, enabling us to make informed decisions and take actions that yield value. Our journey through Data-Driven Transformation is not merely about accumulating data but about ascending this pyramid.

Don't overinvest in technology at first

The subject of data is closely intertwined with technology; still, it should not be the starting point. When we discuss Data Transformation in a structured manner, we often start by consulting the heads of the IT function. However, owing to the background of those involved and a general bias towards tackling easier problems, there is a tendency to focus solely on the technology and infrastructure required to store and process corporate data. Although the technological infrastructure and data architecture are undoubtedly important in our Data Transformation journey, starting only from these choices can lead to premature and excessive investment in infrastructure without a clear understanding of the business's needs. After all, how can we determine our technology needs if we still need to determine what we want to achieve through the technology itself?

The risk we face is investing in a cargo plane when a boat would have sufficed, considering the specific requirements of the journey. Although a cargo plane could get the job done, the costs, time and organisational complexities of implementing an 'oversized' technology infrastructure can hinder our true objective: creating sustainable economic value through data. In essence, beginning with a focus on technology appears to be another False Start we must avoid.

Think twice before hiring armies of people

It is natural to feel ill-equipped when starting to work on a subject far from our primary area of expertise and training. Many companies begin the transformation journey by seeking external 'data experts'. However, how can we select the right individuals when we still need a clear vision of our objective? Is it possible that the current organisation already possesses some necessary skills? Moreover, even if we hire the right people, how can they effectively transform the company without first developing a deep understanding of existing processes and challenges?

Focusing first on resource acquisition may be a step towards simplifying the subject's complexities, but it sadly falls within the infamous list of False Starts for a Data Transformation journey.

Avoid thinking too small

Another potential misstep is to believe that Data Transformation only pertains to a single aspect, process or segment of the business organisation. Although it is sensible to make clear choices regarding the initial data activation initiatives (as we will see in a moment), we must not confine ourselves to thinking narrowly right from the start. The impact of Data Transformation permeates the entire company, affecting every individual in their way, and naturally transcends the boundaries of the IT department to influence processes, products and services without clear functional demarcations.

Data Transformation should be viewed instead as a comprehensive strategy that affects all business areas, requiring a holistic approach from the outset. This broader perspective ensures that initial successes in specific areas can scale and contribute to company-wide transformation, fostering a culture of innovation and data-driven decision making.

Be watchful of data zombies

Launching data projects with enthusiasm is commendable, but without a plan for long-term sustainability, these initiatives can become 'data zombies' - projects that start strong but soon fade into obsolescence, as the focus moves erratically to the next project to start. Ensuring each project has a clear path to ongoing value creation, with adequate resources for maintenance and scalability, is essential.

This requires a strategic approach to project selection, prioritisation and integration within business processes to ensure that data initiatives remain relevant and valuable over time. We should design and build every capability to stay sustainable over the long run, with clear ownership and accountability. If not, all the rest may be compromised.

All the False Starts have warned us about the risks involved in beginning our Data Transformation journey by focusing only on one aspect or ignoring some vital ones. This limited approach will jeopardise the search for a sustainable data strategy over time and long-term value creation. Having seen what 'not to do', now it is time to take action and analyse the steps needed to prepare an appropriate Data Transformation strategy.

The Data Transformation process

Before delving into the process that will guide us through Data Transformation, it is essential to reflect together on its three key characteristics:

- It is an **iterative** process. The complexity of the transformation we aspire for our organisation is incompatible with a rigid, linear approach. A traditional 'waterfall' design, consisting of distinct planning and execution phases, may seem simpler with established priorities, responsibilities and resources. However, in our case, it would inevitably lead to failure. Instead, we will adopt an iterative approach that allows for continuous re-evaluation and adaptation based on our discoveries. This balance between flexibility and structure will enable us to transform our company effectively and sustainably.
- It is a **progressive** process. While we may have a general idea of our destination, our journey will unfold in multiple stages. The transformation will gradually address cultural and organisational aspects, progressing through successive improvement steps. Together, we will utilise the Data Maturity Model tool, which will help us assess our current level and focus on the next step, ensuring that our attention remains solely on the upcoming phase.
- It is **focused on deliverables** or, in other words, 'what is produced'. Before embarking on any endeavour, it is crucial to have a clear understanding of our desired outcome. Although this may seem obvious, many False Starts occur when this fundamental rule is overlooked. It is easier to initially consider 'who should do it' by delegating the complexity to others or 'how it should be done' by focusing on acquiring expertise, technology and data. However, it is essential to always begin with 'what' we want to achieve, the specific deliverables we aim for and the business value they will generate. This approach strongly aligns with our operational objectives throughout the transformation process.

So, if we want a sustainable Data Transformation, we must focus on an iterative, progressive process that always targets concrete deliverables. The path that this book proposes to you tries to fulfil all these requirements and consists of the following steps.

1 Selection of the **big bets**, i.e. a handful of initial projects aimed at exploiting data (we will call them **data capabilities**) on which to focus. The term data capability in this context stands for a specific recipe of data use or, phrased

differently, an established use case. Each capability will be defined essentially by what it will produce in practice.

2 Planning the **enablers**, i.e. those more systemic aspects (mostly technological, organisational and cultural) that transform the company and prepare it to create and amplify the impact of data analytics in the business.
3 Execution and continuous monitoring of the **activation** of data analytics projects, i.e. the 'implementation' of all our efforts, focusing on business value and the direct impact on the profit and loss account.
4 Maturity check and strategy update (**replan**), which 'closes the circle', i.e. allows progress to the next level of ambition and reviewing priorities according to new conditions.

In Figure 2.3, you will find a representation of the path in front of us: an initial phase of strategic planning (big bets and enablers) is followed by a series of iterations alternating between execution and updating of the plan, gradually leading us to increasing levels of maturity.

This book is designed to take you through the four stages of the process by providing a series of tools to help you comfortably drive each step and the entire process itself. A preview of the diverse tools we will introduce and how they can help us is given below.

The big bets identification and selection phase will be a collaborative (and hopefully entertaining) process involving a multifunctional idea generation workshop (**Ideation Workshop**). It will be complemented by an analysis tool for classifying the most promising ones and prioritising them (**Selection Matrix**). Those ideas selected and prioritised will then be explored in all their most relevant aspects thanks to another analysis tool (**Data Activation Canvas**) that will force us to come up with the right questions at the right time to make our ideas actionable and sustainable.

Therefore, we will have to naturally move on to another area of strategic planning that will help our big bets come to life and thrive: the **enablers**. We will start the enablers' discussion with the analytical toolbox to familiarise ourselves with the art of the possible in terms of algorithms, better exploring the area of AI and machine learning. We will see each algorithm with its peculiarities (**algorithm selection**) and **trade-offs**. Next to algorithms sits the data, intended as both content and enabling technology: we will go through different architectural models for organising and managing data (**data architecture**)

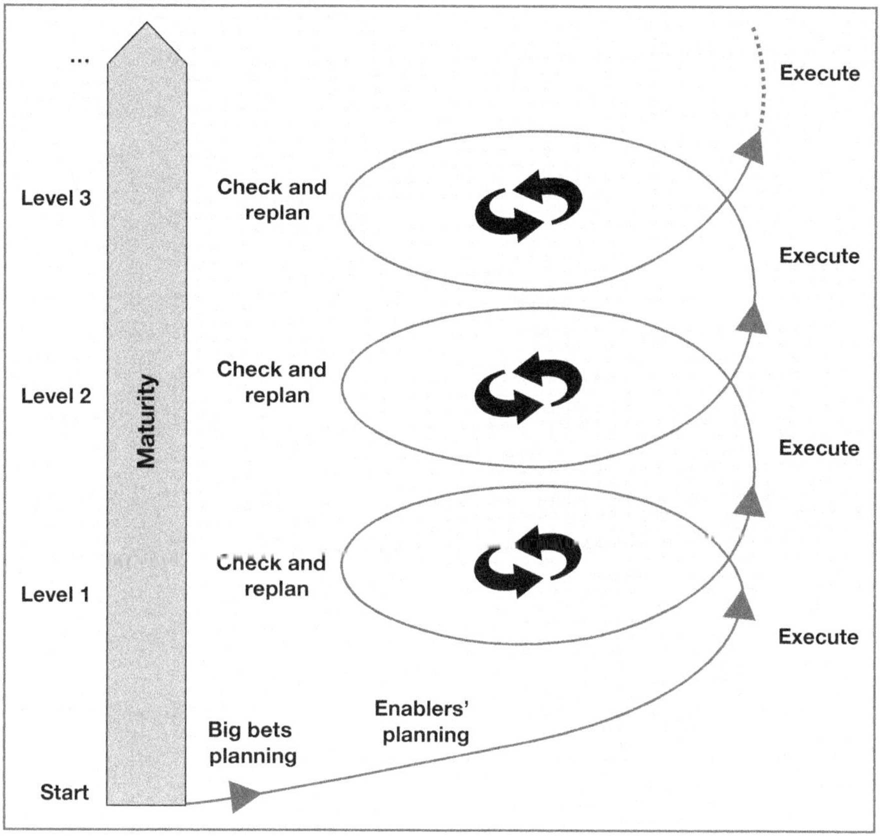

Figure 2.3 The iterative and progressive Data Transformation process. A continuous improvement mindset and disciplined application to current status will help us move across levels

and understand the 'stack' of technologies required to deliver against our business needs.

The other critical enabling factor is people or, better said, personnel organisation. We will analyse the various profiles of professionals required, and their respective competencies (**data roles and skills**). We will review some alternative models of organisational structure so that we can choose the right one for our company (**organisational model**). Finally, we will explore a critical topic, which is effectively managing our data (**data governance**). This will help us balance key aspects such as discipline and agility while keeping value central to our efforts. We will discuss an efficient framework to ensure this becomes more than just a tick-the-box exercise leading to disengagement and failure, as, unfortunately, we often experience.

Once all this is reviewed, an entire chapter will focus on the loop closure regarding execution, tracking and following through your transformation journey. Using a comprehensive tool devoted to measuring your current standing and designing the action plan to move to the next level (**Data Maturity Model**), we will streamline the way forward to define sustainable and continuous progress towards our company's objectives. While doing so, we will also take the opportunity to evaluate ways of working and change management aspects that may foster or hinder your journey.

Our promise, as authors, is to equip you with these tools. It will be your responsibility to determine if and which ones to utilise based on your situation. Examining each of these aspects will provide you with a better understanding of the unique characteristics of your company, which only you can truly comprehend and, therefore, leverage for your unique strategy.

Now that we have reviewed the upcoming path, it is time to begin taking small steps forward. Our first focus should be generating highly valuable ideas to enhance our contribution to creating disproportionate business value.

Ideation: generating game-changing ideas

Choosing our big bets, or the significant opportunities we decide to pursue first, is crucial to ignite our Data Transformation. It is easy to fall in love with ideas that either set unattainable goals or are not challenging enough to make a significant impact. Starting on the wrong foot puts us at serious risk of losing the momentum for change and the support and enthusiasm of those around us, jeopardising the entire journey. To mitigate this risk, in the following chapter, we will approach this decision-making process through four steps: conception, selection, planning and description.

The first step, the **Ideation Workshop**, aims to conceive a wide range of possible ideas for exploiting data, analytics and AI to generate value in the company. This phase should, by nature, be divergent and collaborative. We do not want to bring in structured thinking or constraints, but want to avoid filtering out possible outstanding or groundbreaking opportunities.

It is also vital that we approach this step of the process with a proper multifunctional mindset. Here, we look for diverse experiences and ways of thinking to surface opportunities in areas that may still need to be discovered or clarified to the entire audience. For this purpose, we should gather some colleagues with different areas of expertise and responsibility. For more structured companies, a good choice may be the heads of the various business functions, i.e. the leadership team. For a start-up, we can invite the entire team. This cannot be a siloed exercise, otherwise the output may be biased or narrowed. Whatever you choose, you must ensure that you have enough diversity in the group to achieve a broad and divergent range of ideas.

Before discussing our methodology, it's important to address whether generative AI could enhance or even substitute a traditional Ideation Workshop. Although large language models can indeed spark ideas and simulate some expert functions, the actual value of a workshop lies in its ability to contextualise your unique situation, fostering the creation of ambitious 'moonshot' ideas. This process enhances shared understanding and empathy, crucial for successful change management. Thus, in our experience, generative AI should be seen as a complementary tool, augmenting rather than replacing the human-centric dynamics of ideation.

Back to our workshop, this step in our process is borrowed from the problem-solving methodology called 'design thinking', which is particularly suitable for complex problems and, as in our case, targets innovative solutions. As you often do in design thinking workshops, you must equip the participants with coloured pens and Post-it notes. It will be important to encourage everyone to express any idea, even if they are outlandish or may sound unfeasible. Every idea will bring value to the creative process, and no one involved in the exercise must feel 'judged' or diminished. The ideas generated by each participant individually will be briefly described on a slip of paper and posted in random order on a wall to form a creative base on which to build.

But what do we mean by the term 'idea' in this context? The ideas we are targeting here refer to 'data activation scenarios', i.e. ways in which, through data, analytics and AI, we can impact the way we operate, our products or services or the entire market we play in. At this stage, it is recommended to make optimistic assumptions about what we have at our disposal: we can imagine having resources we do not have yet, like technology or data, being able to use algorithms in a way that seems 'magic' or to control all operational aspects of the impacted business processes effectively.

We are invited to dream big and imagine that anything is possible; we will only come to terms with reality at later stages. On Post-it notes, then, we can write simple or bizarre phrases such as 'I want to predict my orders arrival to increase my service level, therefore delight my customers' or 'I want to offer the most effective assortment recommendations to my customers to maximise my sales' or 'I want to predict if any component of my production line will break in the next 24 hours, to prevent production stop, therefore save costs' or even 'I want to predict if any of my key team members will leave the company in the next 12 months, to reduce risks to my business continuity'.

Although the generation of these ideas does not necessarily have to follow a specific structure, it is helpful to brief or equip each participant with a simple outline, reproduced in Table 2.1. This outline comprises a series of questions

Table 2.1 Opportunities for data-driven value creation. These questions can facilitate our ideation process

Dimensions of exploration	Levers	Example of questions
Impact on the profit and loss account	Maximising revenues	Can I make my products/services more attractive using data and algorithms? Can I improve my customers' experience to increase their loyalty? With data, can I increase my customer/user base?
	Minimising costs	What are the main expenditure items? Can I minimise the use of company resources thanks to the data available? Can I minimise the risk of costly events (waste, damage, theft, fraud)?
	Optimising processes and decisions	Which decisions have the most substantial impact on my profit and loss account? Can I ensure the most value-added processes are equipped with best-in-class data and algorithms to optimise my decisions systematically? Can I speed up the decision-making process by making it data-based?
Types of data analytics	Descriptive analytics	Can I use data analytics to better understand what is happening? Do I know the reasons behind the most significant changes in my business results?
	Predictive analytics	Can I anticipate market trends? Can I predict my competitors' next actions? Can I predict consumer/user reactions to my next moves?
	Prescriptive analytics	Can I use algorithms to 'tell me what to do?' Can I systematically increase the ROI of my investments by optimising my choices? Can I replace some of the more repetitive decisions with an algorithm?

Corporate functions	Marketing	How can I focus my communication towards the most likely consumers? Can I connect my message to the individual consumer's needs through data and algorithms? How can I help my product better respond to unspoken user/consumer needs?
	Sales	Can I improve the purchase and consumption experience by making it personalised? Can I dynamically optimise the price of my services and products using available data? Can I optimise my presence in the desired channels, minimising time or human intervention?
	HR	How can I accelerate the professional growth of my employees by analysing their behaviour? Can I predict their performance and identify top talent? Can I use data to support my employee retention strategy?
	Finance	Can I automate accounting processes? Can I predict raw material costs? Can I optimise my investments by analysing the market in real time?
	Logistics	Can I minimise inventory and increase my service levels by accurately anticipating future demand? Can I optimise the routing of my goods by accurately anticipating traffic?
	PR/ Communication	Can I analyse my social presence in real time and quickly identify risks to my image? Can I automatically assess my brand's reputation with the public? Can I use data to support my sustainability commitments?
	Legal	Can I organise digital legal documents and make their access more usable through algorithms? Using available historical data, can I accurately assess risks and opportunities for legal action?
	Production	Can I prevent breakdowns on the production line by managing maintenance operations using algorithms? Can I minimise my consumption of energy and environmental resources by using sensors and algorithms? Can I maximise the quality of my products by intercepting defects using algorithms?
	IT	Can I prevent or identify cyber-attacks in real time by analysing the traffic on my servers? Can I use algorithms to automatically catalogue, harmonise and remove database duplications?

that allow one to explore in a transversal manner the many directions of opportunities for value creation thanks to data. This outline will inspire the ideation phase, encouraging each person's creativity to wander in directions that had been little explored up to that point.

The first dimension in the framework should be obvious to anyone: business value, particularly the economic impact on the company's business results. This translates into ideas that should help improve or generate revenues, reduce costs, optimise processes and decisions, or improve long-term positioning of company value, e.g. accretive to reputation or brand equity.

The second dimension is also known to us, as we familiarised ourselves with it in Chapter 1. It is represented by the three types of analytical capabilities that data and algorithms can make available to us: descriptive, to understand the past better; predictive, to anticipate the future; and prescriptive, to advise on actions and decisions to be taken by our team or autonomously by the algorithm.

The last dimension is the classical functional areas most of the companies are organised into: from marketing and sales to IT, from production and planning to legal, every business function will be able to benefit from the use of data and algorithms to support the activities under its responsibility. Please note that each participant is called to 'break silos' and explore any functional areas beyond their respective area of responsibility and expertise to ideate as good ideas as they can. Any bridge across multiple functional areas is welcome but also natural if we consider that many breakthrough ideas will impact multi-functional processes and established ways of working.

You can look at the framework as a cockpit, where each dimension of exploration represents a different block of levers you may play according to the type of questions (and challenges) that resonate the most with your situation. You can (and should) improve this ideation model by adding other dimensions that may be relevant to you, such as business units split or product lines split with their related essential questions, to make your cockpit uniquely tailored to your situation and highly relevant to your challenges. You can leverage AI-generated content again to include new questions that may capture external trends or dynamics you would like to keep in mind for your participants.

Once finalised, you can make this inspirational table available to workshop participants to help them in this first brainstorming phase run in 'solo mode'.

Once the ideas have been generated, written and posted on the wall, each participant will be encouraged to look at the other ideas and, if they believe them worthy, to enrich the wall with additional Post-its.

After this cross-inspiration step, the ideation phase is over, and it will have resulted in a series of coloured Post-it notes containing a headline description of a certain number of ideas, even outlandish ones, generated by several people on their own.

Selection: identifying your big bets

We are now staring at the giant wall of Post-it notes we generated – a large number of ideas on the possible usage of data and analytics to create value in the company. How do we select the most promising, or, better said, the right ones on which to focus? First, we need to simplify the list by grouping ideas that are very similar or represent different aspects of the same data activation scenario.

Let us use a few examples to explain how this works. If one Post-it note contains the idea of predicting orders to serve customers better and another suggests using real-time traffic data to optimise customer delivery service, we could bundle them under a single 'umbrella' idea that can take an appealing name such as '*smart customer logistics*'. Organising these two Post-it notes under the same group is legitimate since they both use data to dynamically manage the delivery operations so that the level of service improves versus the current one. Let us imagine an analytical tool that combines the same data, both likely internal and external, to optimise the delivery preparation and the execution while measuring the results.

The delta between the new service level and the existing one can be directly associated with the new capability, and the business value created could be expressed in terms of incremental orders fulfilled, reduction of missed or mismanaged orders or increased customer loyalty (or maybe the three of them). Another example: the Post-it note that refers to the idea of effective assortment recommendations to customers may be joined with the one talking about better customer promotional activities and the one suggesting a breakthrough in store activities execution under the name of '*customer sales booster*'.

The objective is to match, combine and elevate the ideas to generate bigger ones that could impact value generation more or fit better into the company's decision processes. To do that, we will proceed in this 'grouping' activity as a team, perhaps detaching and reattaching Post-its according to their 'affinity'. We will eventually obtain a better-organised structure, an **affinity diagram**. It consists of macro-ideas, i.e. more or less 'homogeneous' groups of ideas that we can use to classify and select our big bets.

To proceed to the selection of our big bets, we must look at each macro-idea about two fundamental dimensions, namely value impact and ease of implementation.

1 The first dimension is the potential value the idea can generate, i.e. its **impact**. At this stage, of course, we will not yet have all the elements to make a precise estimate: we will use the judgement, experience and common sense of the multifunctional team of people we have involved. To assess the impact we expect from each macro, we can ask questions such as: how much direct value would it generate? How much would it save? Would my colleagues' lives be made easier by it? How many in the company would benefit from it? Would it apply to many products/services, or would it only be helpful for a specific case? Could this idea be reapplied by more business units/departments/markets? In short, how scalable is its intrinsic value proposition? In the best case, we will also get an initial estimate and translation of this financial impact. If it is not possible yet, this is not to be considered a barrier to proceed. We can confidently proceed to arrange the various ideas on a scale from the lower end, where we will find the ideas that would impact a minimal part of my business, to the upper back, where there will be ideas that would positively upset our profit and loss account.
2 The other dimension we want to capture is the **ease** with which we estimate we could implement our idea. This feature covers many aspects (like feasibility, costs, time, process fit, risks, etc.) that we will only be able to properly explore in breadth in the later stages of planning. At the moment, however, it is sufficient to make an initial thought assessment that also, in this case, helps us to arrange our ideas in order of ease of implementation. Several questions can guide us through this step: how much would it cost to implement this idea? How much time is likely necessary, and how many people will need to be involved? From a technological point of view, is it feasible? Can we anticipate any risks that might limit its success or adoption? Do we have any experience in this area, i.e. have we already done something similar in the past? In line with what we did in the impact assessment, we also

have to sort our list of ideas by ease for this dimension. At the bottom, we will find the most ambitious ideas that seem almost impossible or at least very complicated to us. In contrast, at the top, we will find ideas that, at first sight, seem easily implementable.

To better understand this critical step, let us take a practical example.

Here is the context: we are assisting a friend with a flourishing bakery chain in our city. The chain has rapidly expanded to include several shops and labs, offering delicious, fresh delicacies beloved by customers. Recently, our friend sought advice on leveraging data and analytics for further growth, leading us to brainstorm and evaluate several promising ideas.

As the first idea, we propose installing a people counter device at each shop's entrance to track customer flow throughout the day. This data will help optimise staff scheduling for peak and off-peak times. The required two way counters are easily obtainable online and can be installed quickly across all locations. After collecting a few weeks' data, we'll analyse patterns using simple spreadsheets to adjust staff levels accordingly, ensuring efficiency throughout the week.

This idea, '*the people counter*', ranks high in terms of ease. The investment required is modest, and the technology involved is readily available. The associated risks are reasonably manageable. The main outcome will be cost optimisation, reducing unnecessary staffing costs while ensuring excellent customer service. Although the value impact can be sizeable, it will not significantly transform the company.

Now, let us explore a more ambitious idea: developing '*the mobile app*' for our bakery chain to enhance the customer experience digitally. This app will enable customer registration, tracking purchases, sending tailored offers and recommending new delicacies for special occasions. Implementing this idea requires significant investment in app development, cloud infrastructure, data storage and analysis. Additionally, integrating this system with our production schedule is crucial to maintaining our commitment to quality and freshness. Implementing our digital ecosystem, including the mobile app, will likely require partnering with a specialised company or consultant for design and setup. The project's timeline could extend from several months to over a year. Once operational, additional time will be needed to grow the app's user base and gather sufficient data for the algorithm to learn customer preferences.

This ambitious project aims to enhance customer loyalty by integrating our bakery's value proposition with innovative digital services, a move yet to be matched by competitors. It promises to boost sales per customer and attract new ones, positively affecting revenue. While 'the mobile app' potential impact significantly surpasses that of 'the people counter', it ranks considerably lower in terms of implementation ease. It is way more costly, time-consuming, and carries a greater risk of failure.

Back to our process: having our ideas sorted in terms of both impact and ease, we can proceed with the identification of our big bets using the **Selection Matrix** tool.

To build our Selection Matrix, we just need to draw a Cartesian diagram like the one in Figure 2.4. Our vertical axis will represent the impact: the ideas at the top are the very impactful ones, those having a considerable potential economic impact for our organisation; the ideas listed at the bottom are those that may

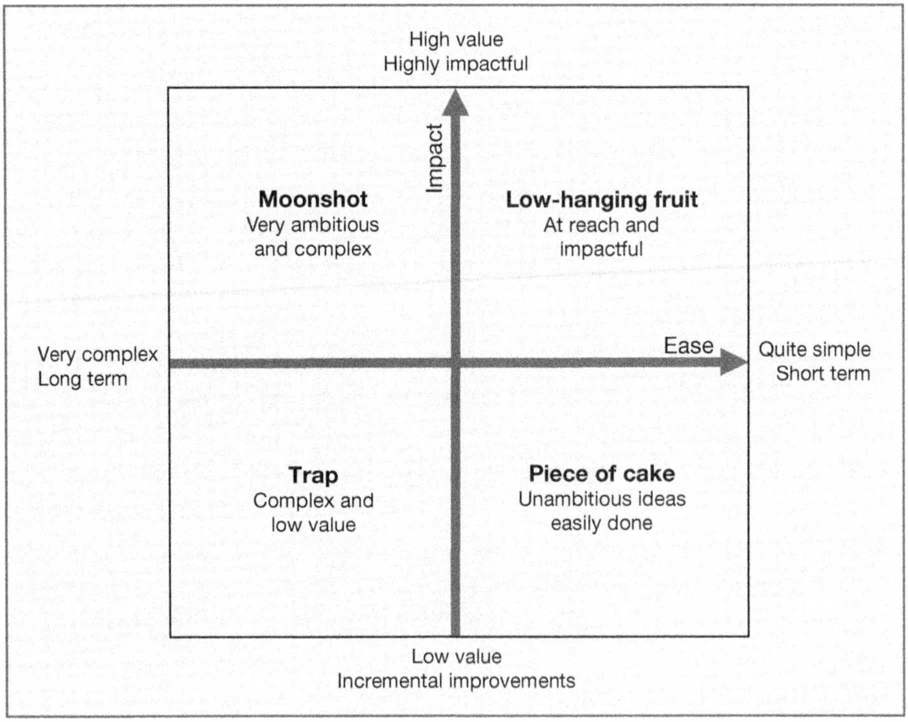

Figure 2.4 The Selection Matrix to be used for our big idea classification. Where would your idea fit in?

have a somewhat exciting nature but, overall, their impact is quite limited. By contrast, the horizontal axis will measure simplicity, which will grow as we move to the right: on the left, will be those ideas that are very complex, costly, risky and would take a long time to implement; on the extreme right, will be those ideas that seem easy and quick to put into practice.

In the above Selection Matrix, we can identify four fundamental quadrants:

- In the top right quadrant, we find ideas that are relatively simple to implement and have great potential. These are the **low-hanging fruits**, really handy ideas with very appealing impacts.
- In the bottom right quadrant, will be the small, easily implemented ideas with a more modest impact. They typically relate to more specific areas and, although they will not turn our business around, they can bring incremental benefits. They are a **piece of cake**, though we should ask ourselves whether they are worth the focus.
- In the top left quadrant, we have the ideas of the century or **moonshots**. They are very ambitious opportunities. They are challenging to pursue but capable of greatly benefiting our company. They touch the heart of the core business and have the potential to be used frequently and generate much value. However, the investment of time and money is considerable, the risk factors are high, and it is mandatory to carefully evaluate whether and when they will produce the expected returns.
- In the bottom left quadrant, we have those ideas that are difficult to implement and generate little economic value. These are possible **traps** to get stuck in, mammoth projects that may get stuck in a swamp, i.e. not have chances of scaling up, have an unclear value proposition or will not significantly impact on our operating model.

Prioritisation: putting your bets into a roadmap

The four quadrants in the Selection Matrix offer us an immediate set of considerations. The first one is that the low-hanging fruits quadrant represents a fascinating starting choice. We are not dealing with significant risks and this route is simple and full of potential. These ideas will also generate some quick enthusiasm and engagement, bringing more supporters to our journey.

The second consideration concerns the trap's quadrant: this is a stay-away area, and we should avoid it at all costs. Why should we embark on complex ventures when little economic return is expected?

The last consideration relates to ideas in the other two quadrants (pieces of cake and moonshots). In both cases, it is necessary to carefully evaluate the ROI on a case-by-case basis, as the dividing line between a successful choice and a significant disappointment is thin.

In fact, looking at our Selection Matrix, we can make a general point about the priorities to prefer. Figure 2.5 helps us better visualise the ideal progression we should follow. We start with the ideas at the top right point, since they are extremely simple to implement and have the highest ROI and move toward the bottom left end, where we imagine we will encounter the worst ideas, i.e. those that are extremely expensive to bring to life and will bring minimal benefits.

Along this path, we will encounter other ideas whose many nuances of costs and benefits must be carefully evaluated. As per the picture, we can imagine

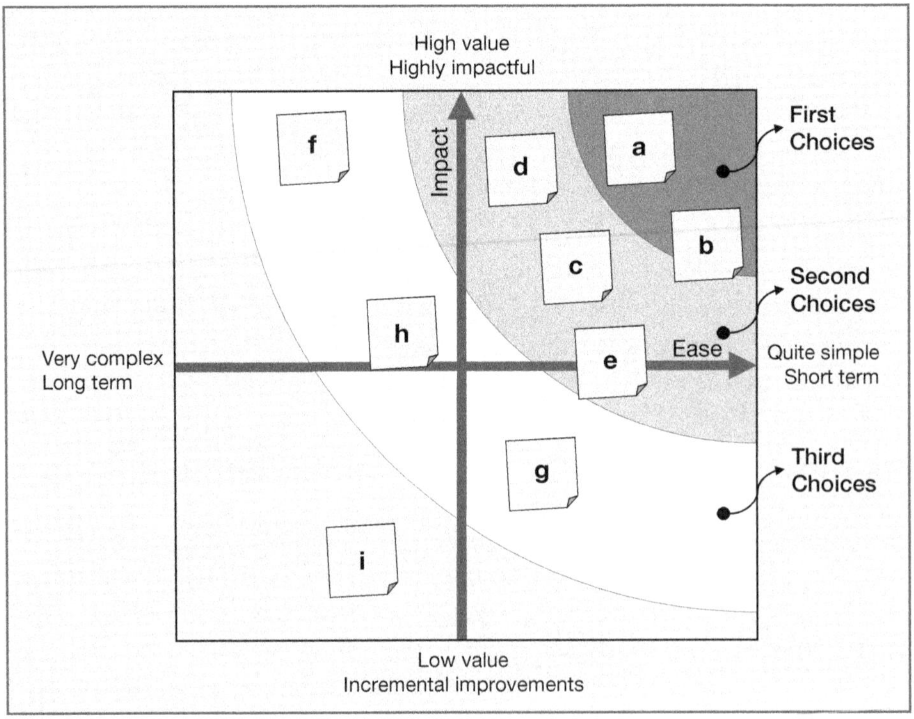

Figure 2.5 The ideas on the Selection Matrix. The most appealing ones will be in the top right-hand corner. Priority will drop towards the bottom left-hand corner

this path as organised 'waves', each delimited by concentric wavefronts and projecting from the upper right-end corner, the point of maximum benefit. Our 'primary choices' will be in the first small wave, and the progressively 'less appealing choices' will be in the larger and larger waves.

By using the Selection Matrix, we can now make an initial hypothesis on which are the big bets to start with and envision the rest of our potential journey or our very high-level roadmap.

It is worth starting our company's Data Transformation now from the low-hanging fruits. In fact, we may have even more potential ideas at our disposal, perhaps higher than the low-hanging fruit in terms of impact or perceived as more urgent from a business standpoint. The insidious risk of starting from these other ideas that are very impactful but require a higher investment and longer timeframes is to lose the momentum, getting bogged down in the quicksand of organisational frustration that comes from 'not seeing the results' of such a costly investment.

The advice is to start small with those ideas capable of impacting our business as much as possible in a short time and, consequently, create the appetite and euphoria to embark on more arduous undertakings progressively. Also, this will give us time to understand if the other ideas can be improved in terms of either value impact, ease or both. This wraps up step one of the preparations for our journey: now we have a shortlist of 'high potential' data use cases, ranked by priority, aligned with key stakeholders via a collaborative, multifunctional approach.

One final observation to note is that, despite the apparent simplicity of this initial stage, conducting a session with senior stakeholders and potential sponsors can be challenging for those who are unprepared or need more experience with the process. There are several risks to consider. For instance, participants may diverge too much, producing high-level and poorly articulated ideas that are difficult to assess. Effective grouping of ideas may also pose challenges, potentially leading to an overwhelming 'solve-it-all' approach that is hard to achieve. Additionally, there is a risk of failing to achieve the desired outcomes within the agreed-upon timeframe, which hinders collective creation and shared ownership of the results. The dynamics of the session may also be disrupted by certain participant behaviours, such as one person dominating the discussion or a lack of interaction within the group. These risks can jeopardise the credibility of the exercise and the promoter's credibility and potentially have negative consequences for the future of the transformation journey. Therefore, adequate preparation or seeking external support, such as that of an experienced, visionary leader, can help ensure the session's success and strengthen the team's trust in the chosen direction.

Before closing this chapter, let us go back to the approach Paulina and the uTrip team took regarding their data and analytics strategy. As an initial step, they have clarified and reinforced their business strategy, refining their priorities and articulating new goals, particularly in mitigating competitive threats and reinforcing their critical points of difference. Building upon this foundation, they engaged in brainstorming sessions to generate ideas on how new data capabilities can support their identified priorities. They could create ideas for eleven different capabilities that were then classified based on their potential for value creation and ease of implementation. Through this classification process, they identified and selected a few capabilities, their big bets, to prioritise and start focusing on. They also envisioned a potential roadmap for the months and years to come. They are significantly motivated to make their data, analytics and AI strategy a further growth engine to outcompete the market.

Now, it is time to introduce new tools and methodologies to help them explore each of these identified capabilities more deeply.

The golden checklist on Data Transformation process

There can only be a valid data and analytics strategy with a real understanding of business strategy and clarity on value generation. Our Data Transformation journey has now been framed and started. In this chapter, we reviewed the fundamental components to approach our Data Transformation journey correctly. Let us check on some fundamentals.

1 **Setting a winning data strategy**
   - Are we intimate with our business strategy?
   - Are we clear on how our data and analytics strategy will enable and augment it?
   - What value are we creating, and how does it fit in the broader company strategy scheme?

2 **Avoiding potential False Starts**
- Have we identified potential mistakes that could set back or derail our strategy and Data Transformation?
- Are we clear why starting from apparently straightforward decisions, such as initiating data provisioning, assembling teams, or overinvesting in technology, is not a winning choice?

3 **Understanding and initiating the Data Transformation process**
- Can we articulate how the Data Transformation process works? Why does it have to be iterative, progressive and outcome-oriented?
- What are the steps to bring the Data Transformation process to life?
- Can we ideate and identify our value-generating, winning ideas, a.k.a. big bets? Do we know how to run a multifunctional Ideation Workshop successfully?
- Can we classify, select and prioritise our big bets? Are we familiar with any tool that can facilitate this exercise, like the Selection Matrix?

We have completed the initial phase of the Data Transformation process. We now have established a preliminary set of significant initiatives or big bets. We are prepared to proceed to the next stage, which involves describing and converting them into actionable operational plans.

In this chapter, we focused on the breadth of thinking, encompassing the richness and complexity of our company needs and opportunities. The next chapter will introduce tools and methodologies to delve deeper into each idea, ensuring its alignment with our overarching goals.

CHAPTER 3
DESIGNING YOUR DATA BLUEPRINT

In this chapter

- What elements should be considered when defining a data capability?
- What analytics methods, data, technologies and skills are needed?
- How can one assess the overall value of the investment?
- What factors enable the 'implementation of the idea?' What can go wrong with them?

In his esteemed work *Lord of the Flies*, William Golding profoundly stated, 'The greatest ideas are the simplest'. This axiom holds even in the realm of grand and intricate ideas. The clarity and precision in articulating these ideas are paramount to unlocking their potential and achieving success.

This chapter aims to facilitate a comprehensive analysis and articulation of the critical data capabilities we have identified – our 'big bets' – through a structured, coherent and impactful approach. By leveraging a straightforward yet actionable framework, this guided process will enable us to concretise the components of data capability, delve deeply into each aspect, evaluate their business impact and devise a strategic plan for implementation if deemed sufficiently promising.

The idea's components description will not only be helpful to make it become a new company capability, but it will also give us the ingredients and requirements needed to support our entire company's Data Transformation process. Once the framework is implemented for our array of potential data capabilities, we will gain a comprehensive understanding of the necessary transformations (ranging from data acquisition to technology, from fostering a decision-making culture to organising human resources) that will facilitate the initial wave of big bets and, undoubtedly, numerous data activation initiatives in the future years.

The Data Activation Canvas model

The Business Model Canvas, developed by the Swiss researcher and entrepreneur Alexander Osterwalder, is a popular strategic planning tool that accompanies start-ups, entrepreneurs and managers.

We have adapted this tool to serve our Data Transformation journey: you will find the **Data Activation Canvas** illustrated in Figure 3.1. It follows the 'block-structured' approach of its more famous brother. It guides us to draw, i.e. analyse, design and document, the critical components of our data capability. Each empty box represents an invitation to think, analyse and describe one of the nine crucial components to be considered when planning each data capability.

To ensure the robustness and relevancy of the exercise, we should approach the Data Activation Canvas as a multifunctional effort involving the different

Data Activation Canvas	Name: ______ Owner: ______	Version: ______ Sponsor: ______
Value proposition	**Enablers**	
1 Activation scenario	2 Analytical methods	3 Data requirements
4 Scalability strategies	5 Business integration	6 Technology requirements
7 Revenue streams	8 Cost structure	
9 Law, biases and ethics		

Figure 3.1 Data Activation Canvas, our blueprint to define each data capability

skills available in our organisation to capture any aspect that may influence the success in the activation and growth of our data capability.

Before delving into each of the boxes of the Data Activation Canvas, let us focus on the frame and its vertical macro-blocks, that are splitting most of the Canvas into two halves: on the left, we find the 'value proposition' elements of the data capability, i.e. all these components that will help us answer the question: 'What will we achieve when the capability comes to life?'; on the right, we find the 'enablers', i.e. those factors needed to keep our value proposition promise, summarised by the question: 'What must occur to leverage this capability in its full effectiveness?'

While moving to the following paragraphs, a clarification: the numeration and sorting beside each Data Activation Canvas title box represents a recommended gradual path forward. It should also clarify upfront some aspects that may create a dependency on other boxes. Nothing prevents us from following a different sequence or from going back to previous boxes and reviewing them appropriately, considering what has been clarified and described in the following ones. This is, instead, a good practice.

After these premises, we are ready to explore our Data Activation Canvas, with a set of questions that will facilitate us in filling in each box.

1 Activation scenarios

The first and most important thing to secure for our data capability is ensuring it is applied and adopted to deliver its value. This means we should think about the circumstances in which we apply the data capability and in which data is put into action, generating an outcome.

To start with the right approach and mindset, let us begin with the end state in mind: we remove all the constraints coming from other boxes and, for a moment, avoid thinking about technology, data and organisation and visualise the capability in action. We will use the following groups of questions to describe the activation scenarios better.

- **What** business process are we impacting and how? What is the exact point of the operating model that will benefit from the data capability and what is the value it will bring? For example, if we are talking about improved decision making, what is the decision we are talking about? Which process is it part of? What is happening today? What would the alternatives be if the data were unavailable, or we did not implement the new data capability?

- **Who** is involved? Who will use this capability? In which function or department? How many users do we envisage once the adoption is established? What are the skills required to operate or exploit the capability? Sharpening our 'who' understanding will help us clarify the people we must involve in our design and implementation phase and, later, during the data capability lifecycle.
- **When** is it used? Does it imply a one-shot, an ad-hoc, or a recurrent usage? What is its frequency of usage? We can also use these questions to understand the non-functional requirements better and leverage them for optimised planning and cost balance.
- **How** is it used? How is the data capability interacting with the user(s) and vice versa? Will it have a user interface, e.g. an application interaction screen, a web page or a dashboard? Or will it not require any human interaction at all? Answering these questions will bring us ahead of the game and allow us to start thinking about technology, resources and skills to implement during and after our capability build.

Figure 3.2 quickly summarises of the four sections that help you explore your activation scenarios.

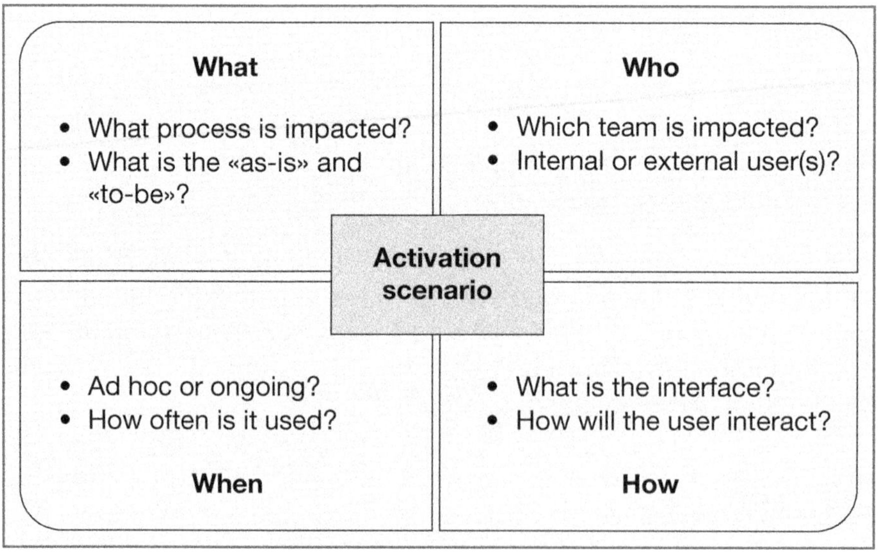

Figure 3.2 Identifying the activation scenario through a simple set of questions

We will use an example to get more acquainted with the process. Let us go back to our friend's bakery chain example we used in Chapter 2 and try to help him with a new idea: generate an automated 'daily menu of delicacies' leveraging data and algorithms to maximise the daily profit per store.

In this case, the process we would like to impact is the daily menu preparation of each bakery store (our **what**). Today, each store manager manually takes care of this within a prescribed assortment rotation established at the beginning of the week, considering the raw ingredients available. Tomorrow, this will be dynamically generated, using data and algorithms to consider each store-specific feature: historical sales, local inventory status, store position, points of interest around the store, demographic profile of the area, weather forecast and local and special events.

The new capability will target the bakery store manager, the pastry chef and the staff (our **who**), all of whom are internal users. It will be used once per day, the evening before, for the following day (**when**).

The menu recommendation will be shown to the pastry chef via a web app on a tablet or touchscreen monitor, where they can confirm or change some of the suggestions. The store manager will sign off the menu and confirm the daily novelties the bakery's customers will find the next day (**how**).

2 Analytical methods

Once the activation scenario of our data capability is clear, we can start thinking about how it should genuinely work from an analytical standpoint. In particular, we seek to understand what analytical methods should be applied within our data capability to generate the expected output. This step has critical implications for our choices for the several other boxes of the Data Activation Canvas, such as technology choices, data requirements and process integration needs. To understand and describe the analytical methods of our data capability, we can use a checklist in the form of the following three macro questions (see Figure 3.3):

- What **types of analytics** do we need to produce our output? As we have seen in Chapter 1, do we want to show, slice and dice what happened (*descriptive analytics*)? Are we interested in forecasting something or predicting possible outcomes (*predictive analytics*)? Should we recommend what to do or even let

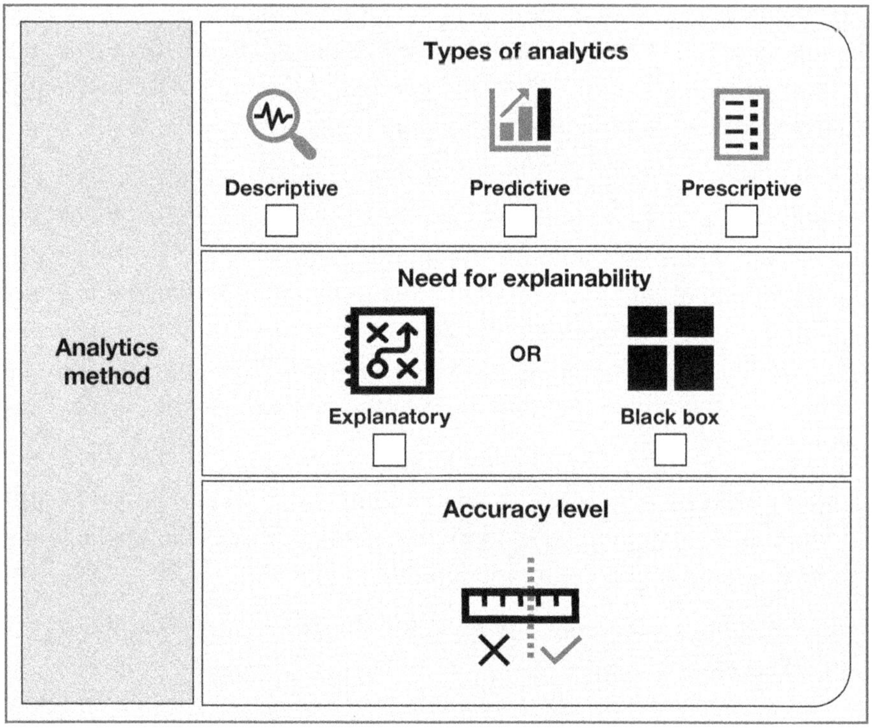

Figure 3.3 Checking the right elements that help define the analytics method required by our data capability

the machine make optimised decisions (*prescriptive analytics*)? Establishing our choices will avoid pitfalls in identifying the correct methodology and data requirements or choosing the proper architectural stack.

- Do the reasons for our output **need to be explainable** to a human user? When providing predictions or recommendations to a user, is there a chance they will need to know 'why' these were suggested (*explanatory model*)? Or is the best possible outcome from the recommendation most important, without the need to understand the underlying drivers (*black box model*)? Having a clear cut on this choice is paramount, given that timings, costs and other critical factors, such as the adoption of the overall capability, may be at stake.
- What level of **accuracy** is needed in this data capability? We are often tempted to answer this question: 'as much as possible' or 'totally accurate', forgetting the implications regarding both timings, cost and, sometimes, overall feasibility. We can look at this aspect by answering the following

question: what is the minimum level of accuracy that would justify the (build and) usage of this data capability? Accuracy very often has a counterbalance of complexity and time. Once the capability is established and successfully adopted, we will always have time to increase that accuracy to new targets and redefine our ambitions.

In our bakery example, we can approach the analytical method needs description as follows.

Our new daily menu of delicacies will predict our customers' demand to propose an automatically generated daily menu that maximises our store-level profit. As such, our **types of analytics** will be both predictive and prescriptive.

Given both the pastry chef and the bakery store manager are often busy, they do not **need to explain** the recommendations. They can revise and replace them according to their experience so that we can choose a black box model.

Defining **accuracy** requirements means understanding the current business scenario. Let us assume the current bakery delicacies production has an average percentage error of ±20 per cent. If our data capability helps bring this down to ±10 per cent, we make a significant difference by sensibly reducing waste or missed sales opportunities.

3 Data requirements

We are now approaching the data requirement box, which should help us understand what data we need and how we should obtain them to satisfy our activation scenario via our chosen analytical methods. Again, we will use a set of questions to guide the description of this box, organised in two macro areas: what is needed and how/where this is available, according to the need-availability model (see Figure 3.4).

- **Need → History:** what data do I need to describe my past or present? We use this data to describe and learn from events through descriptive analysis, statistical modelling or machine learning. When we think about historical data, we refer to business transactions associated with our operations (*transactional data*), variable events such as sales, orders, purchases, billings, registrations, web page visits, search history and more. However, we also need reference data (*master data*), which is more stable information collected to describe critical entities such as products, customers, suppliers, locations, employees,

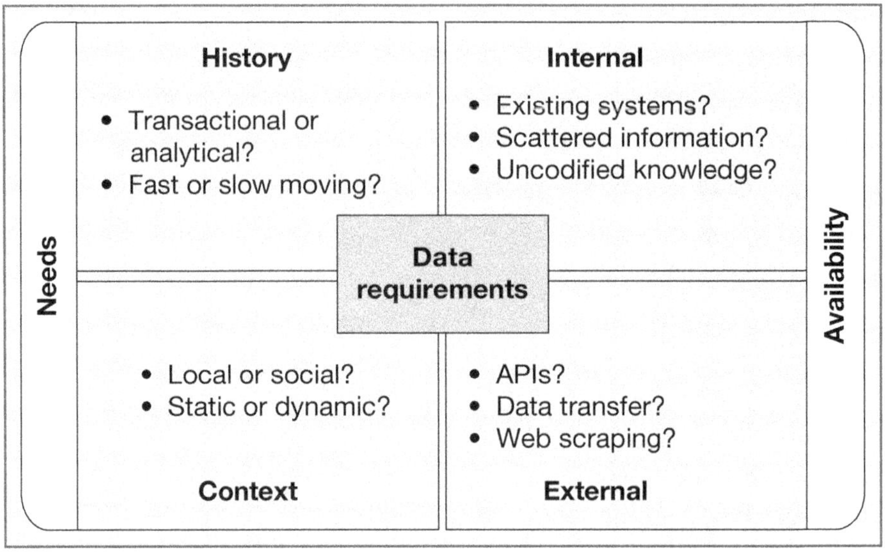

Figure 3.4 Defining data requirements through needs–availability model

etc. Another lens to consider is the logical level of data we need: transactional level data is granular, volatile and typically comes from transactional systems, like enterprise resource planning (ERP), customer relationship management (CRM), e-commerce websites, and many others. Another option is to use a more aggregated form of data (*analytical data*) already present in the company to drive strategic decision making, performance tracking, market research, or other forms of analysis.

- **Availability → Internal:** what data do we have within our internal environment? Much data is captured via the company IT ecosystem and may serve our purpose. In that case, it is essential to identify the source system and its owner and begin documenting the data's attributes (such as frequency, retention, latency and granularity) and the available options for accessing them securely. Furthermore, our data may not be confined to a single system but dispersed across multiple systems, necessitating its integration, transformation, and blending to ensure it is usable for our objectives. Additionally, valuable information might not yet be digitised and may require a more structural approach.
- **Need → Context:** what data enables us to understand the context in which we operate? How can we account for external factors that may impact our business? Acquiring contextual data that captures ongoing activities and

accurately describes our operational environment is extremely valuable. Such data may include local environmental descriptions (such as geographical information or points of interest near a specific location) and social dimensions (such as socio-demographic indicators). When analysing this data, it's also important to consider whether it is stable or dynamic. For instance, dynamic contextual data, like the fluctuating number of pedestrians near a store at different times, can significantly influence customer footfall. Conversely, more static contextual factors, like the socio-demographic composition of a neighbourhood near an insurance agency, may not change rapidly but still profoundly affect the policies favoured by customers in each area.

- **Availability → External:** how will we access data that is not yet available internally and is necessary to enhance our data capabilities? With a vast array of data accessible externally, how can we ensure this data will always be available on time and meet our requirements? To address this concern, we need to assess the accessibility of the data, which may depend on the data provider.

  We can consider three primary methods: first, programmatic access via **application programming interfaces (APIs)**, which allows us to retrieve data as needed; second, a data transfer protocol, where the data producer makes the data available for us in a secured space; and third, web scraping, which involves using programmatic scripts or automated tools to extract content from websites for further use. While web scraping may seem an easy and cost-effective option, there are several important factors to consider, ranging from legal and ethical issues to sustainability concerns. The web's dynamic nature can lead to rapid changes that our strategies must take into account.

  Additionally, modern data platforms may offer other alternatives, such as data marketplaces, where you can explore third-party data offerings and sometimes test samples before making a purchase decision.

Let us apply this approach to the bakery chain example.

A promising opportunity would be to utilise the point-of-sale data from our bakery stores collected through the cash registers. By analysing **historical sales**, we can gain insights into what was purchased and when including details about quantities and prices of products at each store. We can enrich these transactional data with reference information about each store, such as its address, number of employees, operating hours, and product-specific data like ingredients, allergens, recipes, classification and special attributes (e.g., organic, vegan, gluten-free).

Cash register transactions and master data are typically **internally available** and accessible data sources. The bakery store manager maintains electronic records of the ingredients and other helpful information for each menu item. The pastry chefs can also contribute by codifying and standardising recipes across stores, making them digitally accessible. Lastly, this could be the opportunity to electronically capture the surface size of each store, which can serve as a proxy for the shop's clients' hosting capacity.

Our analysis will benefit from **contextual data**, like geographical information. This includes the store's city location and classification, urban district definitions, economic descriptions and nearby points of interest. Other valuable datasets for our analytical model are socio-demographic indicators, which help define the potential customer base in each store's area, weather conditions and traffic or people footfall data, which are potential drivers of our store's sales performance.

The contextual data sources we have identified are (**externally available** and) conveniently accessible through APIs that can be easily integrated into our data landscape. Some sources, such as weather, points of interest and district classification, can be accessed with minimal to no investment. However, others, like average spending in the area, footfall or traffic data, may be more costly and require a thorough evaluation of their added value.

4 Scalability strategies

Although having a 'think big' mindset is essential, we must also consider the balance between risks and a sensitive approach when implementing our ideas. We advise developing a data capability that 'starts small' and gradually expands to become more sophisticated, accurate and re-applicable in various areas. This growth potential, or 'scalability', is a crucial aspect of our value proposition, and it should be considered from the beginning in our Data Activation Canvas. In essence, we need to foresee the possible evolution of the capability over time, anticipating its growth and possible limitations (see Figure 3.5). To help us clarify our ideas, here are three sets of questions to consider.

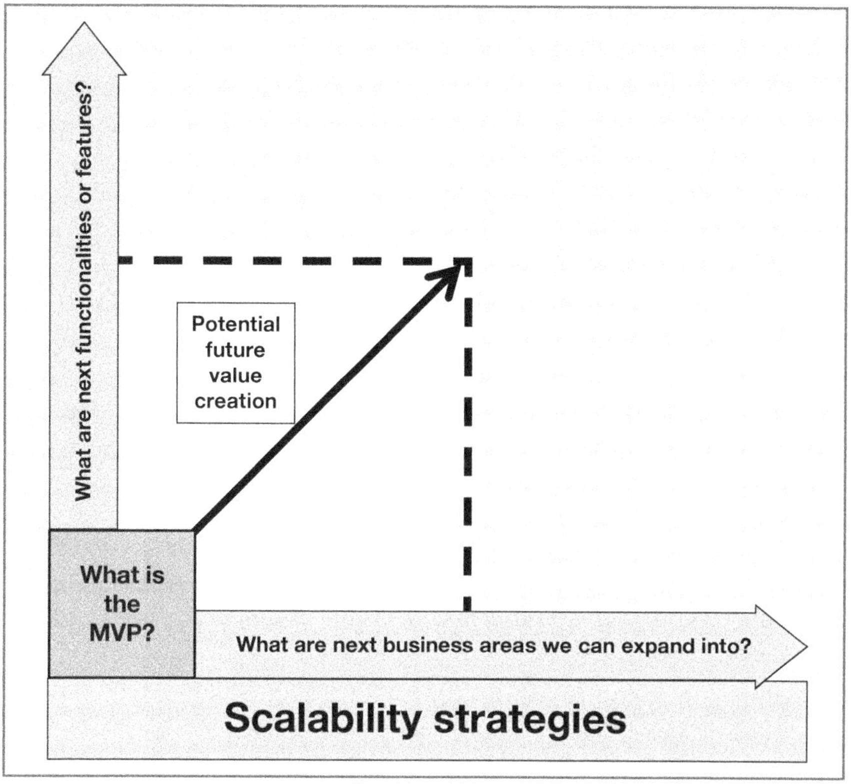

Figure 3.5 Scalability strategies could produce more value by bringing more functionalities to our minimum viable product (vertical scaling) or by deploying it to more units, i.e. business, markets, etc. (horizontal scaling) or both

- What is the **minimum requirement** to get started? What are the essential and sufficient criteria to showcase the value of the capability? By eliminating non-essential aspects step by step, we can determine the *minimum viable product* (MVP), i.e. the simplest version of the new tool to be implemented and run, which can already demonstrate its potential. Having a well-defined MVP enables us to begin with a tangible outcome quickly, minimising the risk of discouragement and losing momentum, which often occurs in overly ambitious projects.
- What **additional functionalities** can we incorporate? Now that we have established our MVP, it is time to consider the potential functionality expansions and their prioritisation and gain an initial understanding of the additional value our capability could bring in the future. As we increase the depth

of our capability's functionalities, we can refer to this as a 'vertical scaling' strategy.

- Can we expand the idea to **other areas of our business**? How much modification would be required to scale the capability? At this stage, it is crucial to determine whether the idea we conceived can be effectively adapted to a broader range of scenarios. This means assessing our capability's re-applicability to other markets, product branches, company functions, geographic scope and business units, including associated costs. Since we are talking about the breadth of coverage of our solution, we can consider this a 'horizontal scaling' strategy.

Returning to our example of the bakery chain, our **MVP** could be an application limited to one restaurant that only bases the recommendation on historical transactions, calendar events and weather forecasts.

Our **vertical scaling** strategy will supplement the application with further functionalities, such as generating price recommendations per item, promotional product combinations, stock optimisation, automated raw material reordering and price optimisation.

The **horizontal scaling** will happen by extending it to all restaurants in the chain. Here, we see a few complexities to be managed: for instance, the cash registers used by different restaurants may not have been purchased together and thus may store data in various formats. Therefore, a common scaled solution must manage data harmonisation, or we need to buy a single cash register model.

Once again, the Data Activation Canvas has proven invaluable in clarifying our data capability. This section has enabled us to effectively plan the initial stages of our capability development and gain insight into its future evolution. By anticipating the potential for scaling, we become proactively receptive to new opportunities that may arise.

5 Business integration

Modern management recognises effective change management's essential role in successful transformation efforts. When adopting data analytics in companies, the primary barriers are often rooted in organisational and cultural factors. Despite data, analytics and AI being technological topics, the most common reasons for failure in Data Transformation processes are not technical but rather

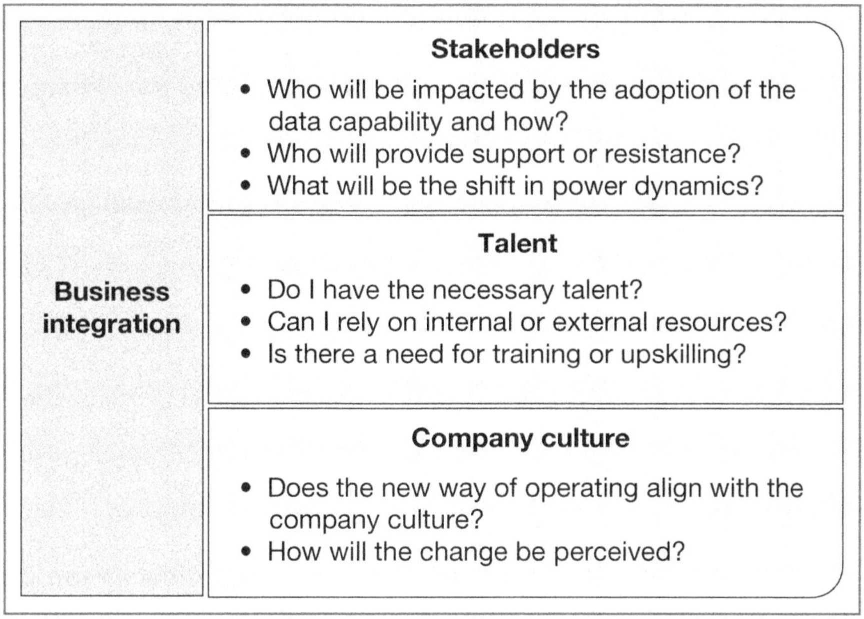

Figure 3.6 Business integration can be defined via stakeholders, talent and company culture impact assessment

'human' in nature. These can include the commitment of senior management, the organisational model supporting the change, and the company's decision-making culture. As we compile the Data Activation Canvas, it is crucial to focus on these significant aspects and ask the right questions to ensure success, as recapped in Figure 3.6.

- Which organisations will be directly or indirectly affected by the data capability and how? Who can provide support or resistance? Will there be a 'shift in power' within the company due to this innovation? It is essential to identify the **stakeholders**, a comprehensive list of individuals with vested interests that must be kept informed and engaged throughout the process. It is important to note that our evaluations will not solely rely on logic. We must also consider emotional aspects, such as the perception of previous experience becoming obsolete in the face of algorithms or the fear of being replaced by technology.
- Do I have the necessary **talent** to achieve the desired outcome? Can I rely on internal resources, or do I need to seek external expertise? Is there a need for training or upskilling? The availability of appropriate know-how is a

common barrier in transformation processes. One obvious scenario is the lack of knowledge in developing the capability, requiring external consultancy or acquiring technical skills from the labour market (such as hiring a data scientist). Another less apparent case is when managers in the company lack proficiency in data analytics and its potential. Here, a challenge arises in making informed decisions and setting a role model for the rest of the organisation. This highlights the importance of fostering 'data and analytics literacy' throughout the company, which we will explore further in our journey.

- Does the proposed new way of operating align with our **company culture**? How will the change be perceived? These questions allow us to anticipate potential cultural challenges that our company may encounter by introducing the new data capability. For instance, consider a scenario where our managers are used to making decisions based on thorough analysis of past data and explicitly explaining the cause-and-effect relationships of previous choices. How will they embrace an analytical capability that utilises **big data** (beyond the comprehension of a single human mind) and relies on a highly efficient numerical model that is not easily explainable? To what extent are our business managers willing to take this risk? This is a typical example of a cultural conflict that should be acknowledged at this early stage.

Although these organisational aspects may be more evident in complex, big- or medium-sized organisations, the same questions should be raised for smaller companies. Let us use again the example of our bakery chain to assess this aspect.

In the current setup, menu generation is an activity for the bakery store manager and the pastry chef (our main **stakeholders**). Above all, the latter may feel deprived of his role as a decision maker about the delicacies he and his team would bake. We should keep these people involved during the first capability tests so that they can give advice and share responsibility for the success of the transformation. It may also be sensible for the chef to retain the opportunity to select which menu to adopt from several equivalent choices generated by the algorithm. It is essential to consider these human aspects when compiling the Canvas.

Regarding expertise and know-how (**talent assessment**), currently, our bakery chain needs more analytical capabilities to develop the desired solution internally. Therefore, it is logical to consider engaging a small local consultancy firm. However, it is essential to proactively plan for the development of our internal resources from the start. This involves identifying a select group of employees willing to enhance their skills in this area and help bring the rest forward.

Given the size of our company, we currently do not perceive a pressing need to be concerned about the impact on **company culture**. Even if the Data Activation Canvas prompts us to be mindful of all aspects, including cultural considerations, we may want to stay practical and avoid trivial debates.

6 Technology requirements

It is time to discuss the technology foundation necessary to enable our capability. During this phase, we will translate the functional and methodological requirements we have identified into definite technological specifications. This will guide our decisions regarding the architecture and systems needed to support our capability. The technological aspect is extensive and warrants a thorough examination, which we can delve into in a dedicated chapter. For now, let's focus on the critical questions that will help us complete the Data Activation Canvas.

- How much **data** should we collect, store and retain? The primary consideration revolves around the volume of data we need to manage, a crucial factor in determining the necessary technological infrastructure. Previously, we explored our information needs through the Canvas. We must advance now by estimating the data size and translating it into specific technological requirements.
- What level of **performance** is necessary for our data processing capabilities? At what speed will we operate? After identifying the required analytical methods, we now focus on the power and speed of the technology needed. Complex calculations demand a more powerful machine; the desired speed influences our technological choices. For instance, if our application requires real-time processing of continuously updated data, our technological infrastructure must be specifically tailored for this purpose.
- What are the user **interface** requirements for our capability? Here, we need to specify the requirements for the human-machine interfaces. For example, this includes deciding whether a web interface is necessary for user interaction, if verbal conversational interaction is needed, whether data scientists should have the ability to adjust the system with new data or evolving

business needs, or if an administration interface is required for configuring parameters not accessible to end users. These considerations are crucial for effectively planning and implementing the technological infrastructure that supports our capability.

- What level of **security** is necessary? What are the risks if unauthorised users access the capability? Addressing these concerns, we may want to start establishing three essential security requirements: authentication (ensuring the person using the system is who we expect), authorisation (granting access only to a select list of authenticated individuals) and auditing (enabling the tracking of user activities within the system to determine 'who did what').

As schematised in Figure 3.7, having clarity on these four fronts will allow us to orient ourselves in the choice of technological infrastructure to use (if already present in the company) or to equip ourselves with.

In our bakery chain example, the data volume (**size**) is not large, at least in the minimum viable product phase, and the data does not vary in real time.

Our menu recommendation algorithm processes data daily, making a commercial laptop sufficient for our initial needs. We must reassess our **performance** requirements as we expand to more restaurants (scale horizontally) and

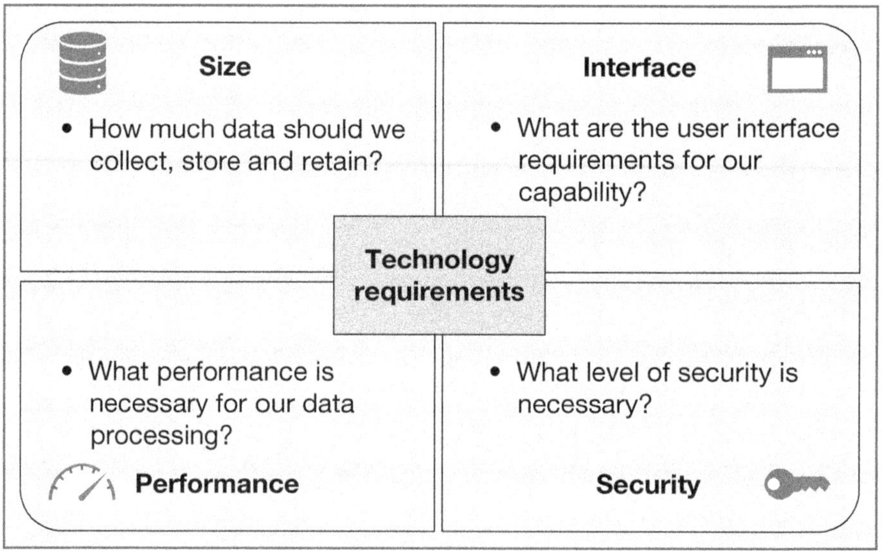

Figure 3.7 To define the technology requirements, we can leverage questions around data size, processing performance, user interface and solution security

introduce additional functionalities (scale vertically). However, we do not anticipate a need for exceptionally high-performance systems.

As mentioned, the **interface** can be limited to one or more interactive web pages displayed in an app. The web pages will require standard **authentication** for access. Regarding **authorisation**, although the risks are not significant, we aim to limit the use of the capability to the appropriate personnel in each bakery store. This approach prevents, for example, a pastry chef in one bakery from altering choices for other locations – no need for auditing trails at this stage.

Even if not detailed, these preliminary evaluations are sufficient to populate the Canvas and define the main requirements of the technological infrastructure.

7 Revenue streams

The upcoming sections of the Data Activation Canvas will guide us in determining our capability's monetary value. This is vital for adhering to the value-driven principles outlined earlier and avoiding the pitfalls of developing solutions based on unclear objectives, mere intellectual pursuits, or external trends. Our previous work with the big bets Selection Matrix has shown how value considerations can set priorities among different capabilities. Additionally, a thorough value assessment will aid in the capability development process, providing a solid justification for the initiative in the face of emerging challenges or helping regain momentum if obstacles arise.

As part of our approach, we will use a set of questions to evaluate the future economic benefits of our capability. We recommend two levels of estimation: a conservative, short-term-focused assessment based on our initial scope (minimum viable product) and a more future-oriented evaluation to gauge the total potential value when our scalability plans are fully realised. This dual approach will help us understand the capability's maximum potential and its strategic significance for our company. Let's delve into the key questions that will help us identify potential revenue streams for our capability.

- How much will our **turnover increase** by adopting this capability? We need to determine its direct impact on our income statement's top-line revenues. Can this capability help us sell more products or services, attract new customers or increase prices? It's crucial to analyse scenarios, comparing the current state (without the capability) to the future state (with the capability fully operational and generating value).

- How significantly can this new tool **reduce costs**? We can directly cut or reduce some costs. Also, by streamlining business processes, decreasing time inefficiency, and automating specific tasks, we aim to boost workforce productivity. We need to quantify how these improvements will enhance our company's profitability and impact the bottom line of our profit and loss account.
- What other **indirect economic benefits** can this capability offer? We need to identify the capability-related value that, while not immediately quantifiable in monetary terms, is nonetheless significant. Let us consider the following: will this capability enhance our decision-making process, enabling faster, data-driven decisions? Can it boost customer loyalty, reduce legal risks or elevate our brand's prestige? Can it strengthen our relationships with suppliers or customers through this data-driven innovation? While these benefits are indirect, they could prove the most substantial, potentially justifying the entire investment in the capability.

Remember to estimate these aspects, summarised in Figure 3.8, considering the capability's potential growth and full-scale deployment across the company, equipped with all envisioned functionalities.

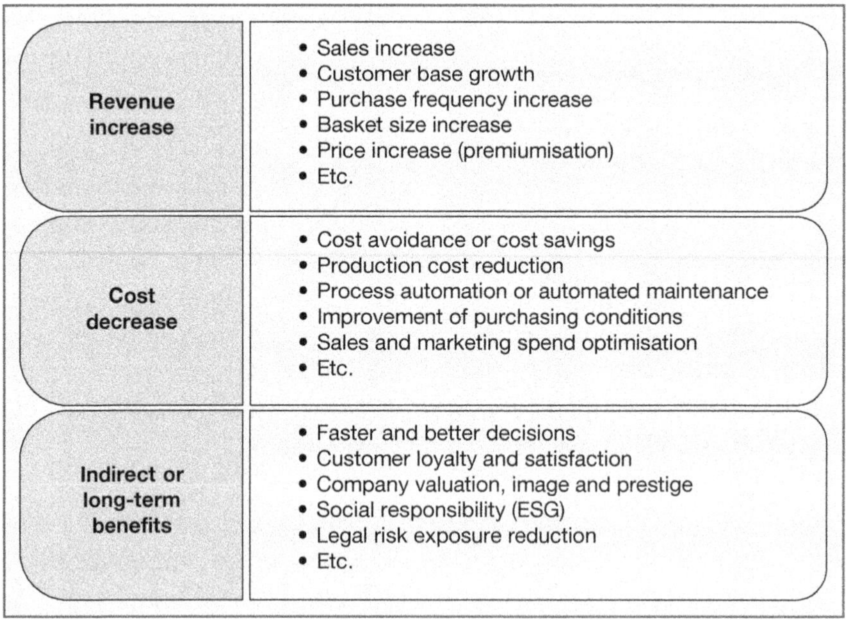

Figure 3.8 Monetary value creation can be expressed via revenue increase, cost decrease and indirect or long-term benefits

In our bakery chain example, the automated daily delicacies menu sounds promising, but we need to quantify its benefits better. We evaluate the current status with our bakery store managers, exploring the impact of a well-assorted daily menu on store revenue. Our analysis suggests that an automated, data-driven pastry menu could lead to an average 10 per cent **increase in store turnover**.

Our findings also show that data analytics can **reduce our bakery's costs** by 5 per cent, reducing ingredient spoilage and product waste without affecting turnover. Since costs currently account for about 65 per cent of revenues, implementing this new capability could boost our restaurant's margin up to 25 per cent, a significant achievement for just an algorithm.

Besides these significant numerical benefits, introducing our new capability will likely enhance **customer loyalty**. Patrons will be drawn to a 'daily experience' in their favourite bakery, with menus tailored daily to suit seasonal events and weather conditions. Moreover, the bakery can promote its progress in **reducing food waste** through improved stock management. While more intangible, these elements are equally impactful and may play an even more critical role in the company's long-term success.

This initial assessment of the economic benefits for each bakery store enables us to quickly estimate the potential impact of scaling the capability across the entire chain. The scale may also unlock additional value through synergies in centralised raw material purchasing and stock management, leading to unprecedented benefits.

8 Cost structure

Evaluating costs alongside revenue stream assessments is crucial to accurately understand the new capability's overall investment and related return. We can outline the cost structure using a simple matrix. The first axis details two cost types – setup costs (affecting only the building phase) and ongoing costs (recurring regularly). The other axis will categorise costs into labour-related (typically the most significant in our cost equation) and goods and services-related. These four categories are illustrated in Figure 3.9 for clarity. Now, let's examine the relevant questions that could help us fill in the Data Activation Canvas.

- What physical or virtual resources are required to implement the new capability? Do we need to invest in high-performance hardware, should we upgrade our existing computers, or can we keep using existing company assets? Is there a need to subscribe to cloud resources for the capability setup, or is there a need to access an external database? Essentially, we must identify the immediate, out-of-pocket expenses of the project phase, covering both tangible assets like computer hardware and intangible ones like software, data, or cloud setup.

- Who will manage the setup, and what are the associated costs? Do we use our internal staff or require external consultants? How many resource hours are anticipated? We must estimate the project team's effort and consider the time commitment of those involved in the transformation, such as participating in testing, verification or training. Refer to the stakeholders identified during the business integration phase and all the people considered in the activation scenario. Determine if their involvement is necessary for implementation and account for their time and cost.

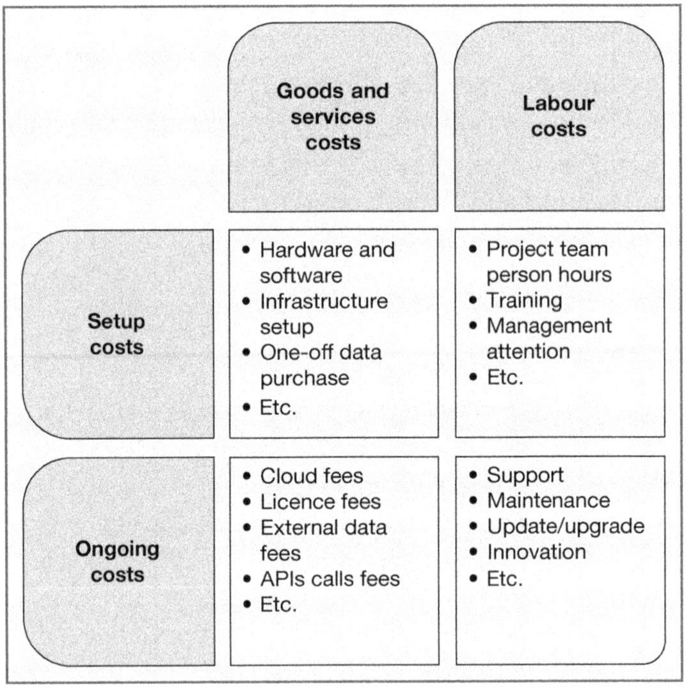

Figure 3.9 Our data capability's cost estimation can be supported by a matrix of cost components, encompassing one-off and repeating costs across labour, goods and services

- Once our data capability is operational, what recurring costs should we anticipate? Consider the expenses for operating and maintaining the acquired equipment and the fees for cloud platform usage. Recurring costs for data access are also substantial, including charges for third-party databases and licences for contextual information that will enhance our algorithms' output.
- What human effort is required to manage and maintain the data capability and its architecture? Once implemented, several roles are essential for the capability's ongoing management, but it is easy to overlook certain maintenance aspects amid the excitement of building something new. Key roles include technical support (to address end-user issues), training (to instruct new users or assignees), master data management (to update customer or product registries), continuous improvement (ongoing optimisation of functionalities) and innovation (advancing the capability to the next level).

Given our limited data volume and modest computing requirements, our automated daily menu example will limit our initial **setup costs** for goods and services. New hardware or cloud services are unnecessary in the initial phase. However, we will require access to calendar events (both national and local), real-time weather forecasts and historical weather data to train our model effectively. Consequently, we should include a cost item in our data Canvas to access this data during the setup phase.

Lacking the required technical expertise and eager to initiate Data Transformation promptly, we have decided to engage external consultants to set up the capability. However, they require in-depth process knowledge, data and other resources. Therefore, we will allocate an internal administrative resource to collaborate closely with the consultant for half their time. This must be accounted for in the **labour cost** of the setup phase.

Since we will leverage existing assets, the **recurring costs** for hardware maintenance are minimal. Still, we must account for the ongoing access fees to the updated calendar events and weather data, which are essential to ensuring our predictive model is retrained effectively.

As part of the project, we plan to have the external consultant train our internal IT staff to handle basic **ongoing support**, calling on external experts only for specific needs, managed within a capped budget for support hours. The administrative resource who actively contributed to the project will train new joiners and serve as an internal subject matter expert.

All these costs, including the labour costs of internal and external resources, must be quantified in monetary terms. They will counterbalance the revenue assessment we previously completed, thus providing the necessary elements to evaluate the return on investment of the capability.

9 Law, biases and ethics: staying on the right side

Directing our efforts toward our business goals, mainly focusing on the value potential of our new data capability, must not overshadow the importance of maintaining moral integrity and ethical consistency. It's crucial to remember that any new capability can introduce new risks, ranging from legal ramifications, which might result in financial penalties, to reputational risks affecting our relationships with customers, partners and shareholders. We should carefully consider whether a capability qualifies to become part of our company's strategic assets or if we need to redefine it to align with more sustainable principles.

While this topic warrants further in-depth exploration, for simplicity in this section of the Canvas, we advise focusing on two key areas: regulatory compliance and human factors. We can analyse and address these through a set of questions that explore both dimensions (see also Figure 3.10).

- Regarding the business process I am influencing, what are the legal requirements? What data security and privacy regulations must I adhere to? Can I ensure that this capability not only complies with the specific regulations but also upholds the underlying principles of these rules? We need to avoid the risk of legal sanctions and the potential repercussions on our company's reputation.
- What is the potential impact of this capability on customers, employees or other human beings? Even when legally compliant, we might inadvertently cause harm, sometimes in ethically questionable ways. For example, consider the transparency of algorithmic processes. While not currently illegal (yet), is it ethical to allow machines to make significant decisions impacting people's lives, like safety in autonomous vehicles or allocation of social and health services, without ensuring transparency and impartiality?

These topics, ranging from regulation to ethics, are extensive and go beyond the immediate goal of defining our Data Activation Canvas. A practical way

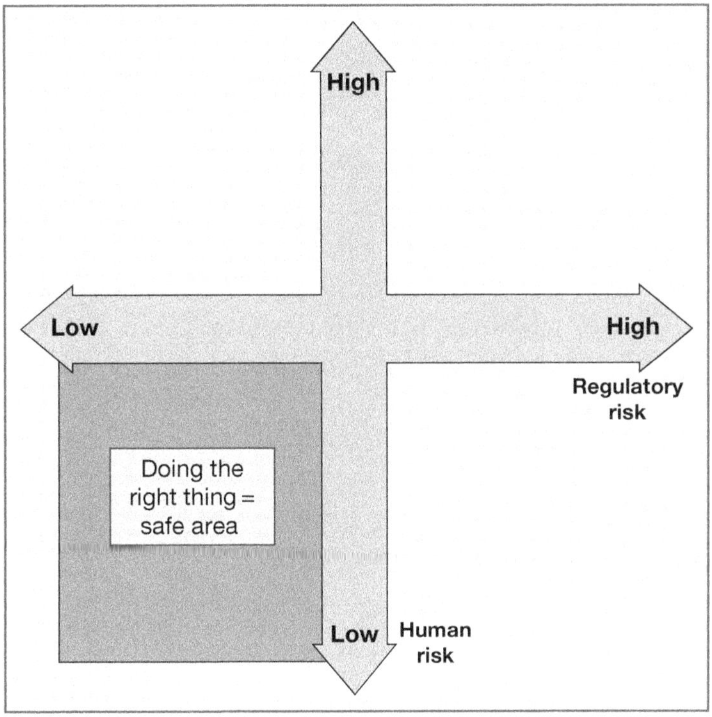

Figure 3.10 An easy representation of the safe side when dealing with human and regulatory risks

to gauge our actions informally is to ask, 'Would I be comfortable seeing my name on tomorrow's front page of the *Financial Times* with an accurate description of what I am doing with my capability?' If we hesitate to answer affirmatively, we should pause and acknowledge the reputational risk on the Canvas. This acknowledgement may be a compelling reason to thoroughly reassess our project, not just for compliance with legal codes but also for broader implications.

Regarding the bakery chain's automated daily menu system, there might seem to be no regulatory constraints. However, we should consider the data management of our cash registers. For instance, if these systems link payment transactions to specific payment methods like credit cards, the data becomes sensitive owing to its traceability to individuals. In such cases, we must adhere to legal requirements for data handling. Ethically, and from a human perspective, we anticipate no significant issues. Nevertheless, it's prudent to conduct the '*Financial Times*' front-page test: responsibly crafting pastry menus based on calendar events, weather conditions, or stock levels does not break our ethical standards, and this reinforces our confidence to proceed with the project.

Headings

Figure 3.11 shows a recap of the Canvas layout with the toolkit supporting its completion. After all the boxes are reviewed and correctly filled in, the last step is completing the Canvas by finalising the header. This step forces us to think and decide about a few aspects that will be decisive for our capability's future success. Here are the four fields we need to fill in.

- **Name:** in selecting an appropriate name for our capability, it is vital to choose one that is visionary, memorable and concise. This name will serve a dual purpose: facilitating internal communication and establishing a 'brand' that embodies the legitimate ambition of our capability. For instance, we might

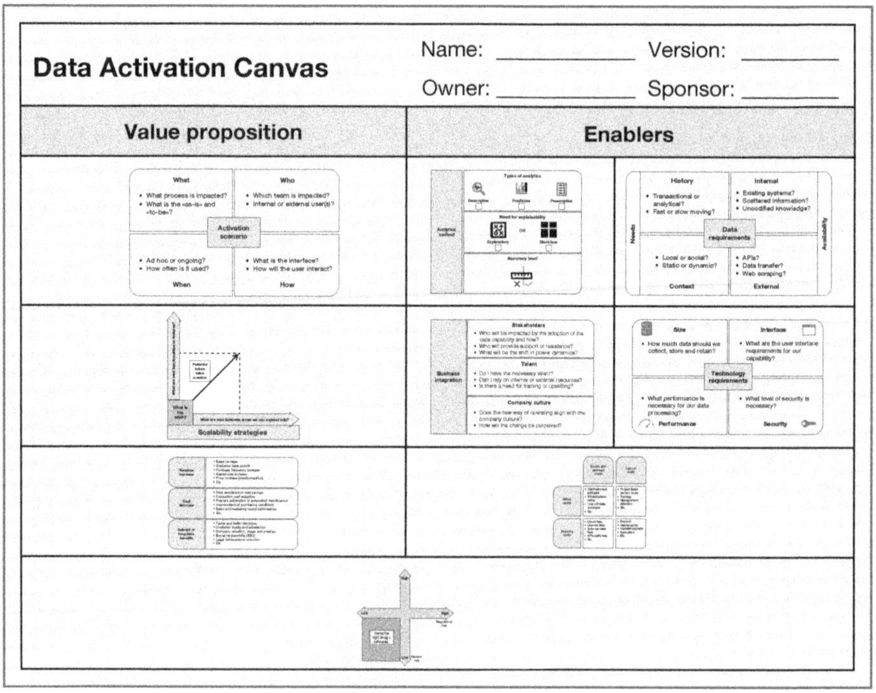

Figure 3.11 Our Data Activation Canvas is accompanied by a set of guiding questions that help in its completion

consider an acronym such as 'ADD' (automated daily delicacies) or a more creative moniker like 'DailyTaste'.

- **Sponsor:** the sponsor for the data capability initiative is typically the business manager with the most significant vested interest in its success. This individual is usually at the helm of the business unit or function most significantly affected by the transformation. The sponsor is crucial in removing organisational barriers that impede the implementation process. In the context of our bakery chain, we can envisage the sponsor as the manager, fulfilling the role of Chief Operations Officer.
- **Owner:** the owner of the data capability is the individual who bears operational responsibility for its description, implementation and ongoing management, including the Canvas periodic revision. Implementing the capability entails managing the project from its inception and maintaining transparent communication with relevant stakeholders. The owner also ensures the capability is effectively operationalised and monitored, proactively addressing necessary corrective measures. In our bakery chain example, the data capability owner could be identified as the head of store managers, who reports directly to the company's Chief Operations Officer.
- **Version:** version tracking serves as a crucial reminder that this document is dynamic and evolving. The Canvas is prepared at the outset to define the data capability before the project starts. However, it is imperative to conduct regular reviews to ensure that the value proposition, enablers and all underlying assumptions remain relevant and accurate in alignment with emerging business needs.

Turning big bets into enablers

Now, we can take a step back and look at our journey so far.

- The **Ideation Workshop** successfully served as a divergent phase, generating various innovative and valuable ideas that align with our business strategies.
- We then streamlined similar ideas into a more limited set of options. We utilised the **Selection Matrix** to identify a shortlist of promising, high-potential ideas that are valuable and feasible within a short timeframe: our 'big bets'.

- Utilising the **Data Activation Canvas**, we accurately described these big bets, clearly defining their value propositions and enablers – the essential factors for their successful delivery and operation.

Having completed multiple Data Activation Canvases for our projects, we can now identify recurring requirements and commonalities for their implementation. This process has brought to light a common thread, which is now shaping our transformation strategy, influencing both organisational design and our medium- to long-term investment decisions. By addressing these systematic needs in a unified manner, we not only pave the way for the success of our initial concepts but also lay a foundation that will likely benefit many future data capabilities.

Imagine if we had taken a different approach, investing indiscriminately in a single factor or focusing narrowly on one isolated capability. Such a strategy could have led us into the pitfalls and False Starts outlined in Chapter 2. Now, with a clearer overall picture, the importance of defining foundational enablers for our Data Transformation strategy is undeniable.

The golden checklist on the data blueprint

At this point, we should be clear on the importance of adequately describing our big bets in a simple yet complete way to ensure our transformation journey is set for success. Let us review a few points that will help meet this objective.

1. **Having clarity on how to describe each big bet**
   - Have we fully adopted the Data Activation Canvas methodology?
   - If not, what alternative methodology are we choosing to capture and document the data capabilities appropriately?
   - Is the chosen approach standard across all data capability ideas so that we can drive comparison and synthesis across our big bets?
2. **Clearly articulating the value proposition**
   - Who and how is benefitting from our new data capability?
   - What value is created by each capability, and in which business process?
   - Can we drive value multiplication by scaling horizontally, vertically or in both directions?

3 **Identifying the key enabling factors**
- What analytical modelling methods do we need to support our data capability?
- Have we captured all the data requirements?
- Are the technology needs clear?
- Do we have the right in-house talents, or have we outsourced the capability development? Have we identified and engaged all stakeholders? Have we assessed the impact on our company culture?

4 **Evaluating the value of the investment and potential returns**
- Is the generated monetary value clear and documented? Have we assessed for short- and long-term benefits?
- What could be the indirect benefits we are also generating?
- What are the expected costs for starting up the data capability and running it on an ongoing basis?

5 **Defining ownership and accountability**
- Who owns the data capability?
- Is the new capability name decided and appropriately communicated?
- Who sponsors this initiative?

6 **Identifying shared needs and potential synergies**
- What are the shared data and technology needs across our capabilities?
- What resources, talent and skills requirements are common among them?
- Are we clear on the winning organisational setup to drive the entire capabilities portfolio?

The questions above are pivotal to staying on the journey's safe path, so the recommendation is to address them adequately. Many of these topics will be explored further in our following chapters, starting from the most fascinating one: how analytics, machine learning (ML) and AI can unlock business value creation.

CHAPTER 4
LEVERAGING MACHINE LEARNING FOR VALUE CREATION

In this chapter

- What do we mean by terms like AI, machine learning, GenAI, and how do they relate?
- What's the 'machine learning way' of doing things, and how does it really differ from the Traditional Way?
- Which family of algorithms can solve which type of real-world business issues?
- How can we manage critical aspects such as validation, overfitting, bias and explainability when evaluating the business fitness of AI capability?

'Machines can learn how to work for you.' This simple statement embodies the attractive promise of adopting artificial intelligence into a business. When we hear and fantasise about AI at work, it's natural to fall into the temptation of thinking that technology can magically solve any tedious business needs, as we confidently delegate them to our digital partners. Well ... unfortunately, it doesn't work this way. As we have already seen when filling the Canvas, humans must do the heavy lifting of, first, realising how AI can offer – if any – an advantage versus the Traditional Way of doing things and then setting up the machines to do the job sustainably over time.

This chapter is about enabling you to do the heavy lifting. We will first shed light on the various terms related to AI that are often interchangeably used in business readings in quite a confusing way. Then, we will meet the algorithms, learn how they work and offer an advantageous way of getting things done in a business. Finally, we will get equipped with a list of the critical points leaders should check when presented with an AI proposition and how to properly manage them.

In this chapter, we will stay well afar from entering the mathematical complexity that comes with an exhaustive understanding of how intelligent algorithms operate. We don't need to comprehend their math details to effectively leverage AI in our business. We have selected a minimal set of concepts that will let you confidently think and talk about AI: don't worry if some aspects look tedious or technical at first – it's enough to grasp the general intuition about them and move on to how to use them.

Let's begin by clarifying the often-overlooked step of defining AI and its associated vocabulary.

A gentle introduction to AI and other trendy terms

In the late 18th century, a peculiar chess player infatuated the courts and intellects across Europe: the Mechanical Turk (see Figure 4.1). Hungarian inventor Wolfgang von Kempelen presented to the world an automaton capable of outsmarting its human counterparts in chess. The Turk, enveloped in oriental garb, its mechanised hands skilfully manoeuvring the chess pieces, was not just a piece of fine craftsmanship; it was a physical manifestation of an age-long human aspiration: the quest to artificially replicate the complexities of human intelligence by using machinery.

As spectators marvelled at the Turk's movements, little did they fathom that within its cleverly constructed cavities, it harboured not cogs and levers of autonomous operation but a concealed human operator, piloting the machine in its gameplay on the chess board. Apparently, not even Napoleon realised the trick, as he lost against the Turk in 1809.

Thanks to today's advances in digital technology, we no longer need tricks. Digital machines, when effectively programmed, are capable of accurately replicating certain aspects of human intelligence. **Artificial intelligence** (AI), a term coined in 1956 but anticipated by English polymath and wartime codebreaker Alan Turing a few years earlier, refers to the ability of machines

Sunny Celeste/Alamy

Figure 4.1 The Turk, as illustrated in 1789. Quite clearly, there was a trick

to perform actions that replicate aspects of human intelligence. These actions include solving logical problems, using natural language for communication, recognising visual patterns, coordinating physical movements and understanding the external environment.

In the vast realm of AI, **machine learning** (ML) is a computational paradigm focused on artificially replicating a specific yet potent aspect of human intelligence: the capacity to autonomously 'learn'. While AI is a broad term encompassing every type of intellectual replication, machine learning is the computing method that allows us to implement something that sounds like magic: machines able to learn on their own and improve from experience. When talking about ML, we refer to the computer algorithms that implement this magic, known as machine learning algorithms.

Table 4.1 AI, GenAI and ML made easy: what you need to know

Concept	Description	Business implication
AI (artificial intelligence)	The use of technology to achieve results typical of human intelligence, such as problem solving, learning and pattern recognition.	Enables automation of complex tasks, enhances decision making and can lead to innovations in products and services.
ML (machine learning)	A computing paradigm that implements AI by enabling autonomous learning from data inputs, essentially generating a program.	Offers predictive and prescriptive analytics and gives AI the ability to adapt to the business context and improve over time.
GenAI (generative AI)	A mix of ML algorithms focused on generating multimodal content, such as text and images, often as a response to natural language prompts.	Boosts personal productivity of employees and offers highly personalised and dynamic customer experiences.

There's another term often encountered: **generative AI**. It refers to the generation of text, images or other outputs by combining various ML algorithms. This is done by correctly interpreting human inputs, usually in the form of natural language texts called **prompts**.

In this book, we are less concerned with academic definitions and more focused on implementing AI to create business value. Table 4.1 summarises these terms and their implications for our businesses.

Now that we have the nomenclature right, let's move on and see the apparently magic ML algorithms at work in the real world.

Algorithms in action: the ML-Way of doing business

AI is not a panacea for all the needs of a company. Our first step is to determine *if* AI, via suitable ML algorithms, can benefit an aspect of our business. Developing an intuition for when and where to apply ML is crucial if we want to generate real value.

In the following pages, we'll encounter various business needs and see two ways to address them. The first is the *Traditional Way*, which is what we'd do using everything at our disposal, including data and IT capabilities, but without involving ML. The second is the *ML-Way* of doing things, where we allow intelligent algorithms to learn how to solve the problem for us, doing so with the scale and speed typical of digital technologies.

Let's start with the first scenario.

Scenario #1: anticipating customer churn

You work for a large retail operator (with supermarkets spread nationwide) and have access to your customer's loyalty card data. Your most pressing business need has lately become churn: many customers (too many, according to understandably concerned company leadership) are abandoning your supermarket chain to start shopping at a new, emerging competitor chain that is growing its share with very competitive prices, sparking a price war. You can't afford to simply lower prices across the board, as it would be unsustainable and unprofitable. You want to leverage the loyalty card data to drive retention campaigns.

Let's see which methods we can apply to manage this.

- *Traditional Way:* loyalty card data analysts identify customers who have been spending much less in recent weeks (setting some static thresholds) and offer them a £10 discount voucher to be used within two weeks, hoping to encourage them to shop with you.
- *ML-Way:* data scientists implement an ML algorithm capable of analysing historical data of customers who have left your chain in the last few months to identify patterns indicative of a high churn probability. By applying this algorithm, data scientists can assign each customer a number (called *propensity score*) proportional to their probability of leaving. Additionally, from the patterns identified by the algorithm, the data scientists deliver a presentation explaining which reasons are more frequent indicators of high propensity to churn. They share very interesting facts with salespeople, such as the finding that coffee buyers are much more prone to leave. The market research team discovered that your competitor has put much effort into their coffee selection, recommending you do the same.

This first example shows the multiple advantages of the ML-Way: it allows us to take 'laser-focused' actions on the customers most likely to leave. It also provides us with genuine 'insights', or additional knowledge, that we wouldn't have been able to observe wandering through the company's big data following a traditional approach.

Scenario #2: personalising experience through customer segmentation

Working for a fashion retail company with a diverse customer base, the aim is to engage customers more effectively by sending regular newsletters on fashion trends. To achieve this, the company seeks to create groups of homogeneous customers, tailoring the message content to fit the unique characteristics of each group.

- *Traditional Way:* in this approach, the marketing team segments customers using static thresholds based on demographics like age, gender and basic purchase history. These thresholds are derived by the marketing team from common sense and a general understanding of customer behaviours. The segments include *active users, dormant users,* 50+ *female users* and so on. The team then crafts newsletters designed to appeal broadly to each of these segments.
- *ML-Way:* here, clustering algorithms analyse customer data, identifying patterns and behaviours that are not immediately apparent. Unlike the static thresholds of the traditional method, these algorithms dynamically define thresholds based on actual customer behaviour. For instance, *high-tier brand lovers who buy only from new collections, singles living in large cities spending more than £ 540 a year, deal-driven customers who buy when the price cut is higher than 45 per cent* and so on. This insight, not explicitly anticipated by the marketing team, reveals unique behavioural patterns and data-based numeric thresholds that tell a lot about customers' preferences.

The ML-Way offers a dynamic and data-driven approach that goes beyond common sense. ML algorithms helped the company gain deeper insights into its customer base, uncovering previously unknown patterns and preferences. This enhanced the relevance and effectiveness of marketing efforts. It also fosters a greater understanding of the customer base, which has general value and can be leveraged for many other business cases beyond newsletters.

Scenario #3: optimising media spending in real time

You work for a company that sells sunglasses, and you are concerned about the drop in revenue in your e-commerce channel despite your continuous investment in digital media. After analysing the situation, you discover that your competitors have diversified their digital presence and found better ways to communicate with consumers, leading to higher conversion rates. You decide to revise your digital advertising strategy to improve your return on ad spend (ROAS) and outperform your competitors.

- *Traditional Way:* the media team applies an A/B/n testing approach to quickly assess what works best and adapt accordingly. This involves creating different combinations of spending across various channels, ad formats and call-to-action texts. After analysing the results of alternate campaigns, the team meets to decide which ones were most successful and diverts the media budget to them.
- *ML-Way:* data scientists leverage an algorithm that can autonomously decide the features of the campaigns, test them live, and adjust them to maximise the ROAS. At first, the algorithm compares random combinations of features, similar to a traditional A/B/n test. In the subsequent iterations, it identifies the most promising feature combinations and focuses on them to progressively improve the performance of the ads served.

Both methods use tests to determine the best way to serve ads, but the ML-Way is potentially faster, cheaper and more effective. The algorithm adjusts its strategy in real time, without the need for human involvement or decision meetings, resulting in fewer ads used during the testing phase. By allowing the algorithm to interact with the media environment, it quickly identifies unexpected and specific combinations of channels, ad formats and content types that may not have been included in the traditional method's static list.

Scenario #4: improving your customer's experience with a chatbot

Working for an insurance company, you aim to enhance the customer experience (CX) for clients who use the text chat channel to inquire about your policies and procedures. A key goal is to improve a vital CX KPI, the net promoter score (NPS), for this channel. This would allow the channel to be reinforced as an alternative to traditional call centres, freeing up their operators for more added-value work.

- *Traditional Way:* a chatbot is implemented which recognises the topics customers want to discuss. Using a well-defined logic, it guides them through the entire tree of possible conversations. This is achieved using an off-the-shelf online chatbot product. A CX team is assigned to define these response logics, clarifying the type of actions and keywords the customer might use (and their various synonyms), aiming to offer an experience not too dissimilar from (and possibly better than) that of the call centre.

- *ML-Way:* this approach utilises generative AI based on large language models to implement a chatbot capable of accessing documentation that call centre operators currently use for case management. The chatbot understands when a case is not resolvable with the available documentation and, in such instances, transfers the call to a human operator (*handover*). When this happens, the case is flagged and used to enrich the documentation so as to handle similar cases in the future.

The ML-Way offers several additional advantages. First, there's no need to invest time and money defining response logic, as it reuses the same documentation used by call centre operators. Additionally, this documentation updates whenever new policies are designed or customer management processes change, eliminating the need for further manual coding work. Finally, the chatbot can identify cases it cannot handle and categorise them for future coding, thereby continuously improving its performance and contributing to a steady growth in NPS.

When the ML-Way wins

The examples above gave us an indication of the cases where the ML-Way outperforms the Traditional Way. Let's summarise this in a list that can help you identify such opportunities in your business. The ML-Way is superior when you need to:

- *make sense* of large amounts of data, too extensive for humans to deal with;
- *spot insightful patterns* across numerous events (such as sales transactions) or entities (such as customers);
- *adapt* the functioning of a business process over time, keeping it up-to-date and compatible with a changing environment;
- *offer personalised experiences* to many individuals, tailoring to their specific behaviours and features;
- *generate* meaningful text and images at scale;

- *automate* reasoning activities to drive productivity and free up human resources for more strategic and creative tasks;
- *predict* future trends and outcomes based on historical data;
- *optimise* resource allocation when numerous variables interact in seemingly chaotic ways.

While keeping an eye on the list above, think about your most pressing business need today: can it be helped by 'going ML' in any of your processes?

Of course, there are many activities where you don't need the ML-Way, and you are better off with a traditional approach. For instance, think about all the cases where you need your company to operate in a fully deterministic and expectable way (like on a production line or in accounting processes). In many cases, the complexity of building and maintaining an ML-powered capability or its associated risks outweigh the benefits compared to a traditional, controlled approach.

ML is not the answer to everything; the key is to determine where it fits best in your business.

Selecting the algorithm that works for you

Not all ML algorithms are created equal. Each has its own strategy for learning from data. In the following pages, you will meet some of the algorithms and recognise the four major approaches they use, which categorise them into four different classes. The purpose here is not to get you through the (many) mathematical details of how ML works but to enable you to select which class of algorithm is best for your business needs.

There are three foundational approaches for machines to learn: **supervised learning**, **unsupervised learning** and **reinforcement learning**. Notably, a fourth hybrid approach mixes the previous three to teach machines how to generate text, images or more: algorithms of this kind fall into **generative AI**.

The four real-world scenarios we used earlier to understand the ML-Way of doing things were not picked randomly: those four cases mirror exactly the four classes of ML algorithms we will look at now.

Supervised learning: learning through examples

Supervised learning algorithms can predict something unknown by looking at previous samples. They can infer the 'relationships' that link an unknown variable (like a quantity or the membership of an element to a class) to the features of known historical examples.

It is called 'supervised' because it is similar to the process of a child learning to recognise colours under an adult's supervision. The adult shows objects of a specific colour while saying the name of that colour aloud. The child starts connecting the sound of that name with the objects of that colour. The unknown variable in this case is the colour, like 'red', 'blue' or 'green'. The child will soon be able to autonomously infer the right colour of an object by looking at it.

When we implement supervised learning in computers, we 'flip' the order of the traditional programming approach, as you see in Figure 4.2. In the traditional approach, you need to write a set of instructions (a computer program) to generate output results starting from input data. In supervised ML, the machine is able, during its training, to infer the program that generates specific results given some specific data. You must provide the machine with data and results during the training phase. The output program (called **Model**, in ML) is a set of rules likely to produce results similar to those seen during training.

The brain of a child learning colours performs a task similar to supervised machine learning: the data is the coloured object, the result is the colour's name and the program is the rule associating the visual signals with the neural concept of that colour.

Let's go back to the first business scenario and see how a machine can learn to predict whether a customer of a supermarket chain will churn using supervised

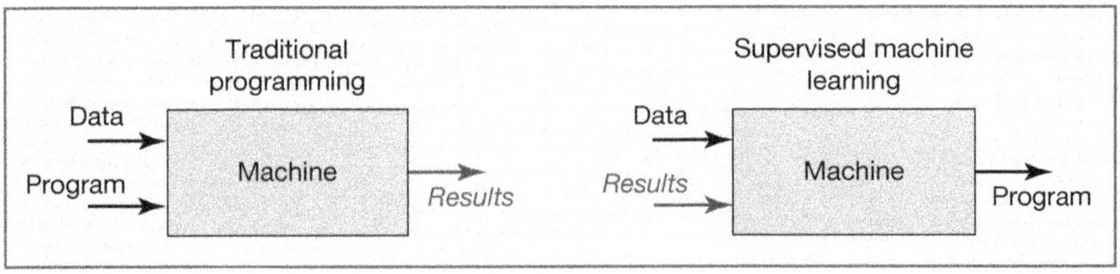

Figure 4.2 Supervised learning enables machines to write programs connecting input data to desired results

AI and biology convergence

Although neuroscientists still need to fully explain how the learning process works, they have already discovered that it affects the physical structure of the brain and how neurons are connected. It is fascinating that one of the most advanced groups of supervised learning algorithms (artificial neural networks, ANNs) was inspired by biological neuron functions. When training an ANN, the strength of the connections between individual neurons changes. Similarly, when we learn something new, the connectors between our brain's neurons (the synapses) adapt their behaviour to retain the new knowledge.

ML. A suitable algorithm for this is the **decision tree**. It learns by processing a table with historical customer data. Such a table would include several columns describing customer behaviours or demographic characteristics (**features**) and one column indicating whether the customer has churned (**label or target variable**).

The algorithm runs through the entire table of labelled data and constructs a decision tree that differentiates between churning and non-churning customers. It works through an iterative mechanism: first, it checks one by one which features better split the customers between churning and non-churning; then it moves to the level below, making a 'finer' split. The output is something similar to what you find in Figure 4.3.

As you can see in the resulting tree, the algorithm has found a set of conditional logic steps that can be applied to each customer to differentiate them between likely churners and non-churners. This logic is the 'program' that the supervised learning algorithm has been able to write by producing its output model. We can now execute this program (apply the model) for every customer every month and build a list of those prone to leave so that we can manage them accordingly with the right retention action.

The algorithm was able to autonomously figure out the features to use at each split and the thresholds to use at each level (like the 47 years of age at the root of the tree). This means that we not only have acquired the predictive capacity to decide who will churn and who will not, but we can also deduce meaningful and data-based insight into the customers' behaviour by interpreting the tree. For instance, it might reveal that customers stopping coffee purchases (branch

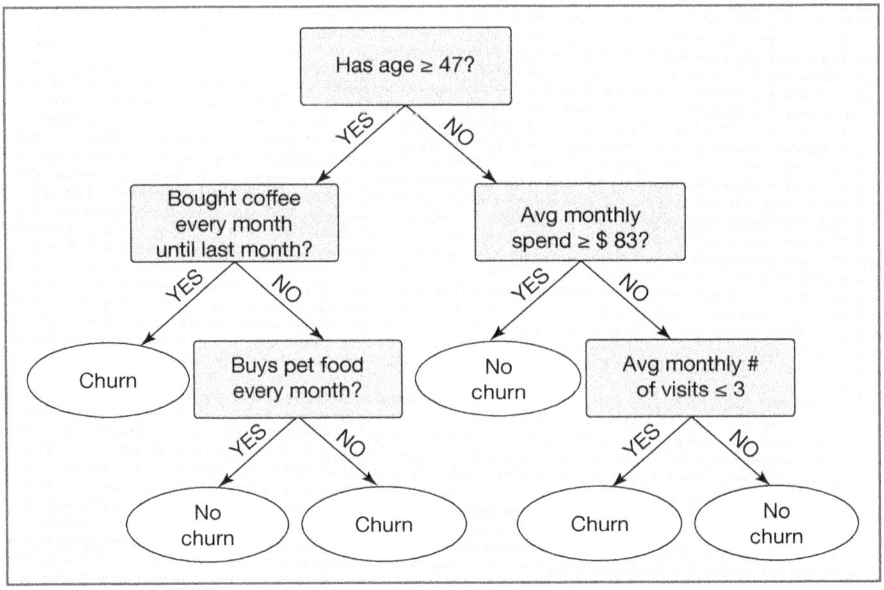

Figure 4.3 A simple decision tree to predict if a customer will churn

on the left) will likely stop visiting our stores altogether, suggesting a competitor's superior coffee assortment. We saw in our scenario that such insight has given the market research department a hint that competitors have a better coffee assortment.

This is typical of supervised machine learning algorithms: they offer predictive power and, on top of that, provide unexpected insights into the phenomena we're predicting (**knowledge discovery**). These insights can lead to systemic business process improvements or data-driven decisions, as our supermarket chain did by enhancing its coffee assortment.

From trees to forests

One way to enhance the accuracy of decision tree models is to use varied samples from the same dataset to generate multiple trees, forming a **random forest**, another notable supervised ML algorithm. A key benefit of a random forest is its ability to measure the 'agreement' among different trees, allowing for the assignment of a **propensity score** to each prediction. In the churn prediction example, this score enables sorting customers by their likelihood of churning, facilitating tailored retention strategies based on their specific churn propensity level.

Supervised ML algorithms fall into two families, depending on the nature of their predictions. For predicting class membership (like churners vs non-churners or positive vs negative patients in a test), you must use **classification** algorithms such as decision trees and random forests. Conversely, for predicting numerical values (like next year's revenue), **regression** algorithms are applied: the well-known simple linear regression is a basic form that finds the 'best fitting' line through known examples. Many supervised learning algorithms, including regression, trees, forests and neural networks, can be interchangeably used for both regression and classification.

Particularly notable types of ML algorithms are **neural networks**. These consist of many layers of artificial neurons stacked one upon each other, forming a deep and complex architecture, which has given rise to a very promising sub-field of ML called **deep learning**. The primary computational challenge in training and predicting with neural networks is matrix calculation, necessitating specialised hardware such as **graphical processing units (GPUs)**. Initially designed for graphical processing in video games, GPUs have become crucial for efficient matrix computations in advanced AI, sparking a global race to acquire these powerful processing units.

Having explored supervised machine learning, which focuses on making predictions of numbers and classes based on labelled data, let's now turn our attention to the second major class of machine learning: unsupervised learning.

Unsupervised learning: finding structure in data

Unsupervised learning is about uncovering patterns and structures in datasets where no explicit labels or outcomes are provided. They can discern intrinsic relationships within data points by analysing the data itself.

Consider the analogy of children playing with wooden toys of different shapes. Without any adult supervision, they can recognise that triangle-shaped toys are similar to each other but different from circle-shaped ones. Similarly, unsupervised algorithms don't aim to make predictions; instead, their goal is to uncover interesting patterns within the data they process.

Let's consider the fashion retail customer segmentation scenario we discussed earlier: we want to leverage our data to discover structures of similar customers that we can manage together. This is a clear example of a task suited for unsupervised ML and, specifically, for **clustering** algorithms.

Clustering algorithms, the most popular one being **K-means**, can analyse the data and identify a given number of clusters of data points that are 'similar' to each other but far from the ones belonging to other clusters. They operate iteratively (like most ML algorithms do). At each pass, the most similar points are grouped together, and the 'perimeter' of each cluster is updated. At some point, this process stops as the clusters converge to their optimal position.

You can observe the output of a clustering algorithm in Figure 4.4. Here, the points are displayed on a two-dimensional (2D) graph, representing just two customer attributes: the average promotional discounts and the average basket size. Although clustering algorithms can function in multiple dimensions, visualising data in hyper-dimensional spaces – say, six dimensions – is challenging for humans, so we have simplified it to two in this example.

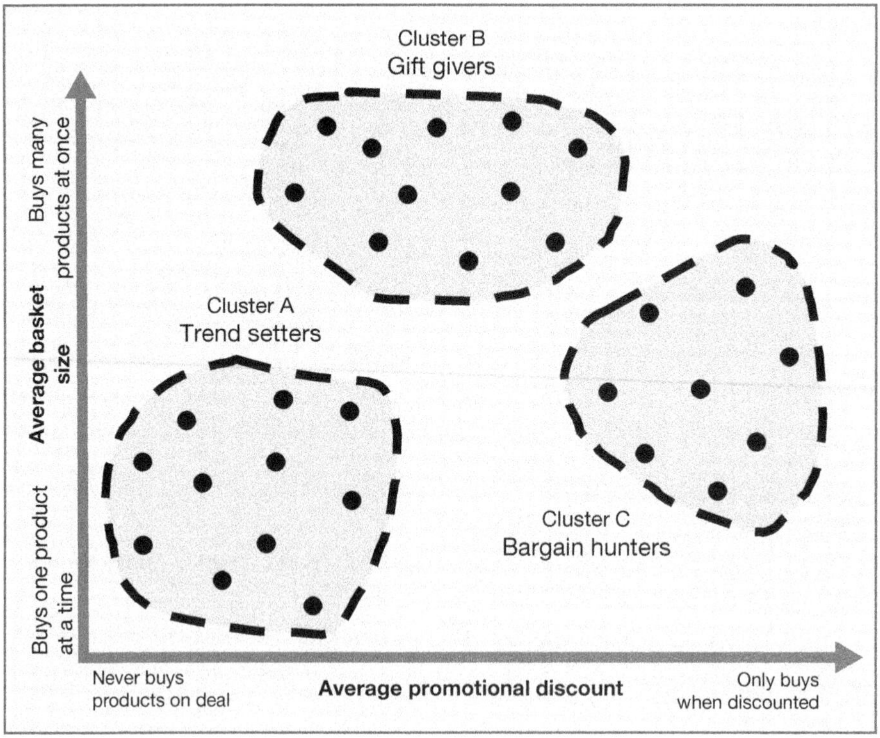

Figure 4.4 We have found three segments of homogeneous customers by applying clustering algorithms

The algorithm has identified three distinct customer segments. By interpreting their position in the chart, the marketing team can assign business-meaningful descriptive names:

- **Cluster A: the trendsetters.** Customers in this group tend to buy new models in small quantities, often as soon as they're released, highlighting their desire to stay ahead of trends and their preference for exclusivity.
- **Cluster B: the gift givers.** This segment includes customers who buy in bulk, possibly for gifting. They are characterised by larger basket sizes and a tendency to purchase multiple items, possibly indicating a focus on value and convenience.
- **Cluster C: the bargain hunters.** This cluster represents customers who predominantly make purchases during aggressive promotions, indicating a high sensitivity to price and deals.

Unsupervised ML algorithms offer a broad range of capabilities beyond clustering. Some are adept at uncovering **association rules** within transaction databases. For example, when analysing the sales history of a supermarket chain, they could reveal statistically significant patterns like '*customers who buy tomatoes and basil often also purchase pasta*'. This analytical approach, known as **market basket analysis**, is instrumental in optimising product placement on shelves or devising promotional strategies.

Other unsupervised ML algorithms specialise in **dimensionality deduction**. This involves simplifying large datasets, an invaluable process in handling big data. It can be achieved by eliminating redundant columns or creating alternative descriptors that encapsulate the same amount of information, effectively 'compressing' the database. This reduction can enhance the performance of other ML algorithms by focusing on the most relevant features.

Reinforcement learning: learning by doing

Reinforcement learning algorithms can interact with the environment and progressively learn how to achieve a specific objective by 'trial and error'. They require little data to start from and operate as autonomous agents, moving their steps towards maximising a given goal.

Following our favourite analogy, think about a child learning to walk. The child tries different ways of standing and stepping and, based on the outcome (success or stumble), they adjust their approach. In the world of machine learning, this is akin to an algorithm learning – essentially – by doing.

In reinforcement learning, the ML algorithm acts as an **agent** and engages in a continuous loop of decision making, action taking, outcome observation and subsequent learning. Much like a child interacts with their surroundings and tries different steps, the agent makes decisions, executes actions, observes the results and learns from these experiences.

Central to reinforcement learning is the concept of a **policy** – the strategy or set of rules the agent follows to make decisions. The algorithm updates this policy as it learns from the outcomes of its actions, evolving to make more effective decisions in the future.

Each action executed in the **environment** produces a **reward**, which can be positive or negative, reflecting whether the action brought the agent closer to or further from its objective. Additionally, the resulting new **state** of the environment is observed and fed back to the agent.

The agent then uses this new state information and the reward feedback to modify its policy, leading to new actions, and the cycle continues, as Figure 4.5 shows. This dynamic and interactive learning process allows the reinforcement learning algorithm to gradually improve its performance and decision-making capabilities, navigating towards achieving its set goal.

Let's go back to the scenario of the eyewear e-commerce company aiming to enhance its digital marketing performance: the reinforcement learning

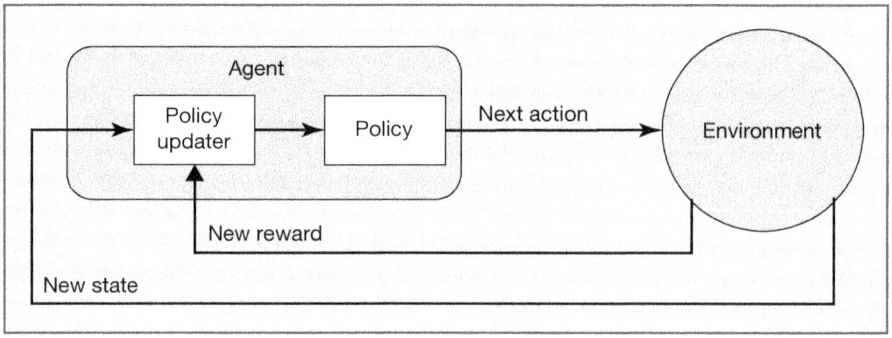

Figure 4.5 Reinforcement learning loop in action. It is all about finding the right policy to have maximum rewards

approach would be a game changer. The agent would utilise a policy incorporating various advertising strategies, including different channels, texts and formats. These strategies are then actioned in the real environment, where a specific number of ads are served based on this policy.

The performance of these ads serves as the reward, informing the algorithm about the effectiveness of its current strategy. Based on this feedback, the algorithm updates its policy, experimenting with slightly different ads to steer towards maximum growth in return on ad spend (ROAS). This process creates a virtuous loop of continuous improvement. However, it's crucial to set appropriate boundaries to ensure the ads align with the company's guidelines and avoid excessive testing costs.

Reinforcement learning can also be leveraged effectively in simulated environments. For instance, an algorithm can make a machine proficient at a game by playing simulated matches against itself, gradually refining its strategy to achieve victories consistently.

When the three foundational ML approaches (supervised, unsupervised and reinforcement) are mixed together, their power can be amplified. Indeed, most of the most advanced AI applications often leverage multiple approaches at once to make the best out of their capabilities. Let's move on to see one notable example of such a hybrid combination: generative AI.

Mastering chess by playing

When Chess World Champion Garry Kasparov lost against IBM's Deep Blue in 1997, it was a landmark event. Deep Blue, a supercomputer designed by IBM specifically for – as cruel as it sounds – beating Kasparov, leveraged immense computing power to anticipate future moves and was programmed by codifying winning chess strategies. It cost IBM an estimated 20 million dollars and 12 years of development to make. The approach shifted drastically with DeepMind's AlphaZero. Unlike Deep Blue, AlphaZero wasn't pre-loaded with extensive chess knowledge. Instead, it played games against itself, starting with random plays. Remarkably, it took only a few hours for AlphaZero to reach a superhuman level of chess proficiency through reinforcement learning, which was significantly cheaper and more autonomous than its predecessor. This is the ML-Way to become a chess champion.

Generative AI: learning how to write and paint

By leveraging generative AI (GenAI) algorithms, machines can learn how to generate text, images or other media in response to human inputs, known as *prompts*, delivered in natural language. GenAI stands at the forefront of AI advancements, repositioning computers from just passive data processors to active content creators.

A prime example of GenAI is found in **large language models** (LLMs) such as **GPT (generative pre-trained transformer)**. During their initiation, called *pre-training*, these models use extensive document corpora to absorb how human language works and amass knowledge from the text. In LLMs, text is transformed into numerical values (by using a process called *embedding*), and such numbers flow through very deep neural networks, equipping the machine with the ability to complete sentences and engage in conversations with a semblance of human understanding.

The intricacy of GenAI stems from mixing various foundational learning methods. The base model is pre-trained by learning unsupervised from a diverse range of human-generated documents – blogs, websites, scientific papers and magazines – assimilating the use of words and contextual applications. You can think of this phase as the model learning 'how to speak' by autonomously codifying the rules of grammar, vocabulary and, more generally, what makes a word 'fit' a sentence in a conversation.

Pre-trained LLMs can infer what is the most likely continuation of a sentence. By adding the best fitting 'next word' to an incomplete sentence, such models can generate text, as you can see in Figure 4.6.

Such a pre-trained model then goes through a semi-supervised learning step, which is a blend of supervised and unsupervised learning requiring only a portion of the data to be labelled. The semi-supervised element introduces a degree of supervision to enable the machine to produce meaningful responses in a conversation. If pre-training was about learning how to speak, this refinement step is about learning how to participate in a dialogue.

Further enhancement comes at the end from methods like reinforcement learning from human feedback (RLHF), involving human input to minimise harmful, untruthful or biased outputs.

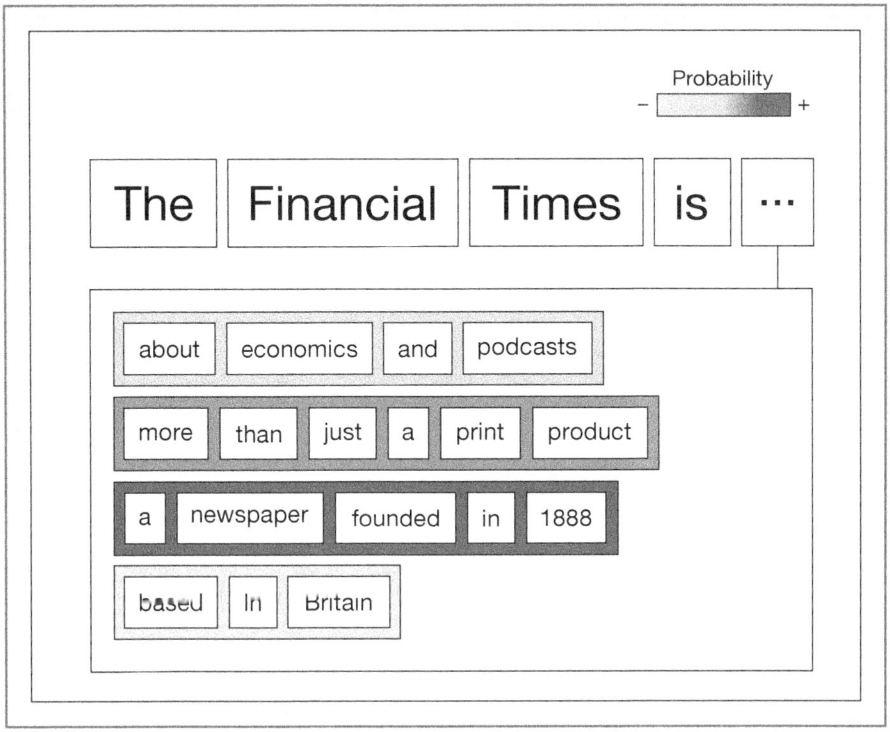

Figure 4.6 LLMs are able to generate text by evaluating the most likely completions of sentences

As you can see, you need to combine unsupervised, supervised and reinforcement learning mechanisms to build tools like the 2022 iconic pioneer of GenAI applications, ChatGPT and its successors.

Organisations must customise these models for specific tasks or enrich them with company-specific knowledge. Two main approaches are used for this. The first is **fine-tuning** the LLM, an intensive process requiring additional training on task-specific data, potentially incurring significant costs.

The second, more economical method involves using a knowledge database, like in **retrieval-augmented generation (RAG)**, to supplement the pre-trained model with additional documents available on demand to inform and customise the content of LLM responses. This last method suits well applications like the call centre chatbot of the insurance company scenario we encountered earlier: by implementing RAG, the model can access existing documentation on how to manage cases, enhancing its responses, saving precious human time, and boosting customer experience metrics like the net promoter score (NPS).

It's important to note that LLMs are *stateless* – they don't retain memory unless specifically designed to do so. Thus, each interaction with them is based solely on the provided prompt. In applications like ChatGPT, the illusion of memory continuity is crafted by enriching each interaction with context from previous conversations. Managing this aspect of 'memory' in real-world applications adds a layer of complexity and cost for programmers.

Acknowledging the limitations and risks of GenAI is crucial. Although powerful, these models can 'hallucinate' or show biases based on their training data. They prioritise 'fitness' – the relevance and coherence of generated content – over the 'rightness' or factual accuracy. GenAI demands meticulous management and oversight to ensure that the output aligns with desired goals and adheres to ethical standards (which often need to be codified).

GenAI algorithms, including GPTs, can also generate images by leveraging mechanisms akin to those used for text. The process behind this image creation involves translating the concepts from the input into visual representations, drawing on vast datasets of images to learn styles, patterns and compositions. However, this capability brings with it a set of limitations and ethical considerations similar to those in text generation. One significant concern is the risk of producing *deepfakes* – highly realistic and convincing images or videos generated artificially, which can be used for misinformation or other nefarious purposes.

Insert token to play: the costs of LLMs

Large language models (LLMs) such as GPT represent some of the most advanced developments in AI, but their sophistication comes at a cost. These models are built upon deep neural networks with billions or even trillions of parameters, necessitating substantial computing resources for both construction and operation. To give you an idea, the process of building these models can take several months and cost millions of dollars. Then, when a human prompt is provided, the neural network is traversed to generate a response; this step is called *inference*. Though inference may take only seconds, it demands significant GPU power and extensive memory. LLM usage is typically charged by the unit of text, referred to as a **token**, that corresponds to the length of a simple word. Providers of LLM services usually charge a fraction of a dollar for every thousand tokens, accounting for both the prompts and the responses. When planning to integrate GenAI applications, you should estimate the number of tokens that will be consumed, adding your estimate to the 'cost structure' section of the Canvas.

Another area of ongoing debate surrounds copyright issues. The datasets used for training these models often consist of extensive collections of human-produced images, the rights to which can be complex and multifaceted. Currently, the question of copyright ownership for the data used in training and the generated outputs remains a topic of active discussion, legal scrutiny and policy regulations.

Every need, its algorithm: the ML catalogue

Selecting the ML-Way to solve business needs is akin to picking from a catalogue of algorithms at your disposal, each suited for different scenarios. This assortment is graphically represented in Figure 4.7, providing a visual guide to the various options available.

FOUNDATIONAL LEARNING	**Supervised Learning** Learn from examples	**Regression** Predict a number **Classification** Predict a category	• Linear regression • Decision tree • Random forest • Logistic regression • Neural networks
	Unsupervised Learning Recognise structures	**Clustering** Find homogenous groups **Association rules** Spot connections across points **Dimensionality reduction** Reduce number of columns	• K-means • Hierarchical clustering • Latent Dirichlet Allocation (LDA) • Apriori • FP-Growth • Principal Component Analysis (PCA) • Singular Value Decomposition (SVD)
	Reinforcement Learning Learn by trial and error	**Autonomous agent** Interact or stimulate	• Q Learning • Proximal Policy Optimisation (PPO)
HYBRID LEARNING	**Generative AI** Generate from learned patterns	**Large language models** Generate text and offer reasoning **Image models** Generate and modify images	• Transformers-based (GPT, BART) • Variational AutoEncoders (VAEs) • Recurrent neural networks (RNNs) • Generative Adversarial Networks (GANs) • Diffusion Models

Figure 4.7 The ML catalogue: which algorithm is best for your business need?

From the figure, it's evident that multiple algorithms exist within each class of ML, and the choice of the most effective one depends on several factors. Understanding these factors can significantly aid in making the right decision, even if you're not a data scientist.

1 **Explainability**: some ML algorithms generate fully explanatory models, allowing humans to understand their inner workings. Decision trees are a prime example, offering clear, interpretable mechanisms as illustrated in Figure 4.3. Conversely, there are **black box models**, such as neural networks, whose functioning is largely inscrutable, even to the same data scientists who trained them. Choosing between an explanatory model and a black box depends on your business needs. If understanding the *why* behind predictions is crucial, opt for explanatory models. However, black box models are more suitable if the priority is maximising predictive power without understanding each prediction's rationale.
2 **Complexity and cost**: simpler algorithms might be less costly and more effective for large datasets, whereas others could be prohibitively expensive when applied at scale. The complexity and associated cost of the model are critical considerations, especially in relation to the size of your data and the specific business need you are trying to solve.
3 **Accuracy**: although more complex and less transparent models like LLMs might offer higher accuracy, they come with trade-offs in terms of cost and explainability. The most accurate models are often more expensive and less explanatory, so it's a trade-off.

With this catalogue and understanding of different ML algorithms, you're better equipped to match business needs with the appropriate ML strategy.

Getting it right: evaluating ML algorithms

Applying ML algorithms to business processes often raises crucial questions: will the algorithm be effective? Can its accuracy and promised value be trusted? Is it suitable for real-world application? Understanding a model's fitness for a business goal involves grasping key concepts that enable critical assessment.

This section will equip you with such fundamental concepts. First, we'll explore methods for measuring the validity of a model and get acquainted with the metrics used by data scientists so you can interpret them in business terms.

Second, we'll investigate the risk of overfitting to gauge the general value of supervised models.

Assessing accuracy

The approach to assess the accuracy of an ML model varies based on the type of learning applied. For instance:

- in **supervised learning**, where predictions involve numbers or categories, the assessment focuses on how close the predicted value aligns with the actual value;
- with **unsupervised learning**, the evaluation becomes more nuanced since there's no singular 'truth' for comparison; in customer segmentation, for example, the aim is to form clusters that reflect meaningful customer behaviours and drive differentiated management strategies;
- **reinforcement learning** involves evaluating whether the agent can efficiently and within set boundaries maximise the reward while interacting with its environment;
- for **generative AI**, the goal is to produce text or images that are fit for purpose, enhancing reasoning or accessing important company information while avoiding hallucinations or biased content.

The evaluation method should start with the business need and work backwards, establishing what must be true for the ML implementation to be successful. Let's see this in action in the case of supervised learning.

Depending on the type of prediction, you can use different metrics to evaluate predictions from a supervised ML algorithm. For example, in the case of regressions (remember, it is when you predict numbers, like revenues or share prices), you can compare the real values and the predicted value of the target variable and compute the 'distance' between them.

One popular metric for this is **R^2**, or **coefficient of determination**. Without getting into the formula, you need to know that if R^2 is low and near 0, the model is very bad. Its predictions are nearly random and independent from reality. If, conversely, R^2 is close to 1, the predictions match well with reality. In all cases, R^2 will be a number between these two extremes and indicates the accuracy of the model: the higher the R^2, the better the model.

Although this is not mathematically rigorous, you can interpret R^2 as the percentage of variability that the model can predict. If R^2 equals 0.8 in a model that predicts future revenues using weather conditions, you can say that the model can explain (through the weather conditions) 80 per cent of your sales behaviour. You can also say that 20 per cent of what happens to your sales is unrelated to weather conditions or is not captured by the model. R^2 is not only a measure of how well a model has been built but also an indication of how much your data can explain your business prediction. If you don't have enough data or its quality is bad, then you cannot have the ambition to predict much, and the R^2 will tell you so.

A further measure for regression accuracy is the **RMSE**, or **root mean squared error**: it gives you a range of the expected error. You can assume that the real value of a measure will fall, in most cases, between the range of plus or minus one RMSE from your predicted value. Another alternative is the **MAPE**, or **mean absolute percentage error**, which tells you the relative extent of the average error you can get (either positive or negative) from the model. Knowing what's behind these three metrics (R^2, RMSE and MAPE) will let you follow technical data science teams' presentations on the strength of a regression model.

The metrics are apparently simpler for classifications (predicting belonging to a category, like churning or non-churning customers). In fact, the most straightforward method to quantify the goodness of a classification is to calculate its **accuracy** as the percentage of times it gets it right over the total number of predictions.

Calculating accuracy might not be enough, though. When you run a binary classification, like predicting if patients are positive or negative for a health condition, your 'error' can go both ways. Imagine you have a classification algorithm (like a decision tree) predicting if a patient is positive for a virus by using blood test results as predictors. You might get cases in which a healthy patient (someone who is actually negative) is incorrectly classified as sick (positive); these patients are called false positives. For these patients, the wrong prediction causes them to perform additional tests or go into quarantine even if this wasn't necessary. Not too bad.

Now consider the opposite type of error: if a sick patient (someone who in reality is positive for the health condition) is predicted as healthy, we have, instead, a false negative. Errors of this kind, in this context, are way more harmful: we would 'send home' an unaware infected patient who will not get the necessary cure and might infect others.

Now you see that accuracy is not a good way to evaluate such a model. In this case, you need to minimise the rate of false negatives. To do that, you use another metric called **sensitivity**, which is calculated by dividing the true positives by the sum of all the real positives (true positives plus false negatives). In the information leaflet of medical tests, you will find no mention of accuracy, but you will find sensitivity instead: this is the measure that counts in the 'business' of making health condition predictions.

After seeing all these different metrics (summarised in Table 4.2), we can conclude that there is no single way to assess the validity of a model. If you are a doctor, you want to maximise the model's sensitivity. If you are a sales manager trying to anticipate how the 'month will close', you want the model to have the MAPE below the typical percentage error that an expert human person would make in the middle of the month. The advice is to always start by visualising how the model's error relates to your business case, then select the right accuracy metrics and interpret them in business terms.

Table 4.2 All you need to know about the most common ML evaluation metrics

Metric	How it works	Example with explanation	
R^2	Goes from 0 to 1. The higher, the better.	Sales prediction model has $R^2 = 0.85$	85% of the variability of future sales can be explained by this model
RMSE	Same unit of measure of the estimate. The lower, the better.	Predicted sales = € 3.400 with RMSE = € 200	Real sales are likely to fall between €3.200 and €3.600
MAPE	Average percentage of error, either positive or negative. The lower, the better.	Sales prediction model has MAPE = 10%	You have an average error of ±10% of the sales
Accuracy	Percentage of correct classifications. The higher, the better.	Churn model has Accuracy = 95%	95% of customers are correctly classified between churners and non-churners
Sensitivity	Prevalence of correct positive predictions across all positives. The higher, the better.	Churn model has sensitivity = 88%	88% of customers who are going to churn can be identified

Avoiding overfitting

Imagine you want to use an ML algorithm to predict something that *will happen* in the future by learning from all the cases in which it *has happened* in the past. What if you realise that the model you build predicts well *only* the specific cases that have already happened in the past? This would make our predicting machine pretty useless.

Such a condition, called **overfitting**, is a common issue in ML: it happens when a statistical model fits too closely to the specific data that has been used for learning. This can result in poor performance when the model tries to predict data it has not seen before. To make business-useful predictions on new data, machine learning algorithms must be able to generalise well beyond the data used for their training.

Normally, overfitting happens when the model built by the learning algorithm is too complex and aggressively adapts to the training data. To illustrate such over-complexity, see Figure 4.8, which shows three alternative models that predict a quantity based on a single input data variable. The models are built using

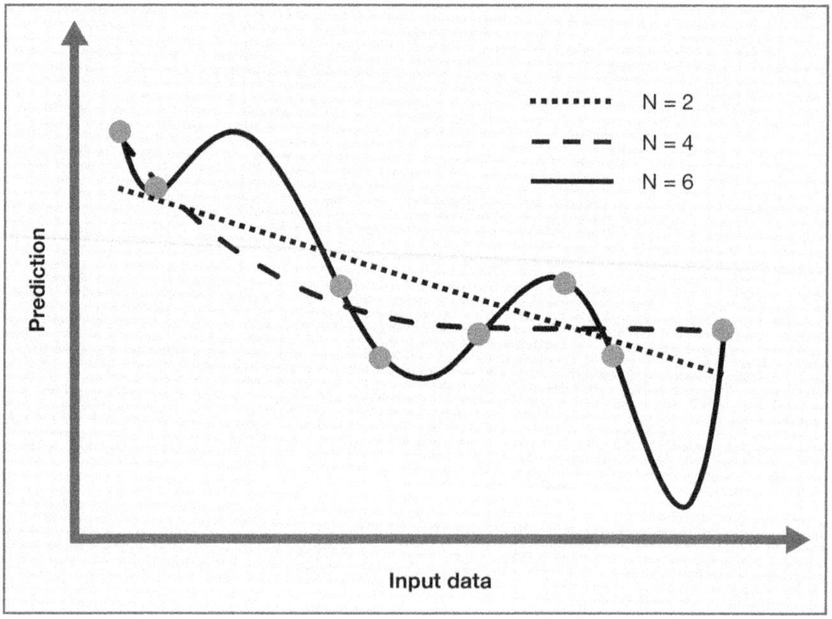

Figure 4.8 Overfitting in action: the N = 6 model is just connecting the (known) dots

the same learning algorithm (called polynomial regression) but using a different number of parameters, N.

Intuitively, if the model uses few parameters (N = 2), it seems 'too simple' and cannot fit well with what the known points suggest: such a model is called **underfitted**. Conversely, if the model uses too many parameters (N = 6), it adapts too aggressively to the known points, making very artificial 'curves' to connect the dots. Such a model is unlikely to have general validity and to anticipate the position of future points that have not been seen during training: this is the typical case of an **overfitted** model. Having high accuracy on an overfitted model is like cheating: we force the model to the known data, jeopardising its ability to predict unknown data.

To obtain a well-fitted model (by looking at the picture, N = 4 seems to be a good bet in this case), we should be able to find the sweet spot between simplicity (if it's too complex, it overfits) and accuracy (if it's too simple, it is not accurate).

Fortunately, there is a way to assess whether a prediction model can generalise. We can split the original dataset into two subsets by random sampling. The first dataset (normally covering around 80 per cent of the initial points) is used for the actual training of the model, and it is called the **training set**. The remaining points are kept aside and form the **test set**: these points are never shown to the learning algorithm but are used to assess the model accuracy, comparing the model predictions with the known reality.

The accuracy metric applied to the test set (R^2, sensitivity, or whatever makes sense in our business case) tells us how good the model is at predicting new data, avoiding any possibility of cheating ourselves with an overfitted model. This is why, as a general rule, the accuracy of a supervised model should always be calculated on a test set only.

The golden checklist on AI

Machines can learn how to work for us. This chapter explained how machine learning can make this happen.

Opportunities and risks in ML are so closely intertwined. You should keep handy a set of critical questions you should ask when considering an

AI-powered business application or evaluating a model's results presented by a data science team.

1. **Choosing ML over traditional methods**
   - Is the ML approach superior to traditional methods in this context?
   - What specific advantages does it offer (automation, accuracy, knowledge discovery, etc.)?
   - How can we measure these advantages in business terms?
2. **Choosing the right algorithm**
   - Does our business case align with the chosen ML algorithm family (supervised, unsupervised, reinforcement or GenAI)?
   - Do we need to ensure explainability or a black box model will do?
   - How can we clarify the algorithm's decision-making process to stakeholders?
3. **Validating model effectiveness**
   - What is our strategy for validating the model's effectiveness?
   - Which accuracy metric aligns best with our desired business outcome?
   - How do we plan to ensure the model's generalisation and prevent overfitting in supervised ML?
   - Are we assessing accuracy on the test set only?
4. **Addressing bias and ethical concerns**
   - How will the algorithm's recommendation impact humans (employees, customers, etc.)?
   - How do we control and educate users about AI limitations, including biases and potential risks of hallucination?
5. **Sustaining long-term effectiveness**
   - What is the plan for regular monitoring and updating of the algorithm?
   - Who is responsible for these tasks, at what frequency will they be conducted and how much will they cost?

AI can potentially be a pivotal ally in the Data Transformation journey. As we have seen in this chapter, ML algorithms can enhance the value derived from data by autonomously learning from it and acting accordingly. The next chapter will explore how having the right technological foundation is crucial in unlocking this 'magic'.

CHAPTER 5
BUILDING A STRONG TECHNOLOGY FOUNDATION

In this chapter

- What recent technological advancements have significantly influenced data management and exploitation strategies, and why are these developments crucial?
- How can we organise data effectively and efficiently, and which practices could facilitate our transformative journey in this area?
- What tools are fundamental in maximising the potential of analytics and AI on a large scale, and what options do we have in this regard?

'Science can amuse and fascinate us all, but it is engineering that changes the world.' This famous quote by Isaac Asimov offers a striking parallel with the history of data science and the acceleration linked to current technological evolution. Many existing ideas and theories, even new mathematical and algorithmic models, have been accelerated by unprecedented technological capabilities that continue to evolve and bring data generation, collection, storage and processing abilities forward.

This chapter will explore the essential concepts representing the backbone for effectively managing and leveraging data in your organisation. We will also discuss how to make sure data is well organised, accessible and valuable, avoiding some of the possible obstacles in our path. Finally, we will analyse the various components of the Modern Data Stack, as well as the physical infrastructure, data platform and applications that can empower your organisation to harness the full potential of the data. With a comprehensive understanding of the critical technological enablers that support a data-driven organisation, you will be better positioned to evaluate, select and implement the right tools and infrastructure to support your Data Transformation journey and unlock the true potential of your data assets.

Laying the groundwork: digital technologies and cloud systems

When we think about modern technologies and take a strategic approach to the discussion, there is often the temptation to look backwards to acknowledge their impressive, exponential development in the last decades. We hinted at this in Chapter 1, as we were grounding ourselves into the reasons for embracing our Data Transformation journey. In this chapter, however, we will avoid a whole narrative on the evolution that has led to the status. Rather, we will scan through the available choices with a forward-looking eye. Nevertheless, we will still touch on a few core principles that set the stage for modern data management and enabled the current landscape to arise.

Two terms, '**digital**' and '**cloud**', have broken into every company's agenda since last century but continue to thrive and increase relevancy, offering new and unprecedented opportunities to increase business efficiency and create value.

Digital is a widely used word in all companies. We often use it in the context of digital marketing and media, online experiences and mobile apps – all areas where data analytics is essential. *Digital technology* is a term that broadly encompasses technologies that operate on information encoded in binary digits or *bits*, powering everyday devices and systems ranging from personal computers and smartphones to smart wearables and digital cameras. Digital content like images, videos and apps, not just hardware, also forms part of our digital lifestyle, fostering interactions through emails, social media and online gaming. The adoption and pervasiveness of digital computing, telecommunication and media have relied on the incredible growth rate of the underlying technologies, governed by the so-called 'Moore's law'.

In the 1960s, Gordon Moore, co-founder of Intel, documented how transistor densities on chips doubled approximately every two years, significantly reducing computing costs and marking **exponential** technological growth. To better understand the implications and size of the phenomenon, let us investigate some practical examples.

- Voyager 2, the first spacecraft launched by NASA in 1977 to run an interplanetary exploration, has a microprocessor frequency of 250 kilohertz (kHz) and is equipped with 69 kilobytes (kB) of memory. An agriculture drone we can purchase online is typically equipped with a CPU operating in the range of gigahertz (GHz) and has several gigabytes (GB) of embedded memory, making it millions of times faster in processing and larger in storage capacity than Voyager 2.
- In 1991, global system for mobile communications (GSM), part of the second generation of wireless phone technology (2G), introduced the possibility to exchange short text messages between mobile devices with a bit rate between 14.4 kilobits per second (kbps) and 64 kbps. The current 5G phone technology can reach a theoretical peak of 20 gigabits per second (Gbps), making it suitable for streaming high-quality videos or playing video games in real time. In approximately 30 years, the bit rate increased by a hundred thousand times. 6G technology, currently in research and development, will bring the bit rate to terabits per second (Tbps), making it a hundred million times larger than the 2G.
- The first commercially available digital photo camera, the Dycam Model 1, released in 1990, had a resolution of 0.1 megapixels (MP) and stored images on an internal memory of 1 megabyte (MB), where it stored 32 KB-sized low-resolution photos. Today, a single smartphone photo goes from a few MB when compressed to hundreds if uncompressed in its raw format, so it is thousands of times larger, but its unit storage cost has drastically dropped.

Although the sustainability of Moore's law has been challenged several times in its pure application to the original context due to physical and financial limitations, a broader interpretation, focusing on overall computational power and efficiency rather than just transistor density, still holds. No other technological area has been going through a similar exponential improvement pattern for a comparably long period. Let's look at the most recent technology trends, such as parallel computing, storage architectures and quantum computing. We can bet that this evolutionary trend in digital technology will continue for the foreseeable years, and Moore's law will continue to apply.

What advantages may a company take from the trends described above? The evolution of digital technology will decrease marginal costs and improve processing performance, and this will have a broad impact on everyone. Yet, these companies truly embracing digital capabilities and embedding them in their operating business model will have a chance to 'surf the exponential curve', bringing disproportionate advantage to their business regarding efficiency and advanced abilities.

The second key term mentioned in this section is **cloud**, primarily used in the expressions *cloud technologies* or *cloud computing*. The first conceptualisation of cloud computing is often dated back to the 1960s when single and powerful computers (*mainframe*) started to be shared on a time basis to allow parallel computation. With the introduction of computer networks and the internet, distributed computing emerged from the need to solve significant computational problems using multiple computers spread across various geographical areas, characterised by autonomous computational entities or nodes, each with its memory, communicating through message passing. The internet, the World Wide Web and distributed processing started thriving in the 1990s when networking technologies and data bandwidth significantly advanced. This progress paved the

Computational innovation in the AI era: from CPUs and GPUs to QPUs

CPUs have followed the expected increase in computational power for decades. Architectural innovation in the processor's design, like for GPUs, has brought new steam to the computational race.

A significant innovation in computational capabilities is expected to come from quantum computing and the *quantum processing unit* (QPU), i.e. the core component responsible for performing quantum computations in quantum bits or *qubits*. Qubits are the fundamental units of information in quantum computing. Unlike traditional bits, they have the unique property of being in multiple states simultaneously, thanks to the principles of superposition and entanglement. This allows quantum computers to perform complex calculations at speeds unattainable by classical computers for certain types of problems.

Although the potential of quantum computing in data, analytics and AI looks promising, quantum technology is still in its very early stages, undergoing significant research and development by tech industry players to make it viable.

way in the early 2000s for the emergence of the first applications purely running on a website and not requiring any installation on local machines. **Salesforce.com** is often credited as the first enterprise to offer such a large-scale service. At the same time, big technology players such as Amazon, Google and Microsoft introduced their suite of cloud services, including storage and computation. As these technologies continued to evolve, they became increasingly integrated into the fabric of modern society and business operations.

Before we get into the new services and business models the cloud has enabled for data management and processing, let's briefly overview *parallel computing* and how *distributed architectures* work. We can use a simple analogy to start familiarising ourselves with these concepts. Let us consider a small local public library that, after the holiday season, receives back books lent to all primary school students during the vacations. The number of books returned is considerable; they span five disciplines: history, geography, mathematics, science and literature. Before the library reopens, all the books must be classified into the proper discipline and sorted alphabetically according to the author's name. The librarian organises the work as follows.

1. The piles of unclassified and unsorted books are split into five subgroups, each randomly assigned to one library volunteer.
2. Each volunteer splits their group of books further into the five disciplines, ending up with five smaller piles of books classified by field.
3. Each volunteer chooses one discipline and collects all the specific piles they manage from the other four volunteers.
4. At this point, each volunteer will have only a group of books related to their discipline. Therefore, they can parallel sort each discipline alphabetically by author's name.
5. Finally, the librarian returns the books to their shelves, satisfied with the collaboration and efficiency demonstrated by the team.

Even if our example is oversimplified, this is how parallel computing works in architectural frameworks like Hadoop or Spark, with groups (clusters) of computers (nodes) working parallel to solve common tasks.

Many cloud services offer the opportunity to 'rent' or use resources we do not physically own and exploit for our benefit through an internet connection. This dematerialisation of physical assets may be a strong advantage for whoever cannot or does not want to acquire costly hardware and maintain it through specialised and expert personnel. So, a cloud provider offers the services we need to store and process large amounts of data, pilot new analytics and AI capabilities, launch new consumer-facing services, or any other scenario requiring storage-intensive or computationally hungry distributed systems. The advantages of such a choice are multiple.

- Limited to no capital investments are required to purchase and set up expensive hardware machine infrastructure.
- No workforce costs are solely dedicated to upgrading and maintaining the new infrastructure.
- Big cloud providers can indeed play economy of scale by implementing massive **data centres**, which bring cost efficiencies and effectively keep performance and security standards aligned to the state of the art.
- Marginal costs and timings are relatively low in case resource upscaling is required by business needs: the cloud provider, if asked, can unlock resources already present in its data centre and adjust service levels accordingly.

However, we should remember the challenges and critical points that cloud computing poses. Exchanging and managing data in the cloud may expose us to further cyber security risks, with new potential weaknesses in the chain that hackers may exploit. Data protection, especially when considering personally identifiable information (PII) or highly confidential data, becomes extremely important as it involves a third party (the cloud provider). National or international data exchange and storage regulations may also represent a challenge if the data centres are not based in our country or if specific local regulations exist about data treatment. These examples already show why the cloud choice may be more challenging and less convenient in some scenarios and instead always requires a thorough assessment.

Technological nephology: look at how many clouds

Managing computing resources in the context of data storage and processing capabilities entails choosing among several options, each with advantages and disadvantages. The choice usually depends on the organisation's needs, budget, strategic goals and technological maturity. However, what are the most common setups? Let us quickly look at them in logical order.

A company or an organisation may decide to keep the hardware and infrastructure they need (servers, storage, networking equipment, etc.) in their physical properties; this is called *on-premise* computing.

Suppose the same company starts getting some cloud computing services on a private internal network, which is exposed only to the company employees or a selected group of users. In that case, it is leveraging *a private cloud.*

If the company prefers to reduce the upfront capital expenditure and delegate some of the core maintenance activities to someone else, the option could be to pay for and use some computing resources 'as a service' over the internet, offered and managed by a third-party provider: this is *public cloud.*

Lastly, *a hybrid cloud* combines on-premise resources or a private cloud infrastructure with a public cloud, allowing data and applications to be shared between them. This may be the choice for organisations that need the scalability and flexibility of public cloud computing but also require a high degree of control over specific data or applications, like on-premise or in a private cloud.

This section does not aim to make us experts in digital and cloud technologies. However, it highlights two technological trends that have profoundly influenced every industry, serving as long-term catalysts for technological and business innovation. We have introduced some essential concepts, such as storage and performance, distributed computing, cost implications and security risks. These are crucial for any wise manager embarking on a Data Transformation journey for their company. Another trend woven throughout our discussion relates to the primary energy source driving our transformational efforts: data. With the emergence of new digital capabilities, increased computing power, and the expanding speed and reach of the internet, our capacity to collect, store, process, produce and even generate data has reached unprecedented levels in human history. This significant phenomenon was recognised and defined in the early 2000s, when the term *'big data'* quickly became a buzzword, drawing substantial investment. The term 'big' refers to the *volume* of data and its *velocity* and *variety*, necessitating specific technology and analytical methods to transform it into value. Indeed, now it is time to explore how we can organise our data and which tools we can leverage to enable our Data Transformation agenda.

Organising data for maximum impact

No matter the size and complexity of the data we are dealing with, more than technology alone is needed to solve our problems and address our needs. It is a must to get data organised so that we can exploit it as efficiently and extensively as possible. We want to capture the real potential of our data, overcoming the restlessness of not being able to exploit all the data in our availability. At the same time, we want to avoid falling into the trap of overengineering our data landscape, including every single source or dataset we will never use to produce a tangible value. Even if we have seen how storage and running costs are decreasing over time, it is pointless to waste resources and time and focus on covering data we do not need or that is not strategic enough at this moment.

How do you select the correct data to focus on? The 'data shopping list' obtained from our data capabilities portfolio review may be overwhelming. Through the Data Activation Canvas, we collected a comprehensive set of data requirements that may or may not overlap across capabilities, with some data shared across capabilities and others particular to a single solution. In any case, we need to get started somewhere and avoid just the data collection and preparation for our strategy becoming a never-ending exercise.

To assess the first and most essential datasets to focus on, we can use the **MoSCoW** methodology, which is also used in project management for requirements prioritisation. MoSCoW is an acronym that stands for:

- Must have: the data we absolutely need in our capability; it cannot be compromised or left out, or the capability minimum viable product (MVP) will not be able to work or generate its business value.
- Should have: data essential to deliver the value of the capability but not critical for the MVP. This may be data tied to important features or functionalities that we can implement in later phases.
- Could have: what data can still add value and improve our final capability? This data supports optional or extra features that could enhance the functionality or user experience in the long term.
- Will not have or, in our case, Would like to have: our intuition, curiosity or simply data availability may suggest some additional data is out there and maybe leveraged. If there is no link to a value outcome, this data should be parked, and the overall need should be reassessed in the future.

Table 5.1 Assessing data needs vs our data capabilities portfolio with the MoSCoW methodology may help us prioritise the data foundation build. In this example, dataset A and E are the right starting choices, but dataset B is also needed to unlock data capability 3

Data capability portfolio	Dataset A	Dataset B	Dataset C	Dataset D	Dataset E
Data capability 1	M	S	W	M	C
Data capability 2	M	C	C	M	S
Data capability 3	C	M	W	M	W
Data capability 4	M	S	C	S	S
Data capability 5	S	C	W	C	C
Priority	★★★	★★	★	★★★	★★

Table 5.1 shows how this approach can be leveraged in the data assessment for a complete set of capabilities.

Now that we have identified what data to focus on, it is time to discuss how to organise it. To make this overview more effective, we will put ourselves in the shoes of Gail, a young manager joining a successful educational toys retail chain, to reorganise the data assets in the company so that they can enable the Data Transformation agenda. This example will help us familiarise ourselves with other essential concepts, critical in defining our *data architecture*, i.e. how data is managed from collection to transformation, distribution and consumption.

Tackling data silos and hubs

Our educational toys chain has rapidly expanded over the past decade, becoming a state-renowned destination for a unique blend of play, shopping and learning. This growth was not solely organic but also driven by acquisitions of smaller chains and shops, which are yet to be fully integrated. The IT department faces challenges in consolidating and harmonising diverse systems that often overlap in function and lack interconnectivity. Upon assessing the IT landscape, Gail identified significant missed opportunities in data management and exploitation due to this complexity. Notably, data is fragmented into its reference systems and very often duplicated.

- The cash register system is linked to a system devoted to storing the sales figures and providing statistics about the store's performance.

- The warehouse management system is linked to the logistic and shipping module but does not integrate with the single store sales data.
- A website with an e-commerce module is managed as a standalone store, without synergies with the physical stores regarding customer experience or product delivery.
- A new fidelity app has been launched to drive customer engagement and loyalty. A registered customer can use his account on the app, the e-commerce website, or in-store, like a fidelity card. They will collect fidelity points based on purchases, event participation and competition results and use them to access premium services and events.
- Lastly, some data related to the physical features of each store are registered in a simple Excel spreadsheet in a shared folder owned by one manager in the headquarters.

The business impact of this landscape is visible to Gail: many managers are complaining because they need to access and become experts in multiple systems to get actionable data support for their decision making. Data collection is as complicated as data collation since different datasets do not always speak the same language and cannot be summarised easily. New use cases on the innovation agenda (their big bets) are delayed or on hold because of the missing data prerequisites.

What we described above is the **data silos** setup: data is organised in separate repositories and exploited 'vertically' by the system owners or the leading unit. Any attempt to collect and consume data 'horizontally', i.e. across silos, ends up in a significant effort and sometimes is not even achievable due to technical and non-technical reasons (ever heard about 'data kingdoms?' Without sovereigns permission, you cannot access the data). Gail knows an alternative is possible by interconnecting the various data, removing unnecessary redundancies and ineffective duplications, and providing a single interface where the business users could access the data. This way of managing data through a shared organisation, access and consumption layer is known as a **data hub** setup.

Gail shares her ideas with her team, setting the expectation that moving from a data silos setup to a data hub setup is not an easy or short endeavour. However, there are a few considerations that she adds to persuade the team further.

- Creating a data hub does not necessarily mean all data must be centralised in a single system. The data hub acts as a middleware among the different systems, making sure they are connected physically or, more likely, logically.

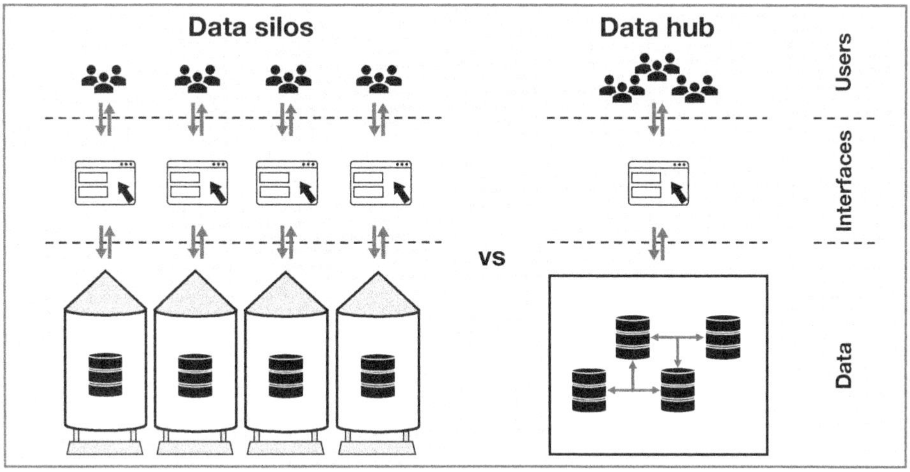

Figure 5.1 From data silos to data hub: centralising the interface to data and bringing data together, physically or logically

- To capture the data hub advantages, connecting data and offering it in a single location is insufficient, but data must be harmonised. For example, a product code in the warehouse management system must be linked to a single product code stored in the sales data from the cash registers and e-commerce system. This means everyone should consume a common dataset of general product information as a reference, i.e. a product *master data* table.

Data silos and data hubs are theoretical definitions, and the literature and industry practice offers many more options. Rather than looking at perfectly implementing a theoretical model, a company should make sure they are pointing in the right direction and, even if through iterative steps or imperfect scenarios, they are landing into the desired data architecture setup to enable their business need, as Gail is suggesting.

Data mesh and data fabric: the modern data architecture

According to Gartner Inc., data architecture has evolved from the concept of a monolithic enterprise data warehouse (EDW), the most successful model in the pre-big data era. New models arose in the new millennium: the 'post-EDW era' in the first decade of the 2000s, characterised by siloed and *fragmented analysis* approach in multiple specialised environments; the 'logical data warehouse (LDW) era' in the second decade, when a more *unified analysis* approach could be adopted thanks to a common semantic layer going across environments; the current 'active metadata era', where *augmented analysis* is enabled for both users and applications, through exploitation of metadata, intelligent engines and orchestrators.

This last phase is close to the **data fabric**, an emerging data management and integration design concept. For many organisations, the data fabric is a natural evolution from their logical data warehouse models because it leverages existing technology and metadata in a modernised data architecture. Its goal is to attain flexible, reusable and augmented data integration to support data access across the business.

Another successful concept is **data mesh**, an architectural approach allowing decentralised data management. Data Mesh architecture bases itself on organising data into specific business domains, decentralising and distributing data responsibility to people closest to the data, and sharing that data as a service. Its goal is to enable the definition, delivery, maintenance and governance of *data products* in a way that makes them easy to find and exploit by data consumers.

Designing the data model

Gail is convinced about the company's approach to setting up its future data management, but her challenges continue beyond a simple pitch. If breaking the silos may be a technical effort only, addressing the causes is not as simple. The educational toys chain's rapid but unchecked growth came at the expense of streamlined operations and organisational coherence. Today, different departments or functions do not share information or cooperate regularly, but only on a need or project basis, leading to inefficiencies or a lack of coordination in data management and exploitation, explaining well why the data silos have proliferated over time.

Now, Gail's idea is to involve the various teams in interviews that may help collect an accurate *data dictionary*, capturing and cataloguing the different data available and its main characteristics, like name, description, source, attributes, update frequency, granularity and coverage, sensitivity classification, contractual details, ownership and many more. This information is the famous **metadata**, literally 'data about data', which can help better understand, operate and govern the company's data assets.

After interviewing the sales, marketing and logistics teams, these are the most critical datasets she discovers:

- *receipts_transactions*: these are the records of each receipt released to a customer, with transactional data organised around a unique receipt identifier code;
- *receipt_details*: this table contains the product information of the transaction for each receipt, organised at the product barcode level;
- *warehouse_transactions*: this captures movements of goods in each store warehouse, organised by store identifier, product identifier (barcode), date/time and movement type (inbound or outbound);
- *product_masterdata*: this is the list of all products the chain manages. In each row of this table, we will find one product barcode and a set of attributes, like the product description, its dimensions and weight, its categorisation and many more;
- *store_masterdata*: this captures the complete store details organised by store identifier code;
- *customer_masterdata*: in this table, we have the list of the fidelity app owners, with their demographics, personal details and consents stored along with the fidelity number.

Now, let us consider a few things to understand these datasets better. Some tables contain transactional events like sales or inventory movements and their details; *transactional tables* are typically larger in volume, more dynamic and frequently updated. A second group, the *master data*, is related to reference data that better describes some entities mentioned in the transactions and helps enrich their understanding.

Every record (or row, for simplicity) in these tables can be identified in each table by one or more unique fields that never repeat in the list. A few examples: in the product master data, there cannot be multiple products with the same barcode; in the customer master data, each row is uniquely identified by the customer loyalty number since two customers cannot share the same number; in the case of the warehouse transactions, instead, the barcode alone is not sufficient to uniquely identify a row, since the same product barcode will be received or shelved multiple times over time and can be present in various stores. In this latter case, our unique identifying fields for each record are the product barcode, the store identifier code, the timestamp and the movement type. In fact, we cannot expect more than one inbound or outbound movement at the same precise time in one store (if this happens, it makes sense to capture it within the same quantity). These fields that help us identify unique rows in each table are called *primary keys* and are critical to combining data present in different tables.

Suppose Gail wants to know the most expensive products in each category and subcategory. In that case, she may combine the receipt details data and the product master data by relating the two tables via the product barcode field. This operation is technically called *join*. Documenting the relationship between the available tables is a critical step to establish how data can be joined and transformed (and before, how the overall database must be designed). The standard way to do that is to draw an *entity–relationship diagram*. This graphical schema explains how the different tables in a **relational database** can be logically related through their keys. In Figure 5.2, you can find a simplified representation of the datasets discovered by Gail.

While creating an entity–relationship diagram with all the related steps may seem merely technical, it has a lot of business value. This output may provide

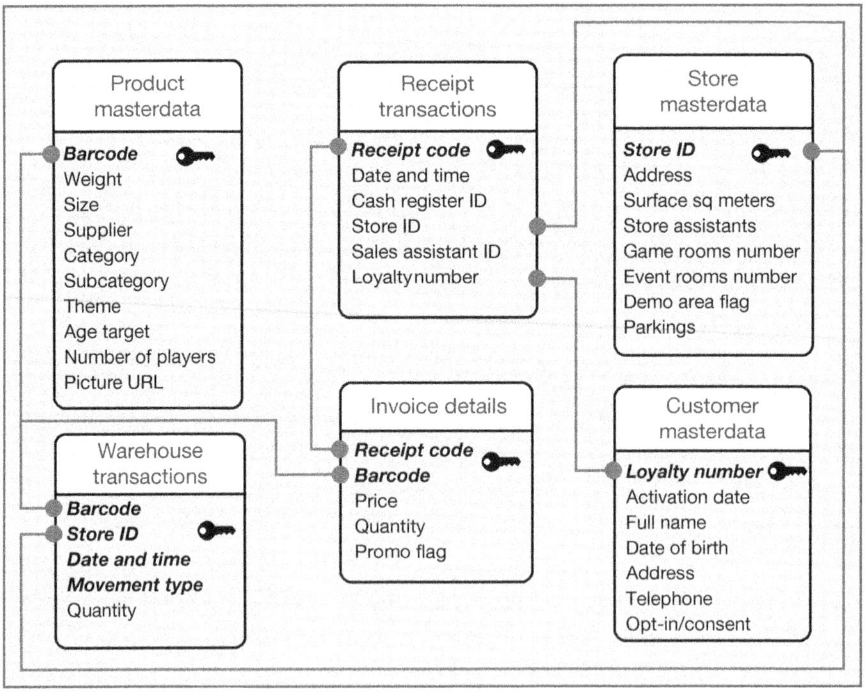

Figure 5.2 Simplified entity–relationship diagram. Fields in bold represent the primary keys of each table

a relatively easy-to-interpret broad view of our information assets model (or simply **data model**) and the interoperability of each component.

Suppose we really want to break the silos and organise our data so that it is tightly interconnected. In that case, we must work hard to understand and standardise our primary keys to join data and derive new value-added insights. This is not an easy task in a siloed data context: some critical table keys may be missing, the standardisation may be overlooked, and even master data may be partially duplicated, leading to possible conflicting data. On the contrary, establishing a standard reference data model will facilitate the convergence of the various stakeholders, help remove duplications and, even in a context of highly fragmented data, offer a target reference status to be achieved with a precise set of actions. This is exactly what Gail realises after creating the first standard data model for the datasets she has discovered and what makes her hopeful her mission can be accomplished.

Treating data as a product

Taking a step back, we realise we are building a data layer that can be exploited across our data capabilities. It is not something we can underestimate in terms of importance or impact. If we fail to set the proper foundation or get it well established and exploited, our data capabilities may fail, and our entire Data Transformation journey may be put at stake. One of the main risks we need to avoid, very often overlooked due to the excitement of the implementation process, is to consider this effort just a project: our data foundation gets established, we hand it over to some operations team, and everyone assumes they will continue to run on their feet. For the post-launch period, this is true; whoever was involved will continue to access and use the data and provide feedback for improvement and new requirements. However, very soon, challenges will arise in the governance and the evolution of the data assets around the potential duplications in other systems due to the lack of awareness and the loss of interest, jeopardising our asset's long-term success.

To prevent this outlook, we could embrace a product management mindset and articulate a few principles we can leverage to secure our data success.

- It should create **value** or support one or more capabilities responsible for value creation. We have discussed this point extensively in the Data Activation

Canvas overview, but it also becomes relevant for the data underlying our data capability.

- A **business owner** must be responsible for defining the governance of this data and promoting its adoption, usage and evolution across the entire lifecycle, i.e. the period data is actively used or can generate value.
- There must be a clear (set of) **consumer**(s) regularly using the data, and adoption and usage have to be measured.

This is a clear mindset shift from the project-driven approach, where we generate the asset and then passively observe if it gets consumed and how. The product management approach implies a change toward a proactive attitude: we seek product success (value generation) by promoting its adoption and usage to existing and new consumers. If these two are not improving, we will intervene in the product evolution, introducing new features or improving the existing ones. This implies that across the lifecycle of our data treated as a product, we will review the backlog of features and their value creation (or impact on adoption), prioritise, implement them according to a roadmap and communicate to our consumer base about our new value proposition.

This same approach can (and should) be applied to each of our data capabilities, especially given that the Data Activation Canvas already clarified many of these elements.

Essential tools for data analytics and AI

So far, this chapter has helped us familiarise ourselves with the technological trends that represent the latent driving forces from the outside, and we clarified the importance of properly organising the data to ensure a solid data assets foundation that sustains our data strategy. We will now analyse the tool landscape we need to explore to activate our portfolio of capabilities from a technical standpoint. In the following paragraphs, through the three-layered model of the **Modern Data Stack**, we will review the available tool choices and how to assess which one best fits our needs.

The Modern Data Stack

Here we come again to the famous big data, discussing the tools that could help manage them effectively. As you may easily guess, there is no simple answer to one question in such a complex domain as data, analytics and AI. Similarly, no single magic tool can address all the needs and entirely enable our data strategy.

To better understand the technological landscape, we will use a simplified model representing our technology across three different layers of the Modern Data Stack. Each layer has its mission and enables the one above in many ways from which we can choose. Let us present each of them.

1 The bottom is the **physical infrastructure** layer, made of hardware components that materially store and process the data. We are talking about machines that must keep running and operating excellently to ensure all the layers above sit on top of a reliable foundation.
2 The middle one is the logical **data platform** layer, where our data gets ingested, organised, modelled and secured before it gets consumed. This layer is also responsible for handling the logical management of the physical storage and compute resources of the layer below.
3 The upper part of the stack is the **application** layer, where we apply the solutions to transform data into economic value. Here, the data assets we organised in the middle layer will be consumed in various patterns through interfaces between data and consumers. These span from business intelligence tools to advanced algorithms and engines producing valuable recommendations, from application consuming data to enrich the end-user experience to data scientists exploring the data to tackle an unmet business need.

Looking at the diagram in Figure 5.3, we can infer a few crucial points.

- Each layer enables the one above but also establishes the requirements for the one below. This means that our requirements must be worked from top to bottom. Starting from the value-generating capabilities we want to activate, we derive the application layer requirements that help identify our data platform requirements that enforce some physical structure requirements. As you can see, our value-driven approach has been reinforced once again.
- Around the stack, you can have many professional roles, acting at multiple levels. *Data architects* design the blueprint for the organisational data framework and set infrastructure-related choices. *Data engineers* build and maintain data assets, pipelines and objects within that data framework. *Data scientists* and *analysts* consume data through data analytics tools to produce valuable business insights via data analysis, statistical modelling or machine learning. Lastly, *business users*, typically non-technical profiles, leverage

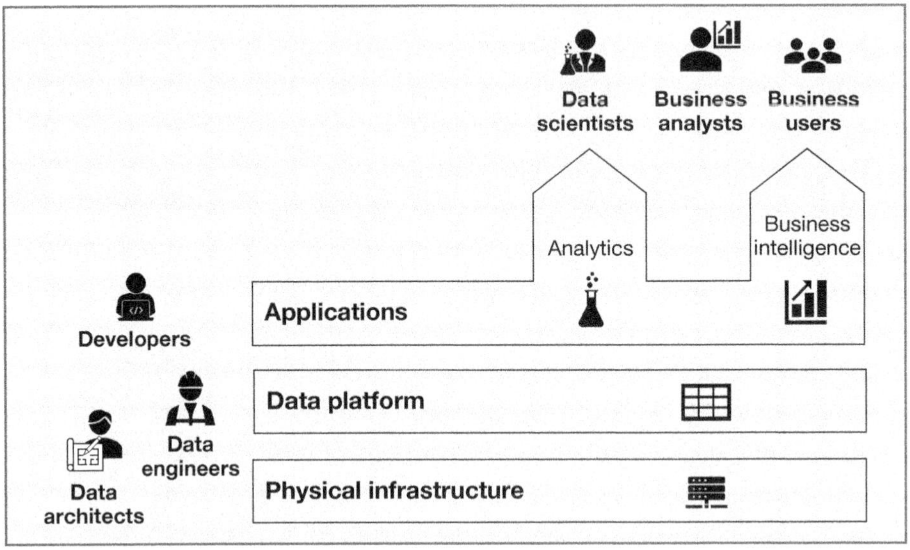

Figure 5.3 The Modern Data Stack. Each layer relies on the one below

business intelligence tools or applications built by *developers* to get insights and drive better decision making. Each figure may be dominantly involved in a particular layer, but this does not mean they cannot stretch across or that other roles may be present (ML and MLOps engineers, for instance). The birth of new roles is continuous, and we will likely see other ones continuing to emerge.

- We already talked about leveraging cloud services to rent IT resources and avoid the complexity of managing these internally. Following this reference model, we can identify three classes of potential cloud services to be considered in comparison to any in-house alternative. If we decide to outsource the bottom layer, we seek an *infrastructure as a service* (IaaS) offer. If we want to delegate the creation and management of the second layer, we are talking about a *platform as a service* (PaaS). In this case, we will focus on a few configurations to get started and then bring in our data to develop the applications and interfaces our business needs. The final choice is to delegate also (part of) the application layer to a third party offering *software as a service* (SaaS). This is quite common when someone else has already covered the business requirements to our satisfaction, and we can focus on exploiting the solution. A few examples beyond analytics are the already mentioned SalesForce application or business productivity suites like Microsoft 365 or G Suite by Google.

Now that we have clarified the Modern Data Stack layers, we can dive deeper into each. We will start from the bottom to understand what is available and what are the main questions we can use to identify the choice that best fits our needs.

Physical infrastructure

When looking at the bottom layer of our model, we are already asked to make a few choices.

- We could attempt to build a parallel computing infrastructure. To do so, we purchase several *servers*, computers devoted to processing and storage, and connect them in a group called *cluster*, sharing common infrastructure. Servers are typically stacked in *racks*, together with other components needed to handle the network connectivity or the power continuity. A *server farm* (another expression for data centre) is the classical place where you can find hundreds or thousands of racks. With a relatively limited investment, we could assemble a small infrastructure that we can supplement with additional resources over time, following the progress of real business needs. However, as we already anticipated, the expertise to set up and maintain it and the cost driven by the energy consumption and server cooling as it scales up may only sometimes play in favour of this choice.
- A different choice could be to take a centralised approach to fulfil our data processing needs and purchase a single costly but very powerful machine, a *mainframe*. This computer is designed for high performance, reliability and robust security. It is a common choice of large organisations for business-critical operations, where potential downtimes may be very costly. Mainframes can handle massive processing loads and manage high volumes of transactions, which is crucial for large-scale industries like banking, insurance and retail. The leader of this technology is IBM with the Z systems.
- If we do not have the budget or do not want to invest significant capital and resources upfront, a third option could be to go to the cloud, leveraging an IaaS provider offering. When purchasing infrastructure 'as a service', we are allowed to exploit a portion of the resources in the provider data centre, tailored to our requirements, with the possibility to scale up or down and paying a monthly fee or 'as we go', i.e. based on the actual consumption of the resources we have chosen.

Data platforms

Once the choices for the physical foundation are clear, we can aim at the data platform layer, which is essential to enabling our capabilities portfolio. To appropriately scrutinise what modern data platforms offer in terms of data storage and management solutions, we should first recall how company data (and datasets) may be really diverse. A company may deal with *structured data*, having a precisely codified structure, with clear rules about fields and keys (previous Gail's datasets are good examples), or *unstructured data*, i.e. not organised in a pre-defined format (e.g. an e-commerce product review, a social media post, a text document or a video). There may be data we are regularly procuring (e.g. data about our competitor's media investments) or data we purchase or collect on an ad-hoc basis, maybe only once, to run a project or solve a problem (e.g. a customer survey to check what they think about our brand tenth anniversary). In a nutshell, given this diversity, there is no 'fits-all' solution, and we need to comprehend and evaluate a few available choices, in this case, too.

First, where do we want to keep our data, and how do we want to manage it? There are two main options we can analyse.

- A **data warehouse** (DWH) can be seen as a very neatly organised data repository with codified rules and relationships. Any new data is ingested based on a specific organisational schema, established a priori, that gets imposed on the data when loaded in the tables (*schema-on-write*).
- A **data lake** (DL) is more like a storage container where data arrives and is 'stocked', very often in its raw format, to be organised only when needed. In this case, its schema will be established a posteriori through the retrieval and reading process (*schema-on-read*).

The choice among these ways of organising data storage and management must start from the expected benefits since both have strengths for specific consumption scenarios and use cases.

A data warehouse will privilege data structure and alignment to defined rules, requiring an effort to design, codify and maintain them over time. On one side, this point allows for better reliability and overall data robustness, as it can enforce **data quality**, consistency, and accuracy (data is cleaned, transformed and structured before being stored); on the other side, it may be more expensive and resource intense to create and maintain. Therefore, a data warehouse is ideal for performing analytics on structured data in organisations with a strong need to integrate data from highly structured transactional systems (like ERP or CRM). It is best suited for business intelligence (BI) and reporting because of its efficiency in supporting large data aggregations, joins and high-performing queries. Finally, a data warehouse is typically accompanied by a range of mature tools for data **extraction, transformation and loading (ETL)**, and it often has more established governance, security and compliance mechanisms.

In contrast, data lakes are preferred when dealing with large volumes of both structured and unstructured data, when there is a need to store data in its raw form for future use, or when an organisation wants to leverage big data technologies for advanced analytics, such as machine learning and predictive modelling. A data lake is often seen as the ideal playground where analysts and data scientists are free to explore, combine and transform data assets with few restrictions on rules and schemas to follow. It also represents a perfect base to build *proof of concepts* or *prototypes*. It has a cheaper storage unit cost and is more flexible in onboarding new data that can be loaded at any time or pulled via standard interfaces from other services (APIs). Data lakes offer flexibility and scalability but require more management and advanced analytical tools to derive meaningful insights.

Table 5.2 recaps the main features of each, but this should give us a different impression than if we were forced to choose between the two options. In

Table 5.2 Comparing data warehouses and data lakes helps understand the respective strengths

Feature	**Data warehouse**	**Data lake**
Type of data supported	Structured data, organised in tables	Structured and unstructured data
Schema	Schema on write (defined a priori)	Schema on read (defined a posteriori)
Data storage format	Cleaned, transformed and processed data organised in tables	Raw format, as it arrives from source
Data unit cost	High	Low
Agility	Low	High
Data readability	High	Low
Data quality and governance	High	Low
Common use cases	Business intelligence, standard reporting	Ad hoc analysis, machine learning, prototyping

reality, most companies embrace both, balancing cost, platform governance and delivered benefit. Additionally, a recent architecture setup, the **data lakehouse**, combines the flexibility and scalability of data lakes with the data management and performance optimisation features typically associated with data warehouses. Data lakehouses are generally built on open file formats and open-source foundations, ensuring compatibility with a wide range of analytics tools and platforms. This architecture seeks to merge the strengths of data lakes and warehouses, providing a unified platform for data science and machine learning workloads (which require raw, unstructured data) and traditional business intelligence and reporting (which rely on structured, processed data).

After this overview, and conscious of the needs we would like to address in our company, what options can we consider?

- On-premise: Teradata, Oracle Exadata, IBM Db2 and Microsoft SQL Server offer renowned solutions for data warehousing. Data lake architectures are typically based on Hadoop Distributed File System (HDFS), often used in conjunction with Apache Hadoop to process large datasets. Data platform solutions like Cloudera CDP and IBM Cloud Pak for Data offer the possibility of being deployed on-premises.
- On cloud: the most significant part of the market is captured by the top three tech cloud giants: Microsoft Azure, which offers Azure Data Lake Storage and Azure Synapse Analytics; Amazon Web Services (AWS), which offers Amazon S3, AWS Lake Formation and Amazon Redshift; Google Cloud Platform (GCP), offering Google Cloud Storage and BigQuery. Two additional mentions: Snowflake, a cloud-based platform offering a unique approach to data warehousing and data lakes, allowing businesses to integrate and analyse structured and semi-structured data efficiently; Databricks, a unified analytics platform built on Apache Spark that is particularly strong in machine learning and advanced analytics, and leveraging a data lakehouse architecture.

Cloud-based data platforms are more and more successful, where no specific data or regulation constraints to adoption exist. They offer the possibility to balance investment and flexibility with the clear advantage of limitless scaling options. However, choosing a PaaS scenario does not mean outsourcing everything to the service provider. Instead, we would have to equip our team with the right expertise and skills to manage, exploit and evolve our data platform adoption based on the evolving business challenges and priorities.

Applications

The highest layer of our stack is where the final user – a data scientist, a data analyst or a business user – can interact with the data assets available in our company, or at least in our data platform. This layer is the actual interface between data and business, and the applications are the vehicle to make this happen. Applications are significant enablers of data activation. Still, when not properly organised, partially effective or absent, the business gets frustrated and disappointed about its ability to generate value from data.

In Figure 5.4, we can see the application needs represented in two prominent families.

- *Business intelligence* (BI) tools cater the descriptive analytics insights to the business users to support their decisions. BI tools include reports, interactive dashboards containing tables and graphs, and management cockpits monitoring the most critical business KPIs. Their mission is to provide quick and user-friendly access to the pre-processed data that can closely represent business facts and help elicit rapid business insights through data *slicing, deep diving* and *drilling down*. These tools are actual data democracy engines since they appeal to both data analysis expert users and non-expert users. The first ones are the business analysts, who use and often design the default BI interfaces that the business users, not necessarily experts in data analysis, can leverage to access the data they need to run business operations and make decisions.

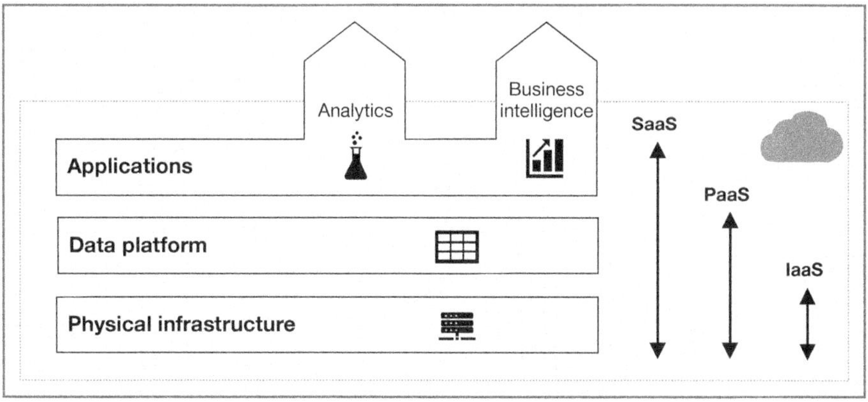

Figure 5.4 The cloud-based service options to manage different levels of our data stack

- *Data analytics* (or simply analytics) tools support the need to extract insights from the data using algorithms that can forecast, optimise and spot patterns and relationships the average human mind could not process through a report or a dashboard. The data analytics tools users are indeed experts, like data scientists and business analysts, who use existing algorithms or create new ones to extract actionable insights and business value from the available data. The analytics tools, as we will see, should allow the expert user to access and explore the data available on the data platform, even at a very granular level, and run their models (mathematical, statistical or ML) on top of the relevant data assets.

Also, in this case, we are discussing something other than two different groups between which we must choose. These complementary tools empower different users with different needs and must be understood and known before making any choice. The business intelligence tools can empower the entire organisation to drive insights from data, truly democratising data access and usage. The higher the adoption, the higher the chance to fully embrace the data-driven decision-making mindset. Parallelly, advanced analytics tools ensure we raise the bar and stay up to the mark vs the industry, generating value from algorithms that can bring augmented and autonomous decision making to life.

For the business intelligence area, famous and successful tools for reporting, data analysis and interactive visualisation are Microsoft PowerBI, Tableau, Qlik, Tibco Spotfire and the open-source alternatives Apache Superset, Redash and Metabase. Most of these tools can connect to our data platform to read and transform the data, run additional data calculations, help define dashboards with a mix of visual and tabular elements, and publish them in a webspace so that the rest of the organisation can access and use them.

On the analytics tools side, the landscape becomes more complex. First of all, the most critical tool data scientists leverage is a programming language that can support both Data Transformation and algorithm development. Broadly used and widespread languages in the data science community are Python and R. Their extreme popularity has made a large set of pre-defined libraries available to everyone, implementing both data manipulation and machine learning algorithms. While these languages ensure versatility and flexibility to their users, in terms of the ability to cover emerging needs, they require solid coding skills and experience. Also, they need an integrated development environment (IDE) where code can be developed and run. Two very common environments serving this purpose are Rstudio for R and Jupyter Notebook for Python. However, R, Python and SQL code can also run in web-based environments that allow efficient interaction with our data platform content: Apache Hive, Cloudera Impala and, the already mentioned, Databricks.

Another exciting set of solutions that serves data analytics purposes but is also addressed to less expert users is the family of low code/no code applications, leveraging a logical approach to replicate what programming language commands would do in a code in the form of a visual workflow that can be built intuitively and rapidly. This is another way to foster data democratisation, offering new tools to users that can efficiently upskill in areas not far from their day-to-day skillset to unlock unforeseen productivity and opportunities. Knime, Alteryx, Dataiku and RapidMiner are relevant solutions in this space.

Given this articulated landscape, it may be challenging to get oriented and make choices, so it is worth summarising at least the strengths of each family of solutions we mentioned and comparing them to see where they can help.

Table 5.3 clearly shows that each family of data analysis and business intelligence tools has its strength and role in addressing business needs, and

Table 5.3 Comparing business intelligence and data analytics applications to differentiate their strengths

Application	Data input / ETL	Machine learning	Data visualisation	User friendliness	Automation	Suitable for
Python Jupyter Rstudio	★★	★★★★	★	★	★★★	Advanced machine learning, capability scaling
Power BI Tableau	★★	★	★★★★	★★★	★★	Interactive dashboards
Knime Rapidminer	★★★★	★★★	★	★★★	★★★★	Prototyping, ETL, Ad hoc analysis, Automation
MS Excel OpenOffice Calc	★★	★	★★★	★★★★	★	Easy data sharing, simple visualisation

there is no magic wand to meet all of them. So, rather than choosing one among the rest, we need to identify the proper toolbox our organisation may benefit from, considering the current status, the opportunity in front of us and our ability to stretch outside our current technical comfort zone.

The golden checklist on the technology foundation

This chapter gave us another important element to unlock our journey: a critical enabler to sustain all the magic delivered by the algorithms and support our portfolio of essential data capabilities. To facilitate the completion of this step, we can leverage once again a simple checklist to ensure all boxes are ticked and we are ready to move on.

1. **Recognising the silent engines of the data revolution**
   - Are we familiar with, and can we articulate how digital and cloud technologies are critical trends influencing the enablers of our Data Transformation?
   - Is our business embracing them enough to benefit from their exponential momentum?
   - Can we leverage them so that our business operating model can evolve?
2. **Effectively organising our data**
   - Are we clear on the data requirements priorities deriving from our data capability portfolio?
   - Have we identified the best possible data architecture for our analytical needs?
   - Have we established a common reference data model for our company's data? Is this available and plain to everyone in the company?
   - Do we know who are the consumers of our data? What value the data is producing? Who is the business owner of the data?
3. **Choosing the right data stack**
   - What are our needs and choices for the infrastructure layer? Will we build and maintain it ourselves, or will we leverage an IaaS provider? Can we explain the rationale behind our choice?
   - What is our data platform choice? Will we implement and maintain it ourselves, or will we leverage a PaaS provider? Can we explain the rationale behind our choice?

- What applications will we pick for our organisation's BI and analytics toolkit? Are we clear on the role of each tool?

Technology is foundational in enabling human progress and a tremendous accelerator of the data revolution we see in our modern society. However, technology is only helpful if the human prerequisites regarding talent, organisation and culture are first met. That is the topic of our next chapter.

CHAPTER 6
NURTURING A DATA-DRIVEN CULTURE AND ORGANISATION

In this chapter

- Who are the main actors of a company's Data Transformation, and how do you define their roles?
- What skills do they need, and how can you develop them?
- What are the common organisational structures you can implement for making the best out of data and algorithms, and which one is the right one for your company?
- What does the CDO do, and do you need one?
- What are the typical barriers to establishing a data-friendly culture within an organisation, and what can you do to mitigate them?

However counterintuitive it may sound, Data Transformation is, first, an organisational and cultural challenge. We find ourselves in a narrative dominated by data, technology and algorithms. Posts and news articles about novel AI algorithms, their billions of parameters and their formidable superpowers often overshadow the unsung efforts (and the sweat) of the people putting these algorithms to work.

Those who have already navigated the joys and pains of this journey know that humans matter most. A recent research study, co-authored by one of us, involving interviews with over 200 managers, identified the most critical success factors in their Data Transformation journey. The top three factors were all very much people-related:

1. hiring and retaining the right *talent* with the necessary skills for the appropriate roles;
2. establishing the proper *organisational structure*, positioning the right talent effectively, and ensuring strong leadership;
3. cultivating a suitable company *culture* supported by the right sponsorship and an open-minded embracement of data capabilities.

In this chapter, you will learn practical frameworks to correctly set up the three data human drivers illustrated in Figure 6.1.

This is no easy ride. Still, if you succeed, you will build a genuine source of competitive advantage. Human readiness is actually scarcer than data and

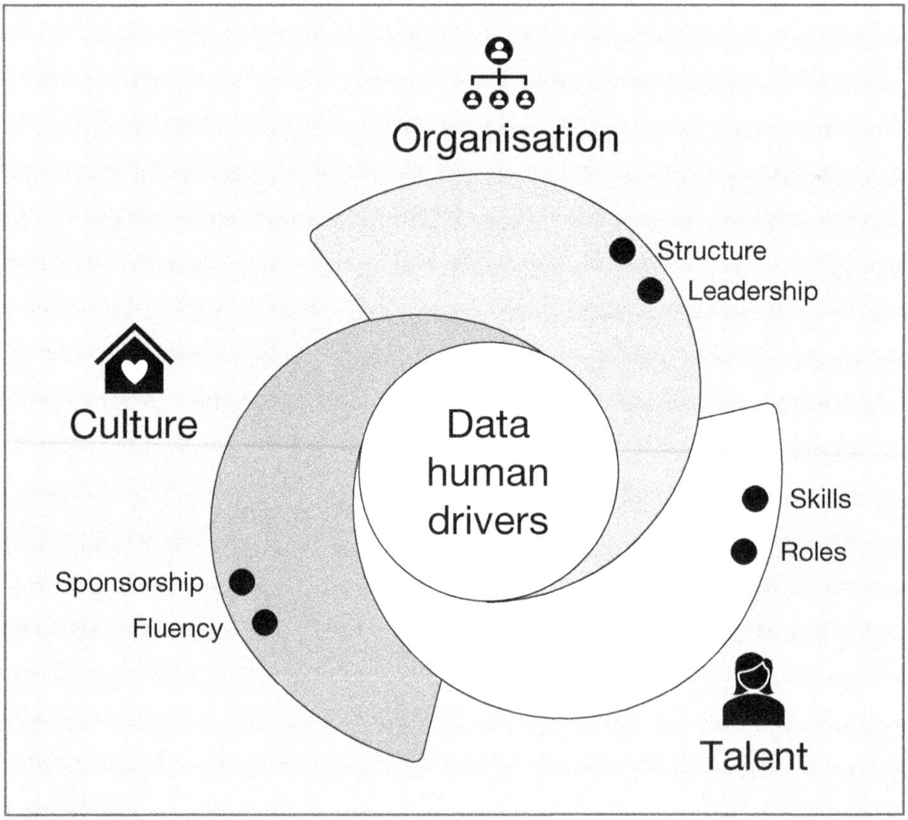

Figure 6.1 The data human drivers: you need to get the right talent, in the right organisation, with the right culture

technology readiness. Although data and technological tools tend to become more and more available over time, cheaper and relatively easier to use, the 'human' factors continue to be the most expensive to set up and the hardest to manage.

This chapter will move beyond the predictable nature of algorithms and technology, delving into the multifaceted and intriguing world of human resources. We will deal with 'flesh and blood' people, with their ambitions, emotions, frustrations, strengths and weaknesses. Buckle up as we begin our journey by envisioning the human talent necessary for success.

Nurturing the right talent

'Data scientist: the sexiest job of the 21st century.' When the *Harvard Business Review* article went out in 2012 with such a fancy headline, the popularity of the new job title reached a new peak. This had somewhat embarrassing – and hilarious – consequences. At that time, many who could crunch numbers in Excel rushed to update their CVs, renaming themselves as data scientists to gain attractiveness on the job market.

In reality, a 'unicorn' professional who can shoulder the entire weight of transforming data into value, like data scientists seemed able to do back in the day, do not exist. Data analytics is, in truth, a team sport involving the collaboration of different and complementary figures deeply integrated within the corporate fabric.

To avoid oversimplification and the risk of falling back into the definition of stereotyped 'super-hero' roles, let's build up the understanding of the talent we need, starting by listing the core data competencies that we, overall, require in our companies. Then, we will use these competencies to describe the professional roles we need to be equipped with to ensure the success of our Data Transformation.

Six core skill sets for Data Transformation

Here is a list of the six core skill sets that are required by an organisation to run Data Transformation at full speed.

- **Machine learning:** this skill set enables the ML-Way by implementing the right algorithms. Skilled professionals in this domain can adopt and repurpose existing algorithms but also innovate methodologies, recognising the potentials and limitations of each, underpinned by robust statistical knowledge.
- **Data analysis and storytelling:** this skill set supports decisions with data-driven insight, which is effectively communicated to decision makers through data storytelling and visualisation techniques. These skills enable the translation of data into business-relevant messages and involve understanding the audience, listening empathically and effectively communicating in business terms.
- **Business understanding:** this involves a deep comprehension of business processes and economic value production. Those with this skill know what the company does to produce economic value, how to navigate the organisation to make things happen, and understand the business landscape, including markets, competitors and regulations.
- **Coding:** is the basic competence of computer science and refers to translating a requirement into the writing of code in one or more programming languages, with Python, R and SQL being particularly prevalent in data analysis.
- **Data architecture:** this skill set enables the management and monitoring of the data technology stack, ensuring data availability and performance to meet business needs. It implies the ability to interpret current business needs and anticipate future ones to prepare – at the various levels of the data stack – the technological architecture required to achieve business objectives.
- **Data stewardship:** this skill set involves taking care of data assets and understanding data governance procedures in a company. It requires recognising the strategic importance of every data asset and algorithm, knowing how to document and use them consistently to ensure high-quality data accessibility.

Although there are many more nuances and specialisation areas not mentioned above, these six skill sets are essential in data analytics.

Four fundamental data job roles

Let's go to the next level and see how such skill sets are 'blended' together in four key job role families in data analytics, namely: business users, data analysts, data scientists and data engineers. Like any other job description, the following ones describe the ideal candidate for each type of role.

- **Business users:** although primarily consumers of data analytics, business users (of any function and seniority level) benefit from a foundational fluency in basic data analysis and storytelling techniques for presenting data effectively. They also understand the potential of AI-powered solutions, anticipating possible ML-Ways of solving their business needs. They recognise the importance of considering data as a strategic asset and ensure adherence to data and AI governance practices.
- **Data analysts:** data analysts (or business analysts) play the fundamental role of uniting the two worlds of business and data. Thanks to their solid understanding of business dynamics, they can proactively intercept opportunities for data capabilities to make a difference. They can also translate business needs into technical requirements and quickly prototype ML solutions (leveraging some coding if necessary) before leaving them in the capable hands of data scientists for scaling. Data analysts are proficient with data analysis (as they need to constantly 'peel the onion' and extract business-relevant insights from large quantities of data) and storytelling (since they want their data findings to make strong impacts and drive action). They know where data is and contribute to the organisation's data stewardship by maintaining the integrity and relevance of data assets.
- **Data scientists:** data scientists are masters in advanced analytics, focusing predominantly on ML algorithms to create predictive and prescriptive models. They excel in coding, which is crucial in developing and scaling complex solutions. Although they understand data analysis, their primary role involves deep technical work rather than business strategy. They contribute to data architecture and stewardship, ensuring that analytics solutions are built on a solid foundation and are sustainable over time.
- **Data engineers:** data engineers (and related roles, such as systems engineers, ML engineers and data architects) specialise in the technical infrastructure that supports data analytics, with a strong focus on data architecture to ensure that systems are robust, scalable and performant. Their advanced coding skills allow them to construct and maintain complex data pipelines. They understand machine learning and play a critical role in data stewardship, safeguarding data quality and accessibility, thus enabling every other actor to perform their roles effectively.

Table 6.1 Data role vs skill set mapping: the more stars, the more important a skill set is for a role

Role family	Business under-standing	Data analysis and storytelling	Machine learning	Coding	Data architecture	Data steward-ship
Business user	★★★	★	★			★★
Data analyst	★★	★★★	★★	★		★
Data scientist		★	★★★	★★★	★	★
Data engineer			★	★★	★★★	★★

As you can see in Table 6.1, the four families of roles necessitate overlapping skill sets. We are far from the somewhat idealised world in which there is a clear division by area of expertise: in truth, data analytics is inherently multidisciplinary. Moreover, the legendary image of the data scientist-superhero appears to us to be far from the harsh reality where we necessarily need several people with complementary roles.

We also notice that literally *everyone* is involved in data analytics. The broad role of the business user family covers all human resources in the company, even those who do not have the word 'data' in their official title. This calls for a universal need to provide basic analytics fluency to everyone: we will come back to this point later.

Data roles in action

To get a clearer picture of the dynamics of collaboration between these different professional roles, it is best to rely on a concrete example.

Jacek, an area sales leader for a utility company distributing electricity in Central Europe, raises an eyebrow when he notices unusually high discounts in the sales data dashboard. In the last three months, some customers have enjoyed up to 70 per cent discount. Concerned about a potential data quality issue, he asks Marta, a data analyst embedded in his business unit, to investigate further.

Marta is able to quickly pull the data and confirm that it is accurate – a few customers are indeed receiving oversized discounts. Diving deeper, she uncovers that this trend extends beyond Jacek's area and could potentially affect the company's profitability on a larger scale. Together with Jacek, she engages the business team overseeing the discounting process, uncovering a flaw in the logic that allows discounts of different sources to accumulate to unprofitable levels.

Recognising the need for a systematic approach to manage this issue, Marta crafts a prototype using an unsupervised ML algorithm to detect such anomalies. Jacek, recognising the potential impact of Marta's work, champions the project to the sales director, successfully securing the necessary funding.

With the project greenlit, Marta pulls Leonardo, a data scientist on the sales team, into the game. Inspired by Marta's prototype, Leonardo develops a more sophisticated system in Python that not only identifies discount irregularities but also analyses their causes, generates some text summarising them, and suggests more profitable alternatives for each affected customer.

Ensuring that this novel capability functions smoothly requires the technical expertise of Priya, the team's data engineer. She constructs an efficient and automated data pipeline that supports Leonardo's alerting system, meticulously cataloguing and documenting the new data assets in accordance with the company's data governance standards.

This brief example helped us 'see in action' the four families of professional roles capable of supporting the Data Transformation. It's a testament to the power of collaboration in the team sport of analytics.

Theory versus reality: data frustrations and how to solve them

Nice story but ... it's too good to be true. In the intricate ecosystem of power, ambitions, miscommunications and ambiguities that any human organisation has, the dynamics across data roles are rarely similar to the idyllic scenario above. Each role within the analytics spectrum faces its own frustrations and shortcomings, often leading to a less-than-perfect execution of the Data Transformation journey.

Let's go through the typical challenges people in a data role have by putting ourselves in their shoes momentarily. If we can recognise their frustrations, we can mitigate them accordingly.

- **Business users:** in the real world, not all business users are as proactive and positive about data as Jacek. Many suffer frustrations due to fragmented systems and siloed data, making it arduous to draw meaningful insights. They might lack the technical know-how to use the tools available to them like Jacek did with the sales dashboard. Often, they may even dismiss data anomalies as 'someone else's problem', contributing to a culture of inaction and finger-pointing. Overcoming these challenges requires organisations to nurture a strong sense of data stewardship from all employees and a broad commitment to learning (and using) data analytics tools. Senior business managers need to role model this by openly showing that they use data analytics tools to make decisions.
- **Data analysts:** unlike Marta, who quickly jumped at the discounting discrepancies and took the initiative to solve them, many data analysts are more reactive as they feel undervalued and overburdened with routine tasks that fail to utilise their full analytical prowess. They often feel trapped in continuous low-added-value requests like extracting data and generating manual reports. They are always in 'firefighting mode' and don't have time for critical deep dives like Marta's quick analysis. To counteract this, organisations must actively involve analysts in strategic conversations explaining their decision-making support role across the business teams. They must encourage them to speak up and articulate the value they can add beyond mere number-crunching.
- **Data scientists:** many data scientists feel they get bogged down by low-quality data or are being sidelined into tasks far beneath their skill level, which hardly resembles the impactful, innovative work they aspire to do (and they studied for). They can be insulated from business realities and are only brought in *after* decisions have been made. Bridging this gap requires an integrated approach where data scientists are involved early in the business problem-solving process, and their feedback is actively sought to refine and drive business objectives.
- **Data engineers:** data engineers may not always be aware of the strategic goals of projects, leading to a misalignment between technical execution and business needs. Additionally, they can be frustrated by the lack of

investment in data infrastructure, which hampers their ability to implement robust solutions. For data engineers to truly thrive, there needs to be clear communication about the purpose and priorities of projects, along with recognition of their foundational role in enabling the sustainability of the Data Transformation journey.

Table 6.2 summarises the typical frustrations people experience and suggests what everyone can do about them. Think about your company and whether you sense some of those frustrations.

To every data professional reading these pages, know this: 'You are not alone. The frustrations you encounter are part of the game. You have a unique role to influence those around you to amplify the value of data analytics in your company.'

To business leaders, the call to action is: 'Recognise the complexity and the ambiguities experienced by data professionals. Role model transformation by learning analytics (keeping this book in your hands proves that you are already doing this) and encourage others to do the same. Empower data professionals in their strategic roles.'

Table 6.2 Typical frustrations in data roles and how to solve them

Data role	What they might feel	What they should do
Business users	Frustrations due to fragmented systems and siloed data	Nurture a strong sense of ownership in data, commit to learning and using data analytics tools, engage in data literacy programmes, ask senior managers to role model using data analytics for decision making
Data analysts	Feel undervalued and overburdened with routine and tactical tasks	Push for involvement in strategic conversations, articulate value beyond number crunching, proactively propose 'low-hanging-fruit' projects on most current business pain points
Data scientists	Slowed down by low-quality data, trapped into tasks below their skill level	Seek clarity on business objectives for every project they get pulled into, show 'graduality' in solutions of increasing technical complexity level, keep others involved during any development
Data engineers	Misunderstandings and under-appreciation, lack of investment in data infrastructure	Advocate for necessary tools and infrastructure resources, explaining their value in business terms, align technical execution with business needs, show the value of data governance with practical examples

Designing the right organisation

Modern organisations are inherently complex. Integrating data talent within their pre-existing matrices of power, accountability and objectives is far from straightforward. It also demands a strategic approach to resource acquisition, encompassing decisions about leveraging and reskilling internal talent versus recruiting from outside the organisation. Equally challenging is the role of the lead executive in the data journey as a CDO.

The following pages will help you visualise three crucial aspects of constructing an effective organisation: selecting the most suitable structure, acquiring the right people and enhancing the potential for leadership success.

Organisational models: selecting the structure that works

Finding the right location of data professionals in the corporate organisational chart is not straightforward. The various organisational units of the company (be it business units differentiated by product, different geographies, or business functions such as Sales, Marketing, HR and Finance) may claim the need to control, more or less directly, the work of business analysts and data scientists to benefit and impact their KPIs quickly.

The difficulty in choosing the appropriate organisational model stems from the existence of two needs that are both legitimate and inherently conflicting.

1 The first requirement is to place analytical skills as closely as possible in contact with business opportunities to ensure a strong link between data and its pragmatic transformation into economic value within a short timeframe.
2 The second requirement is to allow analytical competencies to organise themselves efficiently for scaled development, enabling longer-term ambition to innovate more than what short-term, immediate business needs.

There is a continuum of organisational choices that can meet these needs at different levels. Let's look at the most popular choices.

Distributed model

In the *distributed model*, the analytical talents are totally embedded in the business units (or functions, or geographical markets, as the case may be) and fully integrated into their organisational structure. In this case, data professionals have a solid reporting line to the leaders of their business units.

There is no better way to respond to the first need mentioned above. In a distributed model, data professionals can work hand-in-hand with their business counterparts, getting visibility of what is happening in the business. For example, an embedded data analyst can take part in the day-to-day dynamics of the business unit and can identify (even proactively, if well engaged) opportunities for data and algorithms to impact results.

Over time, these people create vertical domain expertise on that portion of the business, understand its language, deal with ambiguities and conflicts naturally, and know how their business partners behave and anticipate them appropriately. If they play their cards well, others will likely accept them as trusted advisors to the extent that their own recommendations, based on analysis and models, and their proposals for new analytical capabilities are respectfully considered. As artisans, the decentralised data professionals will become experts at building unique and perfectly fitting crafts to meet their organisation's needs.

This model also has side effects. Data professionals will tend to end up working on the most immediate business needs, even if that means going beyond their job descriptions. Data analysts may be asked to solely produce simple reports or data extractions. Their management cannot guide them technically because they are business managers. As a consequence, these data professionals need to rely solely on their personal skill development initiatives and – as we all know – not every person is proactive enough or has the right support to grow their skills in such a situation. Embedded data scientists may not have the opportunity to research and experiment with new algorithms, being 'squeezed' into the need to continually reuse models of proven – albeit limited – success. Data engineers will be asked to focus on building data capacities only for their business units, causing the dissemination of data silos.

In general, distributed analytical organisations tend to be detached across the various business units, which also leads data operators to work in silos, foregoing the opportunity to create synergies and share experiences. Hence, they risk 'inventing hot water' and stumbling upon the same difficulties over and over.

Centralised model

In a fully *centralised model*, the various analytical talents are concentrated in the same team, a *central analytics team* or a *data centre of excellence*, led by a leader with a technical background in data analytics.

Such a centralised organisation will 'look beyond' immediate needs to prepare the company to create a solid long-term competitive advantage using data. The core team will interface with the company's various business units and act as central providers of analytical services, ensuring that data and solutions are 'delivered' according to their specific needs. Working closely together and pursuing a common *vision*, the data professionals assembled in the central analytics team can collaborate at their best: analytics projects are organised into a portfolio of complementary, non-overlapping initiatives, which are executed effectively, generating continuous learning that translates into systematic updates and improvements to the big data stack, at all of its levels.

The central team is also likely to be endowed with the critical mass of people and skills that allows it to maintain a *pipeline* of truly ambitious innovative projects (we called them *moonshots* in Chapter 2) capable of dramatically improving the impact on KPIs (e.g. increasing them tenfold) as opposed to growing them by a few percentage points. Furthermore, a centralised model will allow analysts to grow vertically and specialise in a specific area, thus allowing the entire organisation to benefit from the analytical excellence available. If the decentralised model had 'artisans', the centralised model uses 'factories', representing an industrial system with scaled mass-producing capabilities.

Conversely, this completely centralised organisational model will always be limited in its ability to truly understand the needs of the business it is serving: those in the business units will not always be able to explain what they need (not having the analytical skills to see the opportunities for applying algorithms). The professionals gathered in the core team will also run the risk (very frequent, in our experience) of being pointed at as those living in an 'ivory tower', isolated from the real business needs. They will find themselves in the difficult situation of investing time in continually justifying the value created versus having the time to actually create more.

Hub-and-spoke model

There is a middle-ground alternative to the two extreme models above, the *hub-and-spoke* where a central analytics hub is connected with the various business units through sum peripheral branches in each business unit (BU) called spokes.

This model balances flexibility and standardisation, agility and scaling, tactics and strategy. It supports scaling and innovation without compromising business impact and cooperation. This means that some foundational capabilities will be operated and delivered centrally (by the hub) while the BU execution and business-specific capabilities will be delivered vertically and distributed by the embedded units (the spokes).

This solution is apparently perfect because it takes the best of both extremes. The central team manages the delivery of shared data capabilities, enabling maximum speed and synergy when deploying and maintaining technologies, processes and central solutions, always ensuring the adherence to central standards of governance and alignment with the company-wide data strategy. Through the exchange of knowledge and best practices, the various spokes connect continuously through *communities of practices* (CoPs) and *centres of excellence* (CoEs). At the same time, the embedded teams ensure a constant connection with the business needs, keeping the data organisation relevant and well linked with the company's value chain.

Also, the hybrid model carries its disadvantages. First of all, the embedded BU data teams will have 'two bosses' and will be likely to end up being part of a matrix organisation with priorities that may be in conflict. Also, the reconciliation of the contrasting needs of capability customisation, which is necessary to remain relevant with specific BUs, with the desire to build central systems and processes that are scalable and efficient, can generate major resource allocation conflicts.

As Figure 6.2 illustrates, the three models are all valid alternatives, with their pros and cons, and no specific model wins over the others.

Navigating the organisational maturity evolution

The organisational choices for a data team depend on the evolution stage of the company. Let's go through the typical evolutionary journey of data organisations so we can appreciate this point.

Normally, companies that start their analytics journey follow a fully decentralised model. Every department or BU has a team looking after 'data', which at this stage normally means simple reporting. You can imagine a sales organisation having a handful of people who are more skilled than others with 'Excel' or have already built a simple suite of web-based dashboards reporting revenues by customer type or other sales KPIs.

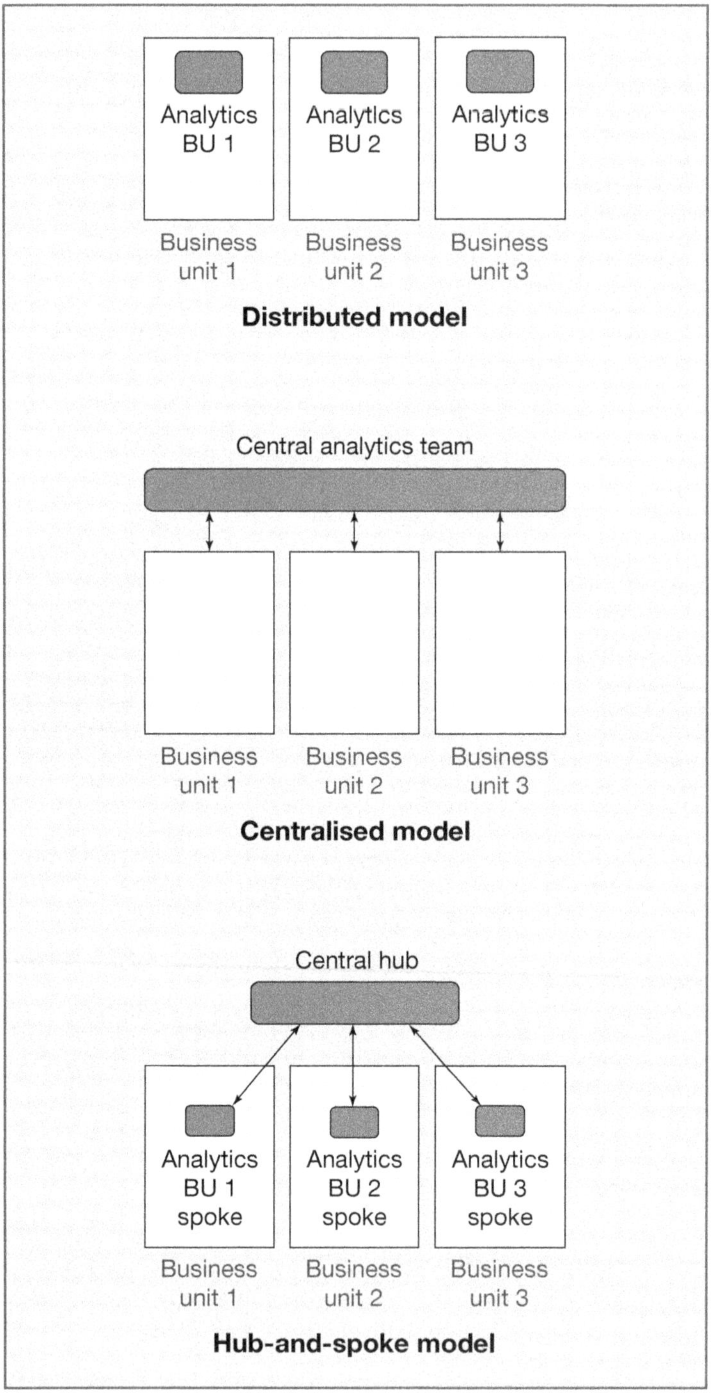

Figure 6.2 Three organisational models for the data organisation

When organisations grow their ambition in the Data Transformation journey, they realise they need a more solid model. At this point, they often build a central data team to work on common 'enablers' such as the data platform, a single pipeline of business intelligence products, setting up data governance standards, data quality tools, etc.

Moving from one extreme to another is not painless. A typical complexity that especially large organisations suffer is that the single BUs do not want to 'lose control' over how data is reported and managed ('information is power', after all, and 'nobody is willing to lose power!'). This creates a lot of conflict and a hard life for the central analytics team: fingers will be pointed at it, suggesting it is in its 'ivory tower' or unable to fulfil basic BU informative needs.

Another complexity to manage at this stage is the existence of *shadow analytics* organisations. In fact, BUs might retain or, sometimes, build their own reporting teams that conflict with the central ones. These shadow analytics organisations could be forcibly moved into the central team, which is normally quite a painful step for both the management and the people impacted.

If the maturity is insufficient, it can be counter-productive to move to the hub-and-spoke model too soon. For example, if the BUs don't know what analytics can truly do for them (besides the obvious reporting), they will struggle with having analysts in their teams. Additionally, if the basic 'enablers' (like governance, technology stack, and so on) are not in place yet, the 'spokes' will be too far from the centre to function properly.

So, to conclude, the organisation's usual journey follows the company's maturity level: you start fully decentralised, then you go centralised, and then you land on hub-and-spoke. Every step can take from one to many years, and it is not recommended to rush. Be aware of your maturity and plan your organisational strategy accordingly.

Talent acquisition: balancing internal and external resources

Knowing which data skills are needed in different parts of the organisation is only the first step. The next challenge lies in acquiring the right talent. Let's explore the options, highlight potential pitfalls and share proven strategies to avoid them.

There are two main routes for acquiring data talent. The first is internal, which involves reskilling current employees and equipping them with the necessary skill sets. The second is external, where new resources are acquired through recruitment or outsourcing activities to third parties. These paths are not mutually exclusive; most companies will navigate both, striking an appropriate balance.

Reskilling internal resources

There are significant (and often overlooked) benefits to identifying and training existing employees to become data professionals.

The foremost advantage is preserving and enhancing existing knowledge, a critical component in creating value. Familiarity with the company's specific business needs and operations is invaluable. Additionally, many organisations already have people working in data analytics within the various business units. Leveraging this existing expertise and integrating these individuals into the new data organisational structure can be more readily accepted by lending BUs.

Identifying the right internal candidates for reskilling requires a structured approach. Being proficient in crunching numbers with Excel doesn't automatically qualify them as prospect data scientists or business analysts. A fair and principled method is essential in selecting internal candidates, focusing on three key elements: skills, motivation and career plan.

To start, you can create a list of the current skills and abilities that exist within the organisation. This can be done through evaluations conducted by managers or self-assessments done by employees. An evaluation form, such as the one found in Table 6.3, can be used to identify specific indicators of the necessary skills.

Table 6.3 Personal evaluation form for pre-existing data analytics skills

Indicator	Score
Regularly creates reports to show business trends through tables and graphs and can redesign the format as needed.	
Knows how to obtain necessary data for analyses, utilising existing interfaces and business intelligence applications.	
Can automate analytical data flows involving the combination of tables, their transformation and aggregation.	
Is familiar with one or more programming languages.	
Is familiar with the fundamental concepts of AI and machine learning.	

Internal candidates for data jobs must be willing to step out of their comfort zones and commit to lifelong skill development (which is crucial in data analytics). Thus, it is important to assess the intrinsic motivation of the candidate, evaluating their genuine interest and passion for data and, most importantly, their growth mindset.

Growth mindset versus fixed mindset

The US psychologist Carol Dweck has carefully studied how people identify the source of their abilities and has thus recognised two extreme cases. On the one hand, those with a *fixed mindset* interpret their abilities as innate and see failure as the consequence of the limitation of their abilities. On the other hand, those with a *growth mindset* see skills as the result of hard work of study, continuous improvement, experiments (even if unsuccessful) and practice. For them, failures are welcome as they represent a further opportunity for growth. Dweck's work has inspired many companies to encourage a growth mindset in their skills development processes, recruitment and reward programmes. Reskilling in data analytics can be an engine for nurturing a broad growth mindset in a company.

The final advice is to develop a robust career map for data professionals, foundational to internal and external talent acquisition. Determine what different job levels look like within each role family (data scientists, analysts, data engineers), including leadership roles. Outline progression routes for vertical (promotion) and horizontal (experience in different sub-teams and business units) growth. Consider pathways to business roles for data professionals aspiring to such transitions in the future.

Career mapping is crucial across all business functions. However, in the world of data analytics, maintaining high motivation and retention rates is tough (considering all the 'frustrations' mentioned earlier in the chapter and the high demand for these skills in the job marketplace). So, the key advice is to look after career progression early on in your Data Transformation journey.

Acquiring external resources

When internal resources are insufficient for your analytical talent needs, you must acquire them from outside. You can do so by recruiting from the job marketplace or outsourcing activities to third parties.

Recruiting data professionals is challenging for a few reasons. First, there's a recognised scarcity of qualified talent in the labour market. Despite the increase in university-level training programmes in data analytics, demand still heavily outweighs supply. As we constantly remind data science and AI students to encourage them when we meet in universities, it is still a great time to enter this field.

Analytical talents in the market are well aware of their value, and they can be 'picky'. They carefully evaluate job opportunities based on several factors, like the role's scope, the skills development programme, the practical impact of their models, the company's prestige, the presence of clear career progression paths, and more. Another hurdle is the relative inexperience of recruiters in dealing with these new professional roles, making it difficult to accurately describe and assess these positions.

To maximise your chances of securing (and retaining) analytical talent, you can adopt several best practices, which are summarised here.

- **Clear role description:** ensure the job description is specific, showcasing the importance of data, AI and analytical roles in your company, along with learning and growth opportunities. Make sure job-seekers understand if and how they can innovate (versus only reapplying proven methods).
- **Innovative recruitment channels:** traditional recruitment channels might not suffice. Consider organising hackathons, data analytics competitions, or other events to attract talent.
- **External visibility:** publicising your company's analytical successes is vital, especially in those industries not broadly recognised as 'data-rich'. Activities like publications, participating in forums and conferences, and media coverage can elevate your company's attractiveness to potential candidates. Data leaders should be externally recognisable and ideally boast some social media followership.
- **University partnerships:** forming long-term partnerships with universities that offer degrees in data analytics and AI can provide early access to the CVs of promising graduates.

Another external source of expertise and analytical staff is outsourcing, i.e. contracting out some data analytics responsibilities to external companies. In some circumstances, it may, for instance, be advantageous to extend one's analytical team by adding consultants with specific tasks (*staff augmentation*), sometimes providing their services remotely (*off-shore*). Another scenario is to outsource a full project to a third-party organisation by carefully aligning requirements with business needs.

There are several advantages to relying on external suppliers. First of all, it is the quickest way to acquire specific expertise, compared to the alternative of waiting for in-house talent to be trained. Financially, it can be a way of not increasing operating expenditure (*OpEx*, *Operating Expense*) while burdening capital expenditure (*CapEx*, *Capital Expense*). Furthermore, especially in the case of game-changing ventures, which have great potential but little chance of success, calling in external personnel may be preferable to augmenting our team with skills that we may no longer need in the near future.

When considering outsourcing for data analytics projects, it's important to be mindful of a couple of best practices which, when overlooked, cause material chances of failure in data projects.

- **Don't underestimate oversight needs:** consultants never work with complete autonomy. Factor in the additional costs related to time and resources that your internal team will dedicate to supporting them. Consider also the support from in-house staff familiar with your organisation's tools, data, people and business processes.
- **Plan for future management of the solution:** you need to carefully envision 'what needs to be true' for your solution to be usable *after* the project ends. Account for the post-project phase, including update to documentation, training of new people, model continuous updating and validation (ML Ops), change management, and so on.

It is wise to follow common sense and ensure all the aspects above are always explicitly included in the project expectations, even when working with trusted partners.

The data boss: CDOs and other tough leadership roles

Emerging organisations, like those in data, must fight hard to establish their roles and gain respect. The boss of such an organisation, like the **chief data officer (CDO)**, faces a daunting task. Today, CDOs hold the unenviable record across the C-suite for the shortest average tenure – just two and a half years. This stems from various factors, primarily: overly high expectations (like the belief that every task can be easily automated in today's digital world), unclear expectations from others (anything 'data-related' falls squarely on the CDO's shoulders), and the fact that CDOs are the 'new kids on the block', often with a weaker political support than their peers.

The ambiguity surrounding data leaders is evident in the naming conventions. There's no universal title or job description for the data boss. Different titles often signal different focuses. For instance, chief data officer (CDO), the most common, indicates a focus on data governance and data technology infrastructure. The chief analytics officer (CAO) or chief artificial intelligence officer (CAIO) lean towards data applications addressing business needs. The chief data and analytics officer (CDAO) tries to blend the roles of CDO and CAO. Since a data leader should take full responsibility for *both* enablers and actual outcomes of data activation, CDAO is possibly a more robust title than CDO for the data leader.

The reporting line of the CDO/CDAO reveals much about this ambition. Many suggest that the data leader should be on the board, reporting directly to the CEO (chief executive officer), to underscore data's strategic importance and ensure robust backing for transformation projects. While ideal, this can be risky for a 'new kid on the block'. Sometimes, the CDO reports to the CIO (chief information officer) or the CTO (chief technology officer), reflecting the role's technical nature. However, this may lead to pigeonholing data analytics into a solely technical challenge. Other times, CDOs report to the CFO (chief financial officer), particularly when integrating a single source of truth and performance management with modern BI is crucial.

The best approach depends on the company's maturity. You should appoint someone who feels at ease with both data and business matters and ensure they participate in and contribute to board activities, even if not reporting directly to the CEO. Ideally, they should build their authority on data by acting also as the primary 'analyst' for fellow top managers.

It is not easy to find a good CDO. They must excel in at least three key areas.

1 **Technical expertise:** the CDO should have a broad and deep technical background in data analytics, be familiar with various analytical techniques and tools, and have practical, first-person experience in organising data and applying algorithms. The CDO should be able to directly support data scientists, analysts and other data professionals, providing advice and alerting them to possible risks and thus – with humility and competence – gaining their deep respect.

2. **Business acumen:** proven experience in the company's sector is vital. The CDO must understand the business, financial dynamics, customer needs and the competitive and regulatory landscape.
3. **Interpersonal and communication skills:** a CDO must command respect from other business leaders and foster sponsorship across functions. This requires emotional intelligence to identify persuasive strategies and an ability to 'sell' analytics potential to even the most sales-savvy leaders. Combining analytics expertise with these soft skills makes the CDO an effective cultural transformer, a true *data evangelist*, capable of impacting and transforming the habits of the entire organisation.

Finding someone with this blend of technical, business and interpersonal skills is challenging. Technical data professionals often shy away from the ambiguous realm of business intricacies. Conversely, business leaders may neglect technical aspects, missing firsthand analytics experiences.

A CDO's origin can be either internal or external. An internal appointee must transcend their functional background to embrace a broad, cross-functional role. An external hire faces the challenge of quickly assimilating the corporate culture, which is crucial given the role's cultural implications but is more likely to carry the multi-faceted deep expertise that such a tough role demands.

Some companies prefer hiring a ready-to-place, experienced *fractional CDO*, focusing on getting the Data Transformation started quickly and forming a permanent leader in the process. Whatever route a company takes, finding the right CDO is clearly vital and should be carefully looked after.

Building the right culture

Every company has a set of unwritten rules, diffused beliefs and accepted behaviours that determine how people interact and make decisions: it's the corporate culture. Having the right people in the right places might not be enough for the Data Transformation to fly. You need to establish a *data-friendly culture* for data and algorithms to actually make a difference.

Assessing whether an environment is data-friendly can be challenging, but it's easy to spot elements of a company culture that are inherently incompatible with succeeding in Data Transformation. Let's examine the most typical cultural inhibitors for data and explore practical ideas on how to reverse them.

Spotting data cultural inhibitors

When a company claims to want to become data-driven, it rarely understands what it is getting into. Its declaration of intent can be in direct conflict with some broadly accepted – or even encouraged – beliefs and behaviours. Researchers have identified some typical 'signs' of such cultural elements that hinder Data Transformation. As we go through them, ask yourself if you have noticed any in your work environment so far.

The dominance of HiPPOs

In many offices, decisions often come down to HiPPOs – the highest paid person's opinions. This catchy acronym reminds us of a common scenario in which hierarchy trumps data. Imagine this: a team gathered around, data charts up on the screen, everyone eager to follow where the numbers lead. But then, the most senior manager, usually the highest earner, chimes in and overrides any data-backed recommendation with their gut feel.

To be clear – this isn't always bad. Balancing instinct and human considerations with data can lead to well-rounded decisions. However, the problem is a lack of balance. In many companies, challenging the boss's view, especially when it contradicts data insights, can be intimidating. This cultural mechanism – called *authority bias* – stifles innovation and can keep a company stuck in 'the way we've always done things'.

Another reason data recommendations are neglected is a basic human protective behaviour: people generally don't like to be told what to do, especially if they don't understand it fully. Managers involved in decision making might be, on the surface, the first ones to say that they are 'data-driven' in their decisions. The same people might also be the first to find smart-sounding excuses to neglect recommendations from data.

The technicality trap

The subject of data analytics often risks being seen as a 'technical' problem, delegated entirely to technical leaders like the CIO or CDAO. This attitude – typical of managers not versed in these matters and often with little intention to become so – is particularly harmful as it limits the potential impact of data on the business.

When we categorise data analytics as a technical domain, we implicitly discourage business people across various functions from getting first-person involved. Non-technical roles may feel exempt from learning about these technologies, missing out on opportunities to spot business-sound ways to apply them in their daily job. This is painful because business people are the best-placed ones to find a use for data and AI, doing a much better job at this than what data scientists would ever do.

As a consequence of seeing data professionals as 'technical staff', they tend not to get involved directly in business discussions, but only pulled in as mere data providers on a need basis. Sometimes, they are asked to find data points to support a decision that has been made already, versus offering novel routes - another missed opportunity to create real business value from data.

The information protectionism

It's an open secret in the corporate world: Information equals power. Imagine a team that's hit its targets and unearthed great insights but, when asked to share the data and make it available for broader use, they clam up. This happens because sharing data can feel like giving away your playbook.

Some managers do not want 'outsiders' looking into how their performance is measured, as this exposes them to unwanted auditing. This mindset clearly builds walls, turns teams into well-guarded silos, and lets suspicion thrive throughout the organisation.

Such protectionism stems from a common role confusion: people often misperceive their duty as *stewards* of a company asset (data) as their right as the sole *owner* of that asset. We will return to the fundamental role of data stewardship in Chapter 7. For now, it is important to recognise the cultural belief that makes overprotective managers defend that their teams are the only ones who should be touching their own data.

Developing your data culture

The behaviours above are clear indicators that you do not have a data-friendly culture. In addition to remaining vigilant and attentive to these signs, the next question becomes: what do I do about them?

We should recognise that the abovementioned inhibitors derive from two major cultural root causes. The first one is the lack of understanding: we tend to be suspicious of what we don't know and understand. The second one is the lack of business sponsorship and integration: data and business running on parallel – and often diverging – tracks.

There is not a recipe and it is impossible to change data culture at once. However, a set of best approaches have been recognised as drivers of a data-friendly culture. They insist on broadening the understanding and integrating data and business worlds.

Data fluency for all

The first set of actions you should implement is related to providing learning and development opportunities on data analytics to all your people. Humans are less scared of something new when they understand how it works. The level of protectionism – and sometimes even Luddism – decreases when you make these topics familiar across the organisation. The other reason for doing so is to build a common language that enables everyone to take part in the Data Transformation. Here is what you should consider.

- Set up a *data fluency programme* for everyone. Be very inclusive. Think about delivery methods that are engaging. Consider town hall sessions, a calendar of online and in-person training sessions, a library of recorded videos, or whatever delivery mechanism you already have in place. The programme should inspire people by showing what's happening in the space, explaining the foundational concepts of data and machine learning, and giving visibility to what the company plans to do in the space.
- Run an *upskilling programme* for data professionals, offering multiple levels and specialisations to provide depth and breadth of learning opportunities to data analysts, data scientists, engineers, and all others. You can offer badges and certifications (internal or external ones) to those who complete the path. Remember that the half-life of data skills is very short: data professionals need to keep learning continuously to stay relevant. If they feel they are not learning enough, they will leave.
- Run a data analytics *learning programme for top management* giving them relevant knowledge to push the boundaries in this space. Executives need to be involved and role model with their participation for the rest of the organisation. Knowing that your boss is learning something new is normally

the easiest way to be convinced that you should learn that too: leverage this mechanism broadly.

These development programmes either can be built internally (many data professionals love to teach and will be happy to take the lead and build quality material) or you can use external help to build or acquire the content you miss. Investing in developing the skills of people normally has a very high ROI, especially in a domain that can easily generate large business value like data analytics these days.

Inclusive data communities

The second set of actions is about building a data analytics integrated community that spans across organisational areas. Since analytics is a team sport, you need to create and build an ecosystem of people that can partner effectively. Here are some options for you.

- Build data *communities of practices* (CoPs), meeting in regular sessions where people can get together and discuss data-related topics, issues and opportunities. CoP activities will also include *share-and-reapply* sessions where the best successes and most useful failures are presented and talked through so that everyone involved in data knows what is happening. These communities should be inclusive and open to both data professionals and business users: what attracts attendees should be their passion for data and AI, not their job title.
- Build a team of *data analytics champions* made of non-data professionals from the various business teams that are passionate about these topics. The champions will get together with the data technical teams and solidify an ongoing partnership, representing their organisation's business needs and bringing back the latest happening around data and AI. Champions will also be actively involved in the development of novel data capabilities, nurturing a culture of co-creation, which breaks the silos across technical and non-technical teams.
- Remember that even people working on the production line and those who welcome your guests at the office reception will have beliefs about data and AI. They might be scared or excited about it and, most importantly, they have the best possible ideas on how to make data and AI a productivity engine – much better ones than any data professional would have. Be inclusive. Invite them to the broader fluency programme and consider organising *idea contests* for everyone to contribute with new thoughts.

Business sponsorship on data projects by design

The third type of activity you can put in place is needed to secure business sponsorship of data initiatives. Here are some proven actions you can consider.

- Business leaders should be, by design, the *primary sponsors* of any data initiative. If you build new data capabilities or run a strategic project on some data enablers, the sponsors of such initiatives should never be people with the words 'data' or 'information' in their job titles. These clearly exclude CIOs, CDOs and all their reports. If a new AI capability is going to game-change a marketing process, the CMO (or someone in their team) should be sponsoring it. Sponsors should be the ones who really 'want' the project to happen and fight for it. Data is business – as simple as that.
- The same business engagement should reflect on the lower levels of the organisation: data teams should have strong ties with business teams who should *co-create* capabilities. Co-creation means that when there is a new opportunity, the technical team sits together with the business team that needs it, and the latter stays fully engaged until it is done. It is not a customer–servant relationship like 'tell me what is needed, and I will do it for you' but a partner-to-partner relationship like 'tell me the business opportunity, and let's work together on making it happen'. Appoint data champions for each business team.
- Leaders should understand that managing data and AI is becoming a new norm of general management. The *manager of the (near) future* will leverage both human and artificial resources to achieve their objectives, orchestrating them carefully, and fostering collaboration between them. They will know when and how to use data and AI for their business needs, and what questions to ask (this book suggests many of the questions they should ask). Make sure this fits in the way you form and select the next leadership of your company, which necessarily needs to be data-savvy. Make this requirement clear and state it publicly, adding to the promotion criteria of managers.

Data culture seems impossible to change, and this can become an excuse not to act. It doesn't need to be this way. Data leadership, together with the company's top management and, obviously, the HR team, can pull this together by investing in the practical programmes mentioned above. It is up to you which one to start from.

The golden checklist on the human journey

People matter. They do, more than anything else. This is true for data analytics, as for any other topic.

In this chapter, we have learned how to deal with the many human challenges that come with Data Transformation. If we get talent, organisation and culture right, we empower our people at best. Let's review the critical elements we need to ensure for this to happen.

- Have you documented the roles and responsibilities of your data professionals, such as data analysts, data scientists and data engineers? Are you clear on the skills they need to possess?
- Which data organisational model are you pursuing? Distributed, centralised or hub-and-spoke? Is it in line with your organisational maturity? Are you preparing for the next phase?
- Have you mapped the availability of data analytics skills in your current organisation? Have you considered reskilling resources appropriately to pursue a career in data?
- What resources do you need to acquire from outside? Do you have a clear role description, effective recruitment channels, university partnerships and the right external visibility to attract the right talent?
- When outsourcing data analytics initiatives, have you considered the oversight needs of external consultants? Have you accounted for the future maintenance needs of the solution once the project is finished?
- Have you defined the role of the data leader (CDO or, better yet, CDAO) well? Are expectations clear and realistic? Has the role received strong and shared business sponsorship from top management?
- Have you planned for a corporate-wide data fluency programme that is truly inclusive for everyone? Do you have an ongoing upskilling programme specifically designed for all data professionals?
- Have you built data communities of practice and appointed data champions who represent the full organisation?
- Are your data projects always sponsored by business leaders? Are sponsors truly engaged and incentivised to deliver business value from data?
- Are managers engaged in the Data Transformation, role modelling their buy-in with the rest of the organisation?

As discussed in this chapter, data analytics is more of a human topic than its name suggests. The way a company manages talent, designs organisations and nurtures its culture determines the overall success of the Data Transformation process. Looking first after your people is – as usual – a very sensible business strategy.

The topic in the next chapter has some major human implications, too. We will soon find out how setting up the right data governance model for enduring value creation is another vital enabler of our Data Transformation ambition.

CHAPTER 7
DATA GOVERNANCE DONE RIGHT

In this chapter

- What is data governance, and what happens if it is not in place?
- What is data quality, and how do you secure it?
- What is a data catalogue, and how do you build one?
- Who does what in data governance?
- How can you set up or revamp a data governance framework in a few months?

Data! Data! Data! I can't make bricks without clay,' said Sherlock Holmes, as he painfully realised he lacked the right data points to solve his latest case. When Sir Arthur Conan Doyle wrote this quote for his fictional character, he anticipated much of the frustration we face today at work when it comes to data. Without the right quality data, in the right place, and at the right time, making effective decisions lacks its main ingredient, as Sherlock vividly foresaw.

We must admit, data governance can be a boring topic. This term is often associated with a defensive approach to managing data, made up of strict rules, static roles, repetitive responsibilities and quite uninspiring compliance procedures and meetings. Fortunately, it doesn't need to be that way.

If we spot the right trade-off between discipline and agility, governing data can be a catalyser of your entire Data Transformation effort. This chapter is all about giving you the essential concepts, tools and best approaches to make data governance work best for you.

As we saw in Chapter 6, many of our data endeavours concern people, their beliefs and the prevalent corporate culture. It is no less for data governance. This is why we had better start our journey by exploring what happens when we don't govern data properly and what cultural convictions are needed to shift gears.

Governing data as an asset

In the bustling office of Closets4all, a mid-sized furniture company, the monthly leadership team meeting had taken a dramatic turn. Linda, the CMO, confidently presented the latest revenue figures on a sleek PowerPoint slide. But before she could move to the next bullet point, Tom, the sales director, interrupted with a raised voice and a printout in hand.

'That can't be right,' Tom asserted, waving his report. 'These numbers don't match our sales actuals.'

A tense silence fell over the room as Linda and Tom locked eyes. Confused murmurs echoed among the executives as they compared the conflicting reports. The CEO, looking baffled, called IT into the room to shed some light on the discrepancy.

The IT manager, Claudia, arrived with her laptop, puzzled about the sales team's separate report. She and her team had spent the past quarter trying to centralise data reports to ensure consistency. Yet, here was a rogue document, throwing all their efforts into question.

After days of digging through databases and code, Claudia's team uncovered the truth. It was a web of data disarray – each department had its own definition of 'revenue'. The marketing team's figures included projected sales, whereas the sales team reported only completed transactions. The discrepancy was compounded by a data glitch in the main sales transaction system, which the Sales team had patched with a makeshift Excel formula. This formula wasn't documented anywhere else in the company. The sales team felt no need to document it. After all – they thought – sales numbers are owned by the sales team.

And there was more. Claudia also discovered that the CRM system was cluttered with duplicate records. The same customer appeared multiple times due to a lack of a unified customer data entry protocol. Additionally, sensitive customer information was found scattered across different spreadsheets with no encryption or access control. With recent privacy regulations tightening, the company was sitting on a ticking regulatory time bomb.

The story of Closets4all is a cautionary tale of how a lack of data governance can create a ripple effect of confusion and inefficiency. Each department's well-intentioned efforts to manage its data independently led to a landscape where critical information was duplicated, definitions were misaligned and crucial data was mishandled.

You might now be desolately nodding as you compare Closets4all to your own company: this scenario is common in organisations that neglect data governance. It's akin to having several buckets - each representing different aspects of data management - underneath a tap of flowing data. Without governance, these buckets have holes: unknown, duplicated, ill-defined and poor-quality data gets potential business value steadily leaked away, as illustrated in Figure 7.1.

Luckily, there are various tools and processes that can be put in place to prevent the problems presented by Closets4all. However, the most challenging aspect of

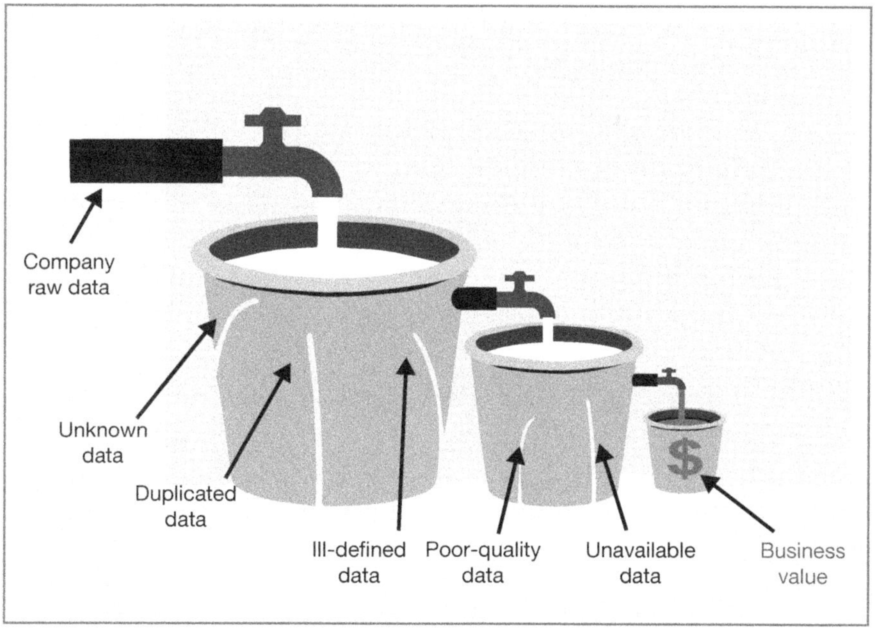

Figure 7.1 The leaking buckets of ungoverned data: when data is wrong, business value is less

this transformation is, as always, the shift in mindset that people must undergo when considering data.

Among the many beliefs data governance experts have identified, we found that the four cultural good convictions that follow below are the fundamental ones to pay attention to.

1. **Data is a business asset:** just like any physical asset, like your work laptop or the office desk, data should be regarded as a company asset, with all the discipline, responsibilities and attention it entails.
2. **Inclusive stewardship over private ownership:** data stewardship implies managing data with care and responsibility as if it were one's own, but ... it is nobody's private property. It is a collective effort across various functions and requires transparency and collaboration.
3. **Business responsibility of data:** the ultimate accountability for data resides with the business side, which must ensure its quality, usability and security, especially when mishandling can lead to significant consequences. IT is there to enable it, but the business leads.
4. **Governance as a multiplier of business value:** data's full economic value can only be realised when it is governed effectively. This involves plugging the 'leaks' in our bucket analogy – ensuring data is accurate, unique and well defined and that all relevant data is available for use. If data is bad, its value is zero.

In the next sections, we will first learn the fundamental elements of data governance (the 'What'), then deep-dive into the people roles and responsibilities to be put in place (the 'Who') and finally see the practical steps we can take to make it happen (the 'How').

Enabling data governance: the unmissable elements

Besides the cultural evolution, you need to leverage a set of tools and techniques to govern your data. For example, you need to be able to define your data assets, understand their flow across systems, and establish criteria for data acceptability. Let's go through the three foundational elements of any data governance initiative: cataloguing, lineage and quality.

Data catalogue: creating an inventory of data assets

A **data catalogue** is an organised inventory of a company's data assets in the form of metadata. As we saw in Chapter 5, metadata describes what a data point represents. The collection of such metadata, the catalogue, functions as a unified reference point, much like a library catalogue, detailing the existence, location and characteristics of various data elements.

Building a catalogue is essential for data governance. If you don't know what data you have, how can you govern it effectively? If you lack a standard definition of a KPI, how can you even check if its value is correct?

A data catalogue is made of two components.

1 **Data dictionary:** the technical description of data elements within tables, including types, sizes and constraints, clarifying the data's structure and properties.
2 **Business glossary:** the business description of data assets, ensuring a shared understanding among all business functions and assigning meaning and semantic context to data.

In its basic version, a data catalogue can be as simple as a shared spreadsheet that describes the metadata for each table or column. Modern data catalogue tools provide a simple user interface where users can look up the data they are interested in and read or update all they need.

Let's see a few practical use-case examples illustrating how handy the catalogue can be.

- **Case 1:** a marketing team uses the data catalogue to learn about customer demographic data stored in different databases and determine how to best leverage it to personalise the upcoming digital campaigns.
- **Case 2:** an IT team uses the data dictionary to integrate two disparate systems, ensuring that data types and formats are correctly aligned.
- **Case 3:** a new employee studies the business glossary to familiarise themselves with key company metrics and data terminologies, speeding up their onboarding process.

Catalogues need to be initiated, populated and then maintained ongoing. Let's review what needs to happen for each of these three lifecycle phases.

1 Data discovery

The first phase is data discovery, which aims to inventory all data assets within the organisation. It employs automated tools that connect to various systems to identify and list data elements, particularly for the data dictionary. These tools scan databases and storage systems to detect and document what exists.

Simultaneously, a manual surveying effort takes place, engaging with different departments to uncover less visible data, such as information tucked away in Excel files. The goal at this stage is not to categorise or evaluate the data but to ensure every piece of data, whether in a sophisticated database or a simple spreadsheet, is accounted for.

2 Catalogue population

Once a comprehensive list of data assets is compiled, the catalogue population phase begins. During this phase, we can fill in the missing metadata, both in the glossary (with the knowledge of business stewards – whose role will be defined later) and in the dictionary (with the support of the IT experts).

We can't populate the catalogue with all data assets at once. This is an iterative process, and we need to proceed by priority. Normally, the most important data is classified as high-risk and high-value.

High-risk data is sensitive and could cause significant harm if mishandled. Think of **personally identifiable information (PII)**, which is privacy-sensitive or highly restricted information. **High-value** data holds the most potential for driving business insights and value. Of course, the amount of unlockable value depends on the data analytics capabilities that leverage those data assets, so this assessment is not trivial. You can leverage the MoSCoW methodology we introduced in Chapter 5 to assess the value of data assets in a structured way. An alternative way to identify high-value data is to analyse the KPIs used in the most critical reports that management uses: if top decision making is based on those data assets, they naturally deserve higher priority in data governance efforts.

Figure 7.2 shows an example of what you can find in a data catalogue. As you can see, every column of the product masterdata table is described with metadata, like the data format, whether it is a PII field, the owner, the sensitivity level, and so on.

1 Ongoing usage and maintenance

The data catalogue is not a static entity but a living document requiring ongoing engagement. As the business evolves, so will the data it uses and produces.

Attribute name	Full description	Data format	Is it PII?	Data owner	Sensitivity level	Last updated
Barcode	Unique EAN (GTIN) barcode identifying the product	13-digit numeric code	No	*Jason Rock* (Inventory team)	Low	15-01-2024
Weight	Weight of the product in kilograms to three decimal places	Decimal number (up to 3 d.p.)	No	*Camilla Brown* (Logistics team)	Low	12-01-2024
Size	Size dimensions of the product (length x width x height)	String (length x width x height in cm)	No	*Camilla Brown* (Logistics team)	Low	18-01-2024
Supplier	Name of the product supplier	String	No	*Erin Poor* (Purchasing)	Medium	10-01-2024

Figure 7.2 A portion of the data dictionary for the product masterdata table, included in the data model encountered in Chapter 5

Regular reviews and updates are essential to maintain the catalogue's accuracy and relevance. This includes adding new data sources, updating metadata and re-evaluating data classifications as business needs change. This ongoing process supports the data's lifecycle and ensures that the organisation can continue to leverage its data assets effectively and responsibly.

Data lineage: tracking down to the source

Data lineage refers to tracking data from its origin (source) through its lifecycle as it moves and transforms across systems within an organisation's data platform. If the catalogue describes a data asset, the lineage tells us where it comes from and what path it takes from source to the eventual utilisation in data analytics applications. It's like having an up-to-date map of all data movements.

Robust lineage information is crucial for quickly resolving data-related problems through efficient root cause analysis, predicting the downstream impact of changes in source systems, and ensuring compliance and auditability. Here are practical examples demonstrating the importance of data lineage.

- **Case 1:** a financial report fails to update the count of the customer base correctly. With data lineage, the team quickly identified a transformation error in the data pipeline, which affected the count of customers in an intermediate transactional system, resolving the issue without manually sifting through extensive code.

- **Case 2:** before changing the definition of store attributes in the data pipeline, an alert is triggered about the potential downstream effects on dashboards, allowing the business intelligence team to adjust the dashboards proactively and prevent disruptions.
- **Case 3:** during a regulatory audit, the company is asked to remove a specific customer attribute from any system immediately. By looking at the lineage, the IT team can track down all impacted systems and ensure compliance in a matter of hours.

Implementing data lineage means adding relevant metadata to the data catalogue that links various data assets and systems. This process results in a graphical representation of the interconnections and dependencies between different data elements, like the simplified version in Figure 7.3. As the picture suggests, the customer data goes through multiple systems before being utilised in BI and analytics applications.

Modern data catalogue tools not only provide visual lineage diagrams, like the one in the figure, but also allow users to interact, deep dive into the assets of interest and visualise the related metadata from the catalogue.

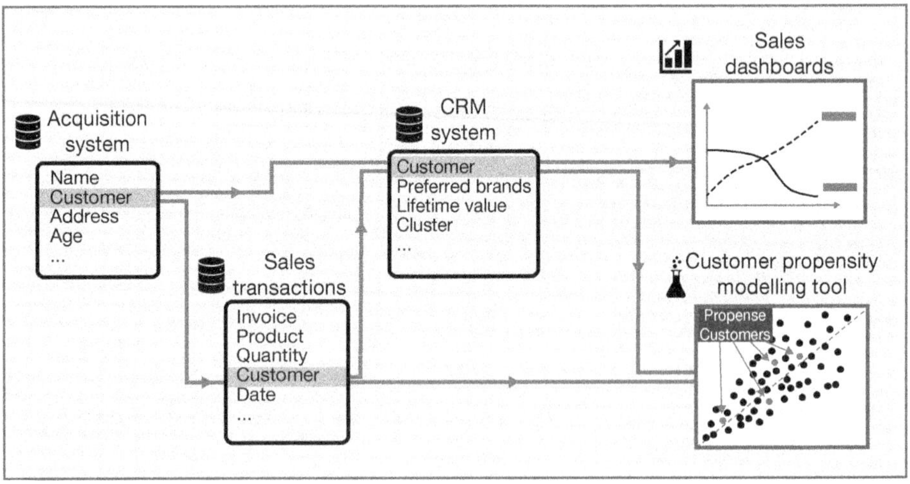

Figure 7.3 An example of data lineage: you can track the route of your data assets, from the source to the capability leveraging them

Make your data FAIR

By keeping a well-organised catalogue and maintaining a complete lineage, you can improve the usability of your data landscape and move closer to achieving FAIR principles. 'F' stands for Findable and is about using clear metadata and common vocabulary to ensure data can be easily located. 'A' means Accessible, meaning that data is available and compatible with common data management tools. 'I' represents Interoperable, meaning the adoption of formal languages and industry standards for uniform data modelling (like GS1 for consumer goods, SID for telcos, BIAN for banking, and so on). Lastly, 'R' stands for Reusable, ensuring that data remains reliable, secure and can be efficiently used over time. Without data governance, your data is hardly getting FAIR.

Data quality: making sure data is right

If the data is wrong, whatever we do with it is valueless. Pursuing, maintaining and measuring the quality of data assets is critical to ensure that data-driven business decisions and outcomes are effective and reliable.

Behind the single word 'quality', there are several dimensions that let us say if a data point is right or wrong. We need to take care of each of such five aspects and appreciate their differences if we want to manage data quality properly.

1. **Completeness:** this aspect checks if all necessary data fields are filled. In a healthcare setting, if patient records are missing critical information like allergy history, it can lead to incomplete patient profiles and potentially hazardous healthcare decisions.
2. **Accuracy:** this reflects the truthfulness of data compared to real-world scenarios. For example, in a retail context, if a sales report inaccurately includes transactions voided due to errors, it distorts the actual sales performance, leading to inaccurate business insights. Sometimes, we use the word '**validity**' to refer to the fitness of a data point to an expected format. An invalid entry, like an ill-formed email address, is, by definition, also inaccurate.
3. **Uniqueness:** this focuses on avoiding duplicates. In a customer relationship management system, having multiple entries for the same client can lead to overestimations in client count and marketing reach, skewing business strategies.

4 **Consistency:** this is about ensuring uniform data across various sources. For instance, if a customer is associated with an email address in the CRM database, having the same customer linked with a different email address in the sales system is an example of inconsistency.

5 **Timeliness:** this aspect assesses that data is up-to-date and reflects the current situation. For example, using outdated financial data in a stock market analysis could lead to incorrect trading decisions.

As shown in 4, there are many ways to 'be wrong'. Fortunately, there are also proven steps we can take to get data quality right. The software that enables us to take care of data quality systematically is called a **data quality management** tool, or **DQM tool**. Let's go through the three phases needed to manage data quality by leveraging such a tool.

1 Quality rules definition

The first phase is about codifying the rules that make a data point right or wrong. Imagine you want to define the data quality rules for a very important KPI, customer sales. By looking at the five aspects of data quality, we can

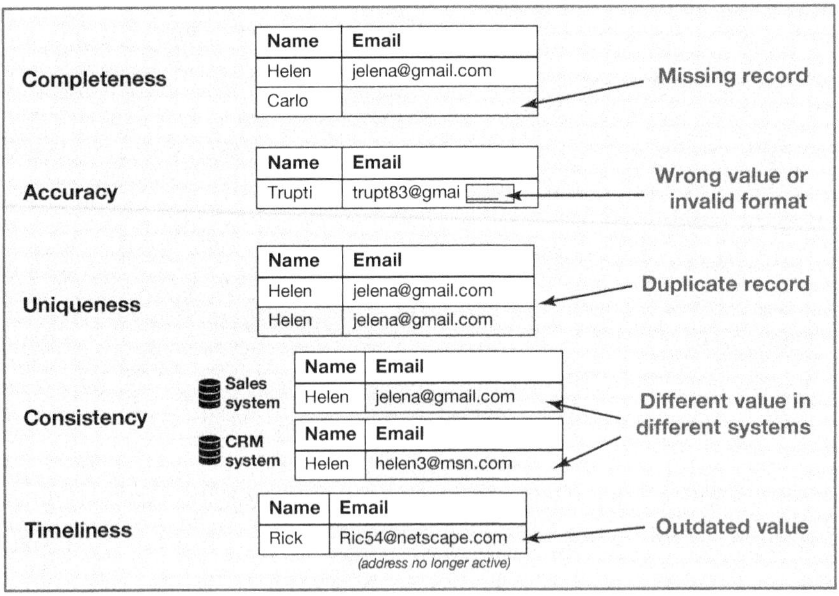

Figure 7.4 The five aspects of data quality: there are many ways for an email address to be wrong

think of several rules that need to be respected for the data to make sense. For instance, one rule can be that no sales transaction can have an empty price field (*completeness*). We can also add that the quantity of products sold in a transaction cannot be negative (*accuracy*). Another rule can be that the amount of revenues generated by all transactions in a given month, as hosted in the sales systems, should always match the monthly revenues recorded in the ERP system (*consistency*). All the rules we have just mentioned derive from a business rationale, which needs to be documented, stored in the glossary and stay ready to be updated whenever needed.

Additionally, to allow the DQM tool to verify adherence to such business rules automatically, we need to 'translate' them into a computer-friendly form. Some of these rules will look as simple as 'checkboxes' to be compiled (like declaring whether a field allows for missing data). Other rules will have to be implemented in a programming language. For example, to check that the sum of monthly transactions in a transaction system matches the monthly record in the ERP system, it is a logic condition that could be described with an SQL query.

2 Quality checks execution

Once the data quality rule is properly implemented in the DQM tool, it can periodically scan the data to assess whether all rules are respected or run this check when a given record is added, removed or altered in any way. Modern DQM tools can run such checks 'in the background' and either issue an alert (like sending an email) or try to fix the issue automatically (like removing the duplicate entry).

3 Monitoring and reporting

The last phase is to monitor and report the level of data quality reached over time across the various data domains. This makes a lot of sense: only what can be measured can be effectively acted upon. Suppose a critical KPI is frequently affected by instances of poor data quality. In that case, we should prioritise fixing it by improving the data acquisition process or enforcing a better calculation method.

A DQM tool would offer reports and dashboards to monitor data quality on an ongoing basis: we could read, for example, the number of incomplete data points by department or calculate the percentage of records affected by inaccuracy over the last months and see whether the situation is improving. Such visibility also drives accountability for data quality, as it lets leaders be aware of what issues they have and act accordingly. Management reports on data quality should spark healthy competition across business domains about whose data is the cleanest.

Who does what? Introducing the data governance actors

The unmissable elements of data governance (catalogue, lineage and quality) gave us a good hint about what needs to be done. Now, it's time to shift our focus to who should do what and introduce the roles and responsibilities of the people making data governance happen.

We have seen how software tools can assist and partially automate tasks such as documenting data assets, tracking their provenance and ensuring their ongoing accuracy. Still, a heavy share of human work needs to happen. We can recognise four fundamental actors in data governance: core team, board, stewards and custodians.

Data governance core team

Sometimes called the data governance programme office, the **core team** runs all the central data governance efforts. It owns the 'project management' of setting up the various aspects of data governance and the process management of all the activities. It should be staffed adequately: these are the 'experts' on how to run data governance and they are fully dedicated to it. This team is led by the top manager of data governance, who could be either a vertically appointed data governance leader or the CDO directly.

The core team builds and animates the data governance community (made of all stewards and custodians), running regular meetings. They look after the ongoing reporting of progress in data governance, track governance KPIs, and communicate through reports and scorecards to all stakeholders, starting from the data governance board. They document all of the processes properly, they know 'by heart' the policies, and they can navigate the technical complexity of the technology aspects related to data management.

Data governance board

The data governance **board** sponsors and supports the data governance programme, being the ultimate sink of every escalation path on this topic. The board's composition needs to be decided depending on your company's organisational structure. Still, this must be senior enough to steer the work. Ideally, the governance board will comprise the top C-level executives of each function and business unit.

They meet in regular board meetings (quarterly is a good estimate of the frequency, but it might vary depending on the maturity of your organisation). Such meetings are prepared by the data governance core team and led by the CDO or the data governance leader.

They are responsible for leading the four cultural convictions of data governance and setting an example for the entire organisation. They assess and approve new policies and procedures, monitor progress, review KPIs such as data quality levels and approve high-risk exceptions to procedures. They also provide executive approval of the budget required for data governance tools and remediations to secure data assets. They appoint stewards for their functions and ensure the active participation of all actors involved in data governance. Finally, they represent their business function in adopting and deploying data governance policies and processes.

Within the data governance board, you have a data governance sponsor, the top executive sponsoring the entire data governance initiative. Often, the sponsor is the chief financial officer. This makes sense because finance is the function that ultimately provides stewardship for the company's assets (which includes data). It also suffers the most from data not being governed properly, with all the financial risk that comes with it. As we said earlier, IT is there to enable data governance. Still, the business is the ultimate owner of the matter, so the CIO is not the ideal candidate to take ownership as the sponsor of the data governance effort as a whole.

Data stewards

The **data steward** is the key representative of a business domain for data. They are people who know the data involved in their line of business well and work with it. To be clear, they are not data analysts or data professionals; they are, and should be, business people who take direct accountability for their business data assets.

Data stewards are required to define the business aspects of a data asset, documenting it in the glossary. They also define the quality rules (although they don't implement them technically by writing code). They are the go-to person with ever-present queries such as 'What does this data mean?', 'Where does it come from?' and 'How is it calculated?' They receive training from the data governance core team on what data governance means, the processes, the unmissable elements, and everything else we see in this chapter.

Data stewards are many, and their scope is separated according to groups of data assets called **data domains**. A data domain is a set of data assets that are logically related to each other. You can think of data domains as high-level categories of data assets implemented to assign direct accountability and responsibility. Large companies will organise data stewards hierarchically, having a senior data steward (sometimes called 'data governor' or 'data owner') to cover an entire data domain and other data stewards covering sub-domains within each.

One important caveat: you should find ways to value the critical role of data stewards, making it appealing and formally recognised. From our experience, what frequently happens is that data stewards are appointed on a part-time basis: governance activities are often assigned 'on top' of their regular business

How do you define data domains?

The approach to defining data domains depends on the way your company operates. One way is to follow the natural definition of business entities like products, suppliers, customers, and so on. For companies that are organised in almost independent lines of business, the data domain structure will follow the splits by BUs and loosely adhere to the business organisational chart (like consumer BU, institutional BU, and so on). For sure, there are overlaps across data domains: when defining them, you will have to make choices based on where you want the stewardship accountability to lie.

responsibilities, without any revision or reduction of the previous workload. This approach will hardly set stewards up for success.

Make sure data stewards are recognised for their job. Progress on data governance KPIs should be part of the performance assessments. Their line managers should support their appointment as data stewards in recognition of their data expertise and be aware of the criticality of such a role. Think about ways to keep their work exposure high.

Data custodians

If a data steward is accountable for data assets from a business perspective, a **data custodian** is accountable for the same asset from a technical perspective. The two roles are complementary in nature. Data custodians are accountable for the technical control of data, including its security, scalability, availability, backup, audit trail and implementation of quality rules. They are normally IT representatives who know how applications, data platforms and ETL processes work, understanding the full complexity of our data points' lineage.

Custodians are the 'main authors' of the technical side of data documentation, like the data dictionary, that they will fill in liaison with their data steward partner. They understand how the data in their domain is created, manipulated, stored, moved from system to system, and utilised in applications. They also have a critical role in data quality as they implement data quality rules by translating business rules (as defined by the stewards) into code and adding technical checks for data integrity.

Some companies assign data custodians by system, and this classification might not be in a 1:1 relationship with the data domains split (that stewards follow). As you appoint custodians, you should try to mirror the data domain structure of the company as much as possible, letting them build over time a trusted partnership with a particular custodian.

Data governance in action

Following the tumultuous leadership meeting at Closets4all, the company embarked on a journey to rectify its data management practices and established a data governance framework. Six months into this initiative, the data management landscape at Closets4all has begun to transform significantly.

Let's have a look at what they have accomplished so far.

- A **data governance core team** was appointed and kicked off the activities, starting from the inception of a simple centralised data cataloguing system designed to serve as a singular source of truth for revenue figures and other critical data. The team has begun to document data assets, starting with the assets that had previously caused the most discrepancies and confusion. They animate the newly created data governance community, running trainings and regular meetings to get things moving.
- The **data governance board** was created with the participation of Linda, Tom and all other C-level executives. The discussions moved from finger-pointing to collectively addressing and systematically solving data-related issues. The board held several meetings to initiate the project, approve new policies, appoint data stewards, and more. In recent meetings, they have started to evaluate the progress of data governance and noted a promising decline in quality issues on the data quality dashboard.
- **Data stewards** covering seven data domains were identified from various departments, including sales and marketing. Their primary mission was to synchronise data definitions across the board, beginning with a joint effort to agree on a consistent definition of the 'revenue' and related KPIs. This crucial step helped eliminate the inconsistencies that had sparked the initial conflict.
- **Data custodians**, members of Claudia's IT team, tackled the glitch in the sales transaction system. This glitch, once temporarily fixed by Tom's team with an ad-hoc Excel formula, was identified as a critical bottleneck in the data lineage, leading to executive reports. By working hand-in-hand with sales and marketing stewards, the custodians implemented a more durable solution that eradicated the need for the Excel workaround yet allowed business teams to input manual adjustments in a traceable and auditable manner.

It seems that custodians, stewards, core team members and board members are off to a great start. Not only did they manage to fix the issues uncovered at the beginning of the chapter, but they also initiated a robust data governance operating model. Such a collaborative effort makes Closets4all data assets safe and accessible: it is easy to imagine how the data can produce real business value through the right descriptive, predictive or prescriptive analytics applications.

As we saw in the Closets4all story, the data governance effort requires the four fundamental actors to operate with clear roles and responsibilities. We can summarise their roles in the RACI matrix in Table 7.1, where every activity is mapped against each role using the following key.

- R is **Responsible** for executing the task.
- A is ultimately **Accountable** for the task and must approve its completion.
- C is **Consulted** about the task to seek inputs.
- I is **Informed** about the task and its outcome.

Table 7.1 A simplified RACI diagram of key data governance activities

Activities	Core team (dedicated)	Board (C-level managers)	Stewards (come from business)	Custodians (come from IT)
Stewards' and custodians' appointment	**R** (prepare proposal)	**A**	**I**	**I**
Policies and procedures	**R** (write proposals)	**A**	**C**	**C**
Training	**R**, **A** (prepare and run)		**R** (attend)	**R** (attend)
Business glossary	**C** (provide template)		**R**, **A** (fill it in)	**C**
Data dictionary	**C** (provide template)		**C**	**R**, **A** (fill it in)
Data lineage	**I**		**C**	**R**, **A** (fill it in)
Data quality rules	**I**		**R**, **A** (define business logic)	**R** (implement the logic)
Data quality tracking	**R**	**I** (regularly review)	**A** (take responsibility)	**I**
Data governance programme implementation	**R** (plan, coordinate activities and report progress)	**A** (review progress and approve changes)	**C**	**C**
Exceptions to data policies	**R** (prepare the case)	**A** (approve)	**C**	**C**
Data governance budget	**R** (plans and prepare)	**A** (approve)	**C**	**C**

While this version of the RACI matrix is simplified and only highlights key activities, it provides a foundation for defining roles and responsibilities. Each company will have its own variation of this view, but what's essential is to have a precise description of these roles and document them in a way that minimises any inherent ambiguities.

Setting up data governance

The Closets4All turnaround gives us hope: a data governance can be set up or revamped within a few months of work. Over the next few pages, we will see what needs to be true to make this happen. Specifically, we will see what documents we need to prepare and publish, what the main phases of an implementation programme are, and what activities we should expect to repeat to keep the model up and running.

Establishing a policy

Good governance of a company is ensured by publishing and enforcing a set of corporate policies that serve dual purposes. First, they act as a declaration of intent, delineating the boundaries within which the company is expected to operate. These policies lay down the rules of the game, clearly specifying what is allowed and what is not, thereby guiding the organisation's actions and decisions. Second, they function as a guide for auditors to objectively verify that the organisation is indeed 'doing the right thing' by operating within the established limits.

Clearly, data governance requires its own policy, serving as the foundation for the entire data governance implementation programme. It outlines the principles, roles and responsibilities and enlists a set of policy controls necessary for effective data management and protection. By establishing a clear and comprehensive data governance policy, an organisation not only sets the stage for how data is to be handled, secured and utilised but also provides a framework for accountability and continuous improvement. It guides the company towards a path of increasing maturity besides compliance.

To provide you with some practical help, let's explore a reusable template for a data governance policy. This template will outline its various sections and potential content items.

Purpose and scope

You should declare the policy's intent, linking it to the higher-level business strategy. You also need to specify the scope of the policy clearly and whether there are exclusions. Here is an example of the text you can use in this introductory part of the policy:

'This policy aims to establish a comprehensive framework for managing, securing and utilising data assets for business value creation, ensuring alignment with the organisation's strategic goals. It applies organisation-wide across all data types and processes.'

Principles

Enlist some general principles that explain the rationale of all the controls you are imposing. These principles should be easy to understand and of general applicability, and they should explain the behaviours and beliefs we expect to obtain by applying the policy. A good start would be using the four cultural good convictions we met at the beginning of this chapter. For example, you can state here:

1 Data assets are business assets and are managed accordingly.
2 Every data asset has a clear definition and owner.
3 The business is ultimately responsible for the management of data assets and their fit for purpose.
4 The potential business value of data assets depends on how well they are governed.

Policy controls

Here, you should explain the controls that are included in the policy and, for each of them, list the fundamental requirements for being compliant. This will be the basis of audits and internal controls, so it must be controllable and measurable.

Here is an example of how you can describe the five data governance controls we recommend establishing:

1 **Data governance roles**
   - Define clear roles such as data stewards, custodians and the governance board.
   - Establish a dedicated data governance team responsible for overseeing governance efforts.
   - Assign roles by the highest appropriate authority to ensure accountability and visibility.

2 **Data catalogue**

- Implement a comprehensive data catalogue tool encompassing a data dictionary and a business glossary.
- Ensure the catalogue includes risk, value and sensitivity data classifications.
- Build and update the catalogue iteratively, prioritising high-value and high-risk data assets.

3 **Data quality**

- Deploy a data quality management (DQM) tool to monitor and improve data quality systematically.
- Define and regularly review KPIs for data quality, focusing on completeness, accuracy, uniqueness, consistency and timeliness.
- Establish procedures for promptly correcting critical data quality issues and ongoing improvement initiatives.

4 **Data integrity**

- Introduce a data lineage tool to trace data origins, transformations and flows, ensuring transparency and trustworthiness.
- Prevent data duplications and ensure single ownership of data assets to maintain integrity.
- Centralise data governance activities to avoid shadow operations and ensure consistent application of governance practices across the organisation.

5 **Compliance and standards**

- Adhere to applicable data protection and privacy laws, including GDPR, ensuring data is handled legally and ethically.
- Incorporate ethical data use principles, promoting respect for individual privacy and data security.

Privacy compliance without data governance?

Privacy compliance, particularly under regulations like the GDPR (General Data Protection Regulation) from the European Union or the CCPA (California Consumer Privacy Act), underscores data governance's indispensable role. A poignant example from the GDPR is the 'right to be forgotten' (Article 17), which allows individuals to request the deletion of their personal data under certain conditions. Without a comprehensive data governance framework, identifying, locating and ensuring the deletion of all instances of an individual's personal data across an organisation's systems can be not only challenging but practically unfeasible. The gateway to privacy compliance is data governance.

This generic template includes all the essential elements of a data governance policy. You can use this template to create your own policy and gain alignment among top management. By implementing a strong policy, data governance will no longer be considered a 'nice-to-have' guideline but rather a set of auditable and externally verifiable rules. Non-compliance with these rules may result in disciplinary action. By adopting a robust policy, you are making clear that everyone should give data governance the attention it truly deserves.

Getting the data governance programme started

After establishing what data governance is, how it works and what controls should be in place, we should go through a playbook for implementing (or revamping) a data governance framework in a company. It goes through different steps, which we could organise into three main evolution phases. However cliché it sounds, the crawl–walk–run model gives us a good framework to envision what to do with data governance.

During the **crawl** phase, you need to initiate the foundational elements and get the programme started. Activities include:

- Document the high-level benefits of what the programme will bring. Start from the known pain points and estimate the value of solving them. You can then add the value of unlocking data analytics capabilities – more to come on data evaluation in the next chapter.
- Draft the data governance policy. You can use the template in the previous section as a base. Ensure you clarify who does what at a high level (with a RACI matrix mapping roles and activities).
- Establish the data governance board, identifying the overall sponsor.
- Establish the data governance core team, starting from its leader.
- Put together a multi-year roadmap for the data governance programme (this crawl–walk–run phasing can be a good base) and estimate the required budget.
- Host a kick-off meeting for the programme with the full board and approve the governance policy and budget.
- Appoint the data stewards and custodians by data domain. People will change over time, and the community might grow, but it's important to build the first layer of it in this phase.

When you get to the **walk** phase, you can begin the actual data governance processes and start equipping the organisation with the right tools for running the processes. Activities you should plan for include:

- Develop data governance procedures required to implement the vision explained in the policy. Start with the critical ones, such as those related to creating and maintaining a data catalogue, lineage and quality.
- Develop data governance training modules and deliver them to stewards and custodians, together with an awareness campaign for everyone in the company.
- Identify priority criteria based on data assets classification (normally starting from high-risk and high-value data) and enlist the top priority data assets based on these criteria and current knowledge (accepting that this list will grow as the programme progresses).
- Identify and procure data cataloguing, lineage and data quality tools. You can run pilots on top-priority assets.
- Kick off the data cataloguing process, having stewards and custodians begin data discovery, create a dictionary and glossary for top-priority data assets and start to document their lineage.
- Kick off the data quality process by designing and implementing data quality rules for top-priority assets and build a first data quality dashboard to track quality metrics. Start from measuring the rates of data quality issues affecting dashboards and analytics products (which should be minimised) and the levels of data availability (which need to be maximised).

During the **run** phase, you will expand the scope of your data governance efforts to the broader list of data assets and implement mechanisms to ensure the programme's sustainability. This includes:

- completing the creation of the data catalogue and the definition of data quality rules, moving to lower-priority assets;
- establishing control plans and an ongoing audit schedule for the data governance policy, identifying internal and external auditors;
- establishing a model to assess the data governance maturity level and establish ongoing procedures to track progress.

For a large company, an aggressive timeline for such a programme should allow for around three months for the crawl phase, then six to nine months for completing the run phase, and an additional six to nine months for the run phase. This means that establishing a full data governance programme can take between one and two years of work. Fortunately, you will not have to wait that long to see the immediate benefits of having the foundation of the governance processes up and running, as the Closets4all team has shown us.

The golden checklist on data governance

Data deserves to be governed as any business asset. Actually, its current strategic centrality in modern business forces us to take care of it even more than what we would do for other company assets. This chapter covered essential concepts, tools and a playbook for establishing and running a robust data governance framework.

Let's review the critical questions we should ask ourselves regarding the way we govern data.

- Do you have an inventory of metadata that describes what data is available in the company? Does it include a business-relevant definition and a technical description of data assets?
- Have you mapped what systems are available in the company and how the data flows across them? Are these systems interconnected, facilitating seamless data integration and accessibility?
- Do you have ways to measure the quality of your data in terms of completeness, accuracy, uniqueness, consistency and timeliness? Do you have formal criteria to determine when a data point is 'right', at least for the most critical assets?
- Do you have a data governance organisation setup, including the core team, the board, stewards and custodians? Is this community actively engaged in fostering collaboration and adherence to governance practices?
- Have you developed a roadmap for implementing data governance processes and tools with a vision for progressively enhancing its maturity? Are there established processes for periodically assessing the success and efficacy of the data governance initiative?

After seeing the importance of disciplined management of our precious data assets, we are ready to move to the next and final chapter of our journey to see how the Data Transformation process can be brought to life.

CHAPTER 8
LEADING THE DATA TRANSFORMATION CHANGE

In this chapter

- How do we assess the data maturity of our organisation?
- How do we prepare to drive the Data Transformation process continuously?
- How do we measure the progress made? How can we accelerate it?
- What aspects should we focus on to ensure the journey is sustainable?

'Without continual growth and progress, such words as improvement, achievement, and success have no meaning,' Benjamin Franklin once said, emphasising the value of continuous advancement in *The Art of Virtue*.

Our Data Transformation journey embodies this philosophy. We described it as an iterative, progressive and outcome-oriented process. We hinted at the necessity to move across different levels of data maturity, continuously assess where we stand, and update and replan our data capabilities portfolio and enablers while unceasingly measuring the value created. It is time to wrap up what we have discussed so far and reach a comprehensive understanding of how we can leverage these concepts and tools along our transformation.

In this chapter, we will first define and leverage a Data Maturity Model that can support our transformation journey, giving us directions and highlighting opportunities to follow along our growth path. We will then discuss the key aspects to be considered when managing the transformation journey and how to drive it continuously. By the end of this chapter, you will be well prepared to lead your organisation through this process and equipped with the key elements to foster enduring growth and development.

The Data Maturity Model: where do you stand?

Let's leverage again the analogy with the journey we have used many times in our discussion: business value is our north star; the big bets are our first main routes to the destination, and the Data Activation Canvas helps us detail these paths; the enablers are our tools and techniques we can leverage across the routes; we also defined how to get organised and manage the journey in terms of people and content (i.e. govern the data).

Our backpack is now full of utensils, and our mind overflows with expectations. How do we make sure we do not get lost along the journey? What we need now to get moving is a compass or, better said, a tool that allows us to check where we are on our journey, if we need to change our planning, revise our toolkit, reshape or update anything in our strategy, so that our process stays consistent, steady and outcome-oriented.

Our compass will be the Data Maturity Model (Figure 8.1), a framework encompassing three critical assessment areas, **people**, **business** and **technology**, to define strengths or opportunities and where to focus on the transformation process, raise the bar and reach the next level. These three areas are helping us identify eight critical success factors that better define the elements of maturity that lead to unlocking the full potential of data, analytics and AI. We will now explore these factors one by one.

Data strategy

In Chapter 2, we discussed the importance of setting a data strategy and how this intimately supports our business strategy in reaching the overall goals the company has set. Let's now look at the Data Transformation ambition. We are dealing with a bold, intentional choice that can only be driven if the top management is supportive and actively sponsoring and makes it central in the company strategy at any level in the organisation.

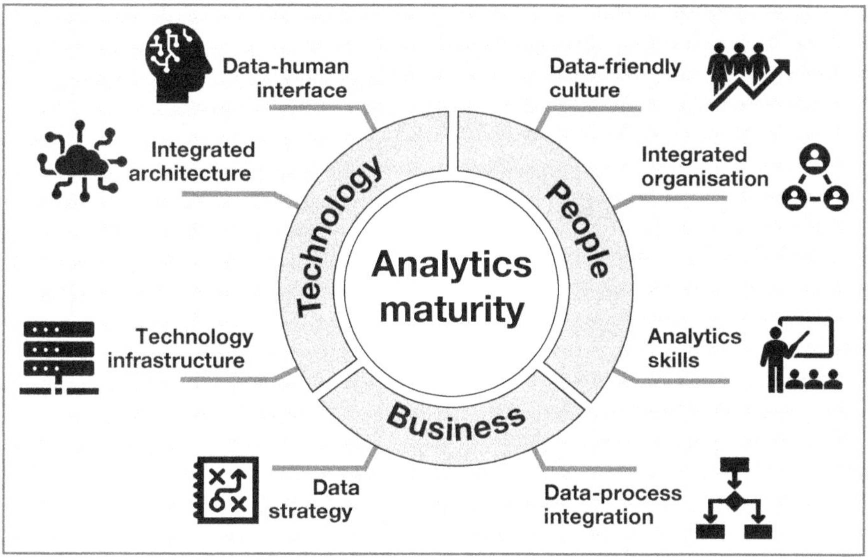

Figure 8.1 The Data Maturity Model, our compass to continuously assess and drive the Data Transformation process

To achieve this, a data strategy is needed. To define it, we can consider a few essential steps.

- Outline a **vision**, a single long-term goal for the next 5 to 10 years that is ultimately linked to the core business goal of the company. This is an exercise of imagination: if 100 per cent of the data, analytics and AI potential is realised, what could be the outcome for the company? It can be a broad and ambitious objective like 'being the most data-driven company in our industry', 'making data, analytics and AI a symbiotic part of our decision making at any level', or 'reinventing the way our company operates, thanks to data, analytics and AI'. It does not matter if the objective seems far in the future or hardly achievable with the current maturity; this is our vision, a universal statement of aspiration that all management should be able to recognise and link to our Data Transformation effort.
- Create a **portfolio of value-driven initiatives** that will support our long-term goals and grant some quick wins or short-term achievements so that you can leverage results to keep momentum and attention from the top management and the broader organisation.

- Establish **enablers** that you can exploit across initiatives to remove barriers to scale and accelerate growth in high-priority areas of your agenda. This will avoid continuously reinventing the wheel and help better manage aspects like total ownership and governance costs.
- Define an organisational **operating model** that will help you sustain your ambitions, empowering the teams in the organisation according to clear expectations and responsibilities so that valuable contribution is maximised. At the same time, inefficiencies and duplications are kept as minimal as possible.
- Set clear **success measures** and report quantitative results on an ongoing basis, especially for your portfolio of initiatives, ensuring an explicit business sponsor clearly owns the accountability.
- Make sure that your strategy is anchored on a solid **ethical and legal framework** to make it sustainable across the years to come.

Once the data strategy is set and approved, it is important to communicate and socialise it as much as possible so that everyone in the organisation (but also outside, if you want) can become familiar with and stay up to date, like for any other crucial strategic initiative of the company.

Data-process integration

Another critical business success factor is the ability to systematically leverage our data and related capabilities in our company processes for a better outcome. Today, every company operating model has a variably intricate set of business processes with diverse digitalisation levels. Different processes may have different levels of data-process integration, depending on the focus, need or historical development. The more we move up in the maturity scale, the more digital capabilities, data and algorithms will be embedded and play a central role.

Here are some probing questions to understand how much data is integrated with a few processes.

- In decision making, are data and algorithms preventively leveraged to simulate outcomes and scenarios? How much is this output leveraged in the decision execution?
- In a customer engagement process, are historical, demographic and contextual data leveraged to improve or personalise the customer experience based on previous iterations?

- In a production process, how much are the production parameters tuned based on algorithmic prescriptions?

The advantage of a completely digitised process is that data is produced by the process itself, meaning that each execution step is appropriately captured in a digital form, creating a digital parallel of the physical process. This considerable amount of data describes precisely how the current process works and serves as the basis for data mining and optimisation.

A way to measure an organisation's maturity on this critical success factor is to map the company's processes and their level of digitalisation by capturing how much data is used or produced along each process. This map of the company processes and their respective digitalisation level must be maintained and revised regularly to identify operating areas that deserve to progress faster because they are more strategic or, simply, behind the rest.

Technology Infrastructure

We now move to the technology area, where the infrastructure is the first critical success factor to be assessed. In Chapter 5, we introduced the Modern Data Stack, and we have seen how the bottom layer is the physical infrastructure to which we delegate the core mission of storing, computing or exchanging data. Being rightly equipped means having the resources needed to cope with significant challenges from the high data volume, velocity and variety our company is exposed to.

This mission can be absolved in many ways, from the scenario where we do everything in-house, with internal hardware, to the other extreme where we outsource this part entirely, delegating a third-party service that would provide a virtually endless amount of resources in the cloud. The strategic choice between these extremes will reflect many needs and constraints, from scalability to agility, cost, control and security. Making informed choices to address these needs will streamline complexity and reduce potential risks.

Integrated architecture

It is essential to ensure our data is efficiently utilised throughout their lifecycle and integrated across the company's operating model and various processes to unlock their full potential. We can achieve this goal by focusing on two key objectives.

- Establish a harmonised and unified data architecture by dismantling existing data silos and cohesively integrating data from diverse operational areas of the company, including sales, marketing, finance, logistics, supply chain and beyond. This involves creating a coherent data architecture where crucial internal and external data sources are interconnected through one or more common data models thoroughly documented and comprehensively understood.
- Transform the data into truly multifunctional assets, treated as any other critical business assets and managed through effective data governance. This entails developing and implementing a comprehensive framework encompassing processes, organisational roles, policies, best practices and metrics to ensure the data's quality, integrity and availability throughout the company.

A robust data architecture lays the groundwork for effectively leveraging data's value, while data governance ensures its sustainability over time.

Data–person interface

Chapter 3 discussed a critical aspect of activating our data capability and generating value: figuring out how users interact with the data. In Chapter 5, we discussed the application layer's importance in effectively accessing our data assets. Indeed, the agility and friendliness of our technological stack in providing effective touchpoints to human beings are significant maturity indicators.

These touchpoints may have different flavours and cater to different user personas. A cornerstone of data democratisation is business intelligence applications, which are critical to ensure business users can autonomously explore, deep dive into, summarise and visualise data in the form of graphs or tables and access the output of predictive or prescriptive algorithms presented for decision making.

Another potential way to interact with the data is via the analytics applications. In this case, expert users like data scientists and analysts are leveraging specialised tools to develop or fine-tune algorithms that can better respond to tailored business needs beyond what could be already covered via business intelligence tools or recommendations from pre-existing algorithms or solutions. Enlightened managers who are open to learning and upskilling in this area can also play this role, considering the lowering of entry barriers offered by GenAI-empowered experience.

Analytical skills

Our last assessment area in our maturity model relates to people. Let us start with the analytical skills essential to support the Data Transformation since they represent the core know-how needed across the journey. In Chapter 6, we presented the six core skills required across the four fundamental data job families a company should consider to be rightly equipped.

These competencies and roles are in high demand and can be challenging to find on the job market, especially as we move up in the skills and experience requirements. Moreover, they continuously evolve to capture and reflect the latest technological and technical practices. Similarly, they may become quickly obsolete; there is a need to establish a continuous and modular learning programme that can update, upskill or reskill our organisation.

The more mature the organisation, the more common, transversal and diffused the data fluency, allowing everyone (including the top management) to speak the same language and continuously learn in the true spirit of a growth mindset.

Integrated organisation

The proper roles and the analytical skills alone cannot deliver on our Data Transformation commitment unless they are well integrated into our company's organisational structure. Balancing immediate business priorities with long-term scaling ambitions often presents a challenge. Yet, a mature organisation can resolve this tension through a model that integrates business operations and analytics, ensuring a cohesive approach to Data-Driven Transformation.

Such a virtuous integration relies on a clearly documented governance, able to prevent challenges and conflicts in critical areas such as:

- Analytics portfolio management, i.e. setting the right priorities for analytics initiatives and related investments to be made. Different company areas may have different visions about the urgency of specific projects. Each business unit or functional team will try to push for their respective agendas, maybe deprioritising or postponing investments that would create a more considerable company impact or a better long-term outcome, like the ones related to data management and infrastructure, master data harmonisation across the company, common reusable data assets creation and many more.

- Career development, i.e. managing the career path of data and analytics professionals in a way that they stay relevant and can continue to grow. This translates into the need to identify, define and promote relevant career models and identify a governance that supports the development of each individual not only with promotions (vertical growth) but also with job rotations across different business units and roles (horizontal growth).

Data-friendly culture

The final success factor in our Data Maturity Model is data culture, a nuanced and subtle area we discussed in Chapter 6. Our intent is apparently straightforward: we want data and algorithms embraced by everyone in the organisation to drive better business outcomes. However, it is difficult to articulate what this means and how it is implemented in our company.

Here is a set of probes we can leverage to determine how data-friendly our company culture is.

- How are the recommendations coming from analytics and AI leveraged in enabling our organisation's decision making? Are they considered and accepted even when contrasting the personal opinion and experience of the decision maker? Are data used to find insights that inform a decision, or are they used to justify *a posteriori* a decision already made? Role models in decision making will make a well-informed (and risk-balanced) decision based on data-driven insights, thanks to their sensible understanding of how analytics and AI work.
- Is data allowed in the decision-making room? Are analysts and data scientists actively involved and contributing to the most critical meetings? To make the data really embedded in decision making, the data professionals' role cannot be relegated to just providing analytical services or, worst case, reports. A data-friendly organisation will have data roles acting as trusted advisors in multifunctional decision teams, where they can bring the algorithms and data expertise.

- Are the data and analytics topics familiar to everyone? Or are they treated as technical and specialistic topics, not open to everyone's understanding? The more we relegate these discussions to the expert circles, the less the actual adoption and trust level will be. How can an organisation fully embrace something they do not understand? This reinforces the need to create and maintain a data fluency programme that allows everyone, no one exempted, to learn and understand the foundational elements of these capabilities and tools and get acquainted with their operation (like you are doing by reading this book).

Table 8.1 offers a simple data maturity evaluation card. For each of the eight critical success factors described above, you can find a definition of the boundary

Table 8.1 Data Maturity Model evaluation card

Success factor	Completely missing *(score 1)*	Maximum maturity *(score 5)*	Score
Data strategy	Non-existent data strategy, neither at single business unit level. Data analytics usage is highly fragmented and not explicitly linked to a committed outcome. The data exploitation is delegated to single individuals. Ethical and privacy risks are not explicitly addressed.	A corporate data strategy is documented, approved and shared with the entire organisation by the top management. There is a portfolio of critical projects, each with a clear sponsorship and execution, and value creation is regularly monitored.	
Data-process integration	Business processes are static and do not include any variation, exception or personalisation that is data-driven. Many business processes happen without capturing transactional logs. The analytical deep dive results do not directly impact the company's working methods.	All critical business processes are completely digitised, and they get executed coupled with a data flow that records their progress and optimises their execution. New process creation or modification happens together with the related information flow update. Company results are recorded and can be analysed in real time.	
Technology infrastructure	The data infrastructure does not match the business dimension. Employees complain about the lack of hardware resources that prevent a practical usage of the information. Systems are vulnerable to cyberattacks.	Computing and storage resources match the current analytics needs. The cloud infrastructure can be quickly adjusted to meet changing needs. Systems comply with the highest security standards and are regularly exposed to penetration tests.	

Table 8.1 *(Continued)*

Success factor	**Completely missing *(score 1)***	**Maximum maturity *(score 5)***	**Score**
Integrated architecture	Data is often stored in physically separate machines, not connected among them. Data formats are not standardised or documented. There is no common master data definition, and joining tables always requires a manual mapping effort. No one in the company knows what data is available and where in the company.	There is a common data model all business units refer to. Key entities such as customers, products and suppliers are managed through a clear master data management process that allows tables to be easily joined. Data governance processes are well documented and carefully reviewed. Comprehensive data catalogue, lineage and data quality tools are available.	
Data–person interface	The interfaces used to access data differ according to the data type and the business unit. Employees do not get any central guidance on how to access data. To obtain data in a format not accounted for in the existing interfaces, you necessarily need to ask for a manual intervention from the IT team.	If equipped with the proper authorisations, whoever in the company can access the largest part of company data through a single business intelligence interface that allows to combine diverse data, create tables and graphs with a high level of personalisation. Data scientists and business analysts can connect their development environment and any application for advanced analytics to the most updated company data at any level of detail.	
Analytical skills	Knowledge about data science techniques is scarce in the organisation and limited to the ones who, thanks to their personal interest, studied them in their free time or at university. Current 'analysts' mostly use their deductive reasoning and base tools (like spreadsheets) to reply to specific business questions. There is no career model for business analysts or data scientists, nor opportunities to develop analytical skills that are considered highly technical and 'niche' skills.	The company has a clear recruiting strategy for data professionals. A formal description of the most important analytical roles exists, and there is a defined standard competencies and career map for each. A comprehensive and modular analytical skills development programme allows each employee (top managers and data professionals included) to deep dive according to business needs, career aspirations and personal interests. All employees, regardless of the respective function, are equipped with base fundamental knowledge about data analytics and can describe their activation ideas.	

Table 8.1 *(Continued)*

Success factor	**Completely missing *(score 1)***	**Maximum maturity *(score 5)***	**Score**
Integrated organisation	Data scientists and business analysts act separately from the business and are considered 'technicians' to be involved only for specific needs. Each business unit uses different approaches to data exploitation, and there are no solid initiatives to harmonise them.	Analysts are fully integrated into the business units: they are in touch with the business challenges and opportunities and can directly impact decisions and influence the strategy. All analysts actively participate in activities from communities of practice of interest, within which they share experiences and codify methodologies of common interest to encourage reapplication. Analysts' priorities and job rotation are managed through a clear and documented process.	
Data-friendly culture	Decisions are usually made by following the opinion of the highest-ranked person, even if this contradicts the numerical evidence. Data is mainly used for retrospective analysis that does not challenge the status quo. The topic 'data' is not considered relevant.	The entire organisation is permeated with widespread knowledge and a keen interest in data and data analytics. Top managers consistently use and trust recommendations generated from data and algorithms; everyone feels authorised to change plans drastically if supported by analytical evidence. Data is considered as a source of competitive advantage.	

scenarios (worst and best case) that you can try to relate to. By assigning a score from 1 to 5, depending on how close we feel to these maturity scenarios, and summing the scores, we can derive our current maturity level and identify possible opportunity areas to move to the next level.

Managing the transformation journey

Transforming a company with data requires embracing new mindsets and ways of working. Responding adequately to a continuously changing business environment, being ready to adopt new technology disruptions and anticipating the next big idea of your industry entirely rely on the organisation's ability to learn, adapt and deliver quickly.

In the following paragraphs, we will look at the most critical aspects to be considered along the process and define how to approach each of them in the context of our journey.

Accounting for data value

We mentioned above in this chapter that business value is our north star. Still, we must elaborate more on how to account for it and subsequently communicate it appropriately.

Before diving deeper into these concepts, let us clear the stage from some terminology. In data and analytics, we often see the terms *monetisation* and *valorisation* used interchangeably. These two concepts are related but have different focuses.

Data monetisation refers to the process of turning data into monetary value, i.e. as a means to generate revenue. It can be a direct monetisation when we are selling data or insights derived from it (as an example, a company may sell some of its customer data to another company interested in the same target). It can also be an indirect monetisation if data is used to improve business processes, make more informed decisions, or enhance products and services, indirectly leading to increased revenue. For example, using customer behaviour data to personalise marketing campaigns, thereby increasing sales.

Data valorisation, instead, is a broader term that encompasses the idea of turning data into a valuable asset for the organisation. It could entail but is not limited to financial gain. For example, data analytics can enhance decision making and gain insights that inform strategic decisions. Or it can improve and streamline operations, reduce costs or increase efficiency. Data can also be involved in innovating products and services or shaping company policies or long-term strategies. Data valorisation is more about the intrinsic enhancement of data's worth and utility in various dimensions.

At the beginning of this book, we anticipated the interdependencies between business strategy and data and analytics strategy, putting the business value generation of our data capabilities at the centre of the chain (see Chapter 2, Figure 2.2). Let's further elaborate on this concept and see how to define and influence the valorisation of each capability and data asset.

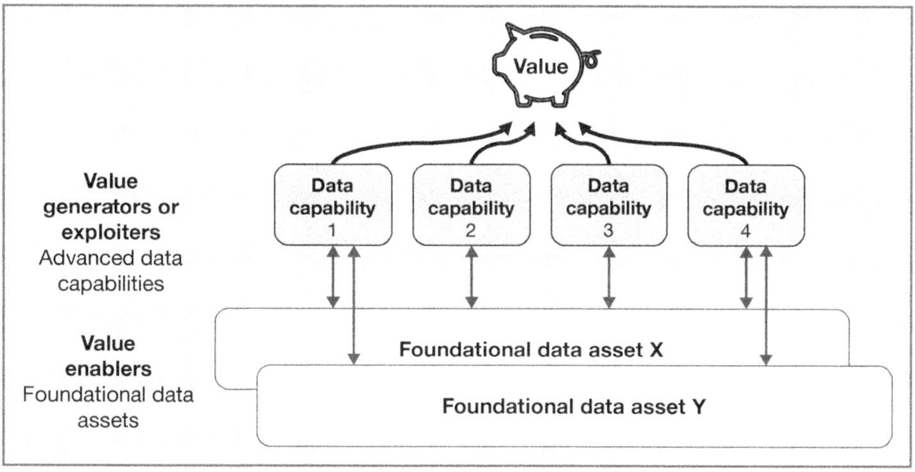

Figure 8.2 Value generators and value enablers are critical to data valorisation. Each capability will produce its intrinsic value, while the value enabled by each foundational data asset is proportional to the number of data capabilities exploiting it

As seen in Chapter 3, the Data Activation Canvas requires explicitly capturing the value creation of each data capability, i.e. advanced analytics or AI solutions that exploit data to produce an outcome linked to business value. In this context, we can call them **value generators**. Similarly, in Chapters 5 and 7, we talked about data assets, which should be treated as any other business assets. Some of them, the important and foundational ones, can be seen as **value enablers** since they carry the critical data needed by the capabilities to work and produce business value. Our total portfolio of capabilities will produce as much value as our organisation actively adopts many capabilities. It means our total value generated is the sum of the value of each capability, as illustrated in Figure 8.2.

Each capability's value can be accounted as its intrinsic value times the adoption. Let us use an example: if my capability is an order recommendation system that, when used, delivers +2 per cent on the average order value, the higher my user base and usage frequency, the higher the value generated. We need to identify levers that can influence intrinsic value or adoption to optimise the value generated by a single data capability. Here are a few examples.

- Capability performance: the better your capability results, the higher the value created or the end-user adoption. Consider the previous example of the order recommendation system: moving from +2 per cent to +5 per cent revenue uplift would deliver more value and attract more users.

- Capability features: the more successful features your capability has, the higher the adoption. Imagine a recommendation system that identifies new product or service opportunities for a customer and automatically triggers dedicated communication to maximise the interest and purchase probability. This case can support both direct value generation and adoption.
- User experience: a better experience, aligned with the user expectations or surprisingly more efficient, will increase the capability adoption.
- Value equation and ROI: working on the correct capability value equation (i.e. revenue vs costs) is critical to ensure the proper adoption. Would you unquestioningly adopt a capability that will increase your costs by 20 per cent while promising a 21 per cent revenue increase? What if your costs increase only by 5 per cent and your revenue promise stays at 21 per cent?
- Data quality: even if all the conditions above are met, but data quality is not ensured, your value will not be realised. Data quality should meet at least the minimum standard required by the capability not to compromise its performance. Any improvement from there may result, for instance, in a more accurate model (resulting in a performance improvement) or better trust in data (resulting in adoption improvement)

Instead, foundational data assets are enablers, so the higher the number of capabilities exploiting them, the higher the re-usage, therefore, cost optimisation and scale. To influence the adoption of each asset by the data capabilities present (or upcoming) in our portfolio, we can think about these levers.

- Richness and depth: do I have all the KPIs my target data capability needs? Do I have the correct data granularity and frequency?
- Footprint and coverage: is my data asset covering all my business units or markets? Are all channels or other scenarios included?
- Total cost of ownership: is my asset affordable for the data capability to adopt it? Do I have the proper cost structure to exploit scale efficiency as the asset gets reused over and over?
- Data governance and quality: is the asset well governed, with clear ownership? Is the level of data quality good enough for my target data capability? Can I guarantee a service level that ensures the capability can run smoothly over time?

Choosing the right methodology for analytics: agile vs waterfall

Our Data Transformation requires a significant effort to be managed, and project management methodologies play a crucial role by providing frameworks to plan, execute, and finalise projects efficiently. Given the unique challenges of analytics projects (rapidly changing requirements, multiple stakeholders involved, need for exploratory mindset, and so on), choosing the best methodology for each scenario is essential.

The classical project management approach is called **waterfall**. It is a highly structured approach, perfectly suitable to manage projects with well-defined requirements and deliverables. It is linear and sequential in nature and, therefore, easier to track and communicate progress to stakeholders.

This high level of control is counterbalanced by low flexibility. Requirement changes are complex to incorporate once the project has started, which can be a significant drawback in analytics projects where requirements may evolve. Also, the fact that testing occurs late in the project may lead to the discovery of issues too late in the process, significantly impacting the timeline. In the waterfall approach, the project scope tends to be preserved at the expense of time and resources.

The waterfall approach is typically preferred in analytical projects with well-defined or low-flexibility requirements. For instance, a project aiming to create reports that meet specific regulatory standards, a project aimed at migrating data from an old system to a new one, or a project aimed at creating a standard financial report that follows a specific format and contains predefined metrics.

The **agile** methodology has been primarily used in software development but has since been applied to various other areas, including analytics. It is characterised by its focus on delivering value to the customer in the shortest possible timeframe, preserving customer-centricity, flexibility and a collaborative approach. Agile projects are divided into small, manageable units known as *sprints* (or *iterations*), each involving planning, designing, coding and testing to produce a working product increment at the end.

In the analytics context, the agile approach accommodates changes more easily, allowing for the iterative refinement of analytics models as new insights are gained. Short sprints and continuous feedback loops enable quicker delivery of new features, which may benefit fast-paced analytics environments. However, agile demands high levels of collaboration and communication, which can be challenging in distributed teams and, given its flexible nature, it has a less predictable outcome and timelines, potentially complicating long-term planning.

A few good examples of where to use agile are the following: exploratory data projects, where insights generation can be iterative, and requirements may evolve as new information is discovered; new analytics models or analytics solutions development, where the best approach is not known upfront and might require experimentation and iteration to refine; projects where ongoing stakeholders' input is required, such as the development of a dynamic business intelligence dashboard that needs to evolve based on user needs; complex projects where requirements are uncertain and both data processing and analytics approaches are discovered through iterative exploration and refinement; projects needing a quick market entry, like deploying a predictive model that addresses a timely business opportunity or competitive threat.

As in many other areas, there is no silver bullet, and the methodology should be decided based on the conditions. Some projects may benefit from a hybrid approach, blending elements of both methods to suit the project's unique requirements and constraints.

Continuously injecting innovation to unleash value

The world of data analytics is very dynamic and responsive to new technology and practice trends. As such, the core analytics technology innovation and the possibility of embracing new algorithmic approaches or leveraging new data sources will naturally come into the Data Transformation agenda. However, how can we embrace a systemic approach to this topic, staying focused on our main plan (our big bets and enablers) and avoiding missing a new opportunity that may translate into a significant value? Here, we propose following a straightforward framework and moving across three logical stages to assess and qualify a new idea as a potential big bet to be added to our portfolio.

First, we need to ensure the idea is viable and there is technical feasibility. To assess that, we can run a **proof of concept (PoC)**, a small-scale experimental project or demonstration run in a controlled, low-risk environment to evaluate our idea's practicality and effectiveness in solving real-world problems. Running a successful PoC means starting with a clear definition of what we aim to achieve (for instance, building a new predictive model, testing the feasibility of a new analytics tool, or the effectiveness of a data integration process). We choose a small, representative dataset and select analytics tools and technologies that align with the project's goals, keeping its potential scalability in mind. Based on the objectives, we develop a prototype that brings the concept to life. The results will determine if the goals were met or if the concept has to be refined further. The idea could even be dropped entirely already at this stage.

If the PoC is successful, we can move to a **proof of value (PoV)** that centres on proving the technology's actual value within the specific organisational context, using deliberate metrics such as return on investment, revenue growth, cost savings, or user adoption. Whereas a PoC primarily focuses on demonstrating an idea's feasibility or technical viability, a PoV aims to establish the actual value or tangible benefits that the solution can deliver to the business. In the case of PoV, the most critical step is identifying and defining the key metrics or indicators that will be used to measure the solution's value to the business. Once this is clear, a detailed plan can be outlined and executed. Compared to the PoC, in this case, we need a significant scale sufficient to produce measurable outcomes that can be used to quantify the benefits and decide whether to move it further.

If the PoV is successful, we can move to the real data capability design and build, starting from a **minimum viable product (MVP)**, that would optimise the time to value realisation and ensure the data capability activation is prioritised, as detailed in Chapter 3.

Although this three-step framework is already quite simple, we do not always need to cross all stages. Jumping from a PoC to an MVP, skipping the PoC and starting from a PoV, or starting straight with an MVP is possible, provided the prerequisites and expectations are precise. Unrealistic aspirations, such as exploiting a PoC's frugality and pretending an MVP's scaling ambitions, should be ruled out at the onset to prevent unnecessary failures.

Co-creating with business partners for mutual success

Our Data Transformation journey aims to drive business value, so it can only be successful if it is fully endorsed and adopted by our business partners, directly impacted by the different capabilities. The best way to ensure success is adopting a customer-centric approach in the capabilities design, with the customer, in this case, represented by our business partner or counterpart. A customer-centric approach would mean actively involving the business partner in every stage of the capability development, from ideation (as we have seen already in the Ideation Workshop in Chapter 2) to design, build and launch, including capability evolution over time. In particular, co-creating analytics solutions with business partners involves collaboration between data scientists, analysts, IT professionals and business stakeholders in a multifunctional approach.

The co-creation approach offers several significant benefits to all parties involved:

- more business-relevant analytics solutions, given the deep business understanding infused in the process and the ability to foster the link with higher strategic business goals;
- more user-friendly capabilities, as the business has been testing its usage throughout the entire lifecycle, providing feedback from the beginning;
- stronger business user buy-in and higher adoption rates among end users, since the engagement of business partners in the development process increases their commitment to and ownership of the solution;
- better agility, because co-creating with business partners allows for more agile development processes where feedback is quickly integrated and solutions can evolve more promptly to meet changing needs;
- better data literacy and culture because the collaborative process helps demystify data and analytics for business stakeholders since the start and encourages a shift toward a more data-centric approach across the organisation.

The co-creation with business partners approach helps us connect the dots between the value focus, the agile methodology and the iterative approach to innovation. It is not just about developing data-driven solutions; it's about fostering a collaborative, innovative and data-informed culture within an organisation. This approach enhances the effectiveness and adoption of analytics solutions and drives tangible business outcomes, innovation and strategic advantage. It's a true win-win strategy.

Driving the Data Transformation: who and how

The Data Transformation process is not a sprint run but rather a marathon. If we want to win in the long run, we need to secure a clear and structured approach, getting organised for success. We need to clarify accountability and responsibilities, setting the appropriate expectations on timings and outcomes.

To keep it pragmatic, let us lay down a playbook of the necessary steps to drive the Data Transformation journey for your company.

- Set up a **Data Transformation board**, a multifunctional team of top managers that takes on the challenge and responsibility of driving the Data Transformation in the company and the related change management. As it should be clear at this point, this cannot be a technical-oriented board only. It will include the head of the technical organisation enabling the change, like the chief data officer and the chief information officer or their equivalents. However, this is not sufficient to drive the real business transformation behind the technical effort. Therefore, other functional heads (marketing, sales, supply chain, production, human resources, and more) or business unit heads impacted or benefitting from the change must be included. Given the high ambition and stakes of our programme, it is not acceptable to tolerate disengagement ('it is not my area of concern') or finger-pointing ('the failure is not due to my team'); therefore, the board has to be a role model of change management, proving with facts the commitment toward its mission and securing the outcome against emerging challenges. Ideally, the accountability of the outcome should be with the CEO, leading the board and testifying about the strategic importance of data, analytics and AI in the company.
- Establish a **portfolio** of projects connected with the Data Transformation programme so the board can see and understand it as a whole. It will include a mix of value-oriented data capabilities projects (the big bets of Chapter 2, described in Chapter 3 via the Data Activation Canvas) and more foundational projects acting as enablers across the other projects or the organisation (think about the technological and data platform evolution, as mentioned in Chapter 5, the corporate data fluency programme, as mentioned in Chapter 6, the data governance inception, as reviewed in Chapter 7, and many more). In a nutshell, we are talking about converting our vision into a tangible set of deliverables, as mentioned in the data strategy critical success factor of our Data Maturity Model. Our Data Transformation strategic portfolio represents the 'action plan' to move from our current maturity level, assessed via the Data Maturity Model, to the next one. In other words, the Data Maturity Models set the stages of our journey; the project portfolio defines the path to get there.

- Schedule a drumbeat of **steering meetings** to ensure the board can play a critical role in ensuring that Data Transformation can proceed as intended. During these meetings, the board will:
  - review the status of each project in the portfolio, focusing on removing possible barriers of any kind, from technical to organisational or resources-related;
  - reassess the maturity level reached by the company, according to the Data Maturity Model and decide on the next iteration – this may mean adjusting the project portfolio, repositioning some of the expected outcomes, or agreeing on the next set of initiatives to increase the maturity in strategic or lagging areas.
- Create a **communication plan** for the broader organisation that includes the vision of the programme, regular updates about the status of the Data Transformation journey, the most significant achievements, and the upcoming milestones. This can be conveyed via newsletters, internal websites or internal social media pages built on a repository of general-purpose documentation that can create awareness and stimulate interaction. Removing scepticism and fear while balancing expectations is vital in managing the change. This can be achieved by leveraging testimonials from sponsors or board members (as well as business users), celebrating success stories, creating educational material beyond the technical training, and actively listening to the organisation, for example, via dedicated surveys or question and answer sessions. In other words, raising the company's interest in Data Transformation will create the organisational substrate for building its success.

As a last point of reflection, Data Transformation is an iterative and progressive process that helps us move toward higher levels of data maturity. This implies we should not underestimate the graduality of the approach to be embraced to avoid pitfalls or failures driven by challenges non-proportionate to our maturity level.

Figure 8.3 captures these dynamics along two axes: the maturity level versus the complexity of the challenges. High challenges in the context of low data maturity are a perfect recipe for failure: we are not ready for them, and this is leading to a potential 'burnout' effect. Similarly, putting a very mature analytical organisation against low-complexity challenges will be detrimental in both outcome and motivation, creating the 'boredom' effect in our team and stakeholders.

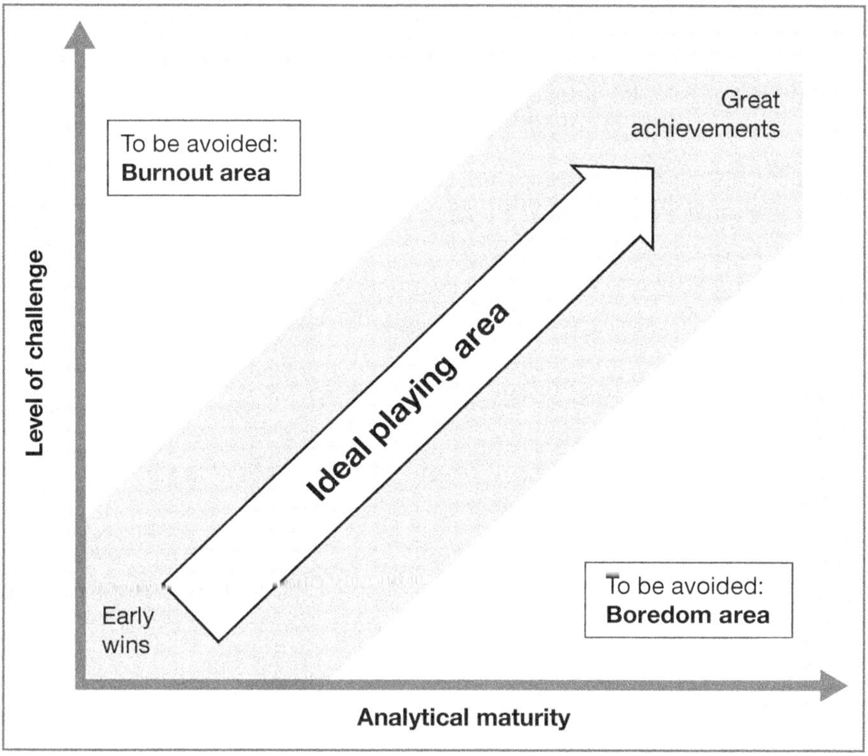

Figure 8.3 Ideal playing area for our Data Transformation programme: we secure our ability to win in the long term by balancing the complexity of challenges with our maturity level

The ideal playing area is where our data maturity level and the complexity of the challenges are proportionate. As our maturity level increases, we can take on more complex challenges. Solving them will also contribute to our maturity growth, creating a virtuous Flywheel Effect that will gradually but constantly unlock higher achievements.

The golden checklist on the Data Transformation journey

We finally reached the end of our path, but we cannot close it without checking on crucial aspects that will help you lead the Data Transformation change.

1. **Assessing our data maturity**
   - What is our way of assessing the data maturity of our company? Are we embracing the Data Maturity Model?
   - Where do we stand now? What strengths and opportunities emerge from the assessment?
   - What does it take to reach the next data maturity level?
2. **Managing the transformation**
   - Where is the value in our project's portfolio? Can we articulate and regularly measure it? What is our strategy to improve it?
   - Are we clear on what methodology we will use to drive our projects? What will be waterfall vs what will be agile?
   - What is our approach to innovation as part of the Data Transformation? How do we balance risks with speed and scale ambitions?
   - What is the role of the business partners in our ideation?
3. **Driving the Data Transformation**
   - Who is accountable and responsible for the Data Transformation in our company?
   - Have we established a Data Transformation board? Do we have an intentional project portfolio, balancing big bets and long-term enablers?
   - What is our process to review the Data Transformation status and drive adjustments? How do we ensure continuous improvement and progress?

This chapter helped us complete our toolkit, and we are now ready to start our own Data Transformation journey. With its critical success factors, the Data Maturity Model allows us to see where we stand and start formulating our ambitions. It does not matter if we are starting from zero or already have a strategy; our objective is to identify a new set of initiatives to make our end vision come closer. The value focus, the right level of sponsorship, and a transversal top management commitment are non-negotiable if we want to make this a transformative outcome; the rest can be adjusted and tailored to our company's reality and needs.

Enjoy the journey – we hope it to be memorable!

READY TO MAKE IT HAPPEN?

What a journey it's been! Let's take a moment to reflect on how much ground we've covered together through this book.

We started from the realisation that the value of data must be viewed using the lens of real business needs and its solution. We've encountered frameworks, such as the *three types of analytics* model, that help us recognise value opportunities within our business and place them within our vision. The *Data Analytics Flywheel Effect* encouraged us: by focusing on the right *enablers*, we can make the value creation process from data self-sustainable.

From framing value, we moved to crafting a *data strategy*, steering clear of the dangerous – but so common – *False Starts*. Through an *Ideation Workshop*, we pinpointed specific value propositions, albeit still at a high level, and positioned them within a *Selection Matrix* to discern their priorities. This led us to question how to transition from high-level ideas to concrete value propositions. We met the *Data Activation Canvas* – a tool for simplifying this process and guiding us in articulating what we want to achieve, why, with whom and how. This Canvas allows us to transform our value proposition into specific requirements.

With clear ideas of data capabilities in mind, we understood the importance of fundamental enablers and examined each one to figure out how to make things happen. Artificial intelligence was the first enabler we found along our way: we learned to define the *ML-Way* of solving problems, drastically different from traditional approaches. We explored the *ML catalogue* to identify the algorithms at our disposal and how to choose the right one based on our needs. We also looked at *key evaluation metrics* to ensure that this ML-Way, no matter how appealing it looks in theory and presentations, effectively addresses our business needs and creates real value.

Next, we ventured into the realm of technology and infrastructure necessary to establish our data capabilities, starting with the *Modern Data Stack* architecture. We saw how *cloud* solutions could help us organise data in ways that fit our purpose, such as *data lakes* and *data warehouses*.

After so much talk of algorithms and technology, we realised that the heart of the Data Transformation is the people who drive it forward. We explored the *role and skillset mapping* of data professionals and how data analysts, data scientists and data engineers stand in our structure, depending on the *organisational design model* we choose. As we did so, we stayed mindful of our company's significant cultural challenges and of the tools, like *data fluency* programmes, available to us for the necessary – yet so hard – cultural shift.

The next stop in our journey was *data governance*, our ally in keeping data – the main asset for our ambitious strategy – organised and fluid enough to navigate the pathways of Data-Driven Transformation. We familiarised ourselves with operational instruments such as the *data catalogue* and *data quality* tools and defined the *data governance roles*. We also outlined the phases of a roadmap that starts with writing a clear and simple *data governance policy* and moves towards its sustainable implementation.

Finally, we learned how to manage the ongoing journey of Data Transformation by acquiring the *data analytics maturity model*, a tool that allows us to assess our current reality, measure the level we've reached, and better plan our next steps.

At the end of such an adventurous, challenging and – we truly hope – fulfilling journey, we'd like to offer two final pieces of advice.

First, *make it happen*. This book is not meant to collect dust on a shelf; its place is on your desk, within easy reach. Begin with small, manageable steps and gradually bring about change. If you're a data professional, recognise your role – you're not a passive observer; you're the main change agent for allowing data and algorithms to create value. If you're a leader or a CEO, there are no excuses; it's time to act and kick off or revamp the journey of Data-Driven Transformation – make it a priority. Don't feel overwhelmed by the magnitude of the task. Remember, this journey is designed to be progressive, allowing you to advance step by step. Start with the low-hanging fruits. If you already have a programme in place, now is the perfect time to revamp it. Use the checklists provided in each chapter as a starting point. Give them another read – do it now.

Second, *stay curious*. You are not at the end but at the beginning of this adventure. Your learning journey is ongoing and will never cease. Keep your curiosity alive by exploring other books and resources. We're here to make it easy for you. On the book's website, you'll find a 'Resources' section for a deeper dive into each chapter's content. We'll also share updates and further insights on our LinkedIn profiles and on the book's website. Please connect with us on

LinkedIn (you'll find the links to our profiles below; do mention you're a reader when you add us), stay in touch, and share your feedback with us – we highly value your input and can't wait to hear about your success stories.

We are incredibly proud of you for completing this journey with us. If you found value in this book, share it with someone you care about – be it a peer, team member or friend. This not only shows you care but will also support your journey by fostering a shared understanding and a common language on topics that – believe us – you'll keep talking a lot about.

Best wishes on your Data-Driven Transformation journey. Now go and *make it happen!*

Andrea and Michele

Reach out to us!

Andrea: linkedin.com/in/andread, www.ademauro.com
Michele: linkedin.com/in/michelepacifico
Book website: www.data-transformation.net

Guided notes

Chapter 1

- The concept of collisions between traditional vs digital operating models was originally proposed by Marco Iansiti and Karim Lakhani. To learn more, see: Iansiti, M. and Lakhani, K.R. (2020) *Competing in the age of AI: Strategy and leadership when algorithms and networks run the world*, Harvard Business Press.
- On the advantage of banks with fully digital operating model: Franzen, F., D'agnoluzzo, V. and Sebastiao, B. (2020) *Digital attacker banks' time has come*, Bain & Company, available at https://www.bain.com/insights/digital-attacker-banks-time-has-come/.
- *Financial Times* senior columnist Tim Harford explains clearly why electrification didn't bring immediate returns to the industrial system: Harford, T. (2017) 'Why didn't electricity immediately change manufacturing?', https://www.bbc.com/news/business-40673694.
- On the advantage of the unit electric engine: David, P.A. (1990) The dynamo and the computer: an historical perspective on the modern productivity paradox. *The American Economic Review*, 80 (2): 355–61, available at: http://digamo.free.fr/david90.pdf and Du Boff, R.B. (1967). The introduction of electric power in American manufacturing. *The Economic History Review* 20 (3): 509–18. JSTOR, https://doi.org/10.2307/2593069.
- For a thorough explanation of how the shift from central drive to group and then unit drive made a significant impact on industrial production, see: Devine, W.D. (1983) From shafts to wires: historical perspective on electrification. *Journal of Economic History* 43 (02), 347–72, https://doi.org/10.1017/s0022050700029673.
- To learn more about the impact of ICT capital investments on productivity, see: Brynjolfsson, E. and Hitt, L.M. (2003) Computing productivity: firm-level evidence. *Review of Economics and Statistics* 85 (4) (2003): 793–808, available at: https://dspace.mit.edu/bitstream/handle/1721.1/5417/4210-01.pdf.
- To learn more about the organisational complements driving the contribution of information technology to productivity, read: Brynjolfsson, E and Hitt, L.M. (2000) Beyond computation: information technology, organizational transformation and business performance. *The Journal of Economic Perspectives* 14 (4): 23–48, http://www.jstor.org/stable/2647074.

Chapter 2

- On the definition of a full business strategy and the explanation of the framework presented in this chapter, you can refer to Lafley, A.G. and Martin, R.L. (2013) *Playing to win. How strategy really works*, Harvard Business Review Press. It is worth reading the paragraph 'Six strategy traps' (p. 214), where the most common mistakes like non-making choices or making bad choices are commented on. It is quite impressive to see how these have a straight parallel with the potential data strategy traps.
- A significantly extensive overview of business strategy approaches is documented in Koch, R. (2021) *Strategy. How to create, pursue and deliver a winning strategy*, Pearson, Financial Times Publishing. Chapter 4, 'Strategic ideas concepts, tools and techniques', contains over 150 pages of definitions and invaluable examples to familiarise yourself with vocabulary, models and concepts your business may benefit from.
- In various discussions, the expression 'Every company is a data company' has become widely recognised. Noteworthy insights on this topic can be found in the following sources: J. Yueh and R. Bean discuss interesting perspectives in their article titled 'Every company is a data Company' on Forbes.com, https://www.forbes.com/sites/ciocentral/2018/09/26/every-company-is-a-data-company/#78f38ba75cfc; A. Orad also provides valuable insights in his article on Forbes.com titled 'Why every company is a data company', https://www.forbes.com/sites/forbestechcouncil/2020/02/14/why-every-company-is-a-data-company/.
- Identifying big bets or valuable use cases has been at the heart of this chapter. In the article 'A ninety-day plan to build a data and digital strategy', Boston Consulting Group partners and experts M. Schuuring, L. Quarta, A. Sawadogo and C. Koral offer an interesting example (exhibit 2) of a big bets overview and prioritisation across the full value chain of a clothing e-tailer: https://www.bcg.com/publications/2022/how-to-build-a-data-and-digital-strategy.
- For a definition and description of design thinking, you can leverage a short but complete digital guide by Emily Stevens: https://careerfoundry.com/en/blog/ux-design/what-is-design-thinking-everything-you-need-to-know-to-get-started/. To better understand how design thinking can bring quantifiable value, you can look at a Forrester case study on IBM's design thinking framework, available at: https://www.ibm.com/downloads/cas/Z4WBDR8Q.

- The American Society for Quality offers definitions, examples and resources to help better comprehend the potential of the impact effort matrix: https://asq.org/quality-resources/impact-effort-matrix.

Chapter 3

- The Data Activation Canvas has been inspired by the Business Model Canvas. For a more detailed comprehension of its application through real-life examples, we recommend Osterwalder, A. and Pigneurr, Y. (2010) *Business model generation: a handbook for visionaries, game changers, and challengers*, John Wiley & Sons.
- Data Activation is a widely used term, especially in the context of sales and marketing. A good process overview is provided by J. Boudet, B. Gregg, J. Heller, and C. Tufft of McKinsey in this article from 2017: https://www.mckinsey.com/capabilities/growth-marketing-and-sales/our-insights/the-heartbeat-of-modern-marketing.
- The importance of data in the retail and consumer industry is well recapped by this opinion of H. Thomas, executive director of the *Financial Times*: 'The supermarkets' next big product is your data', https://www.ft.com/content/26959b97-90ad-4bc1-b9df-1b7461ba71f9.
- For a better understanding of the key factors and features of a minimum viable product, you can read Lenarduzzi, V. and Taibi, D. (2016) MVP explained: a systematic mapping study on the definitions of minimal viable product, *42th Euromicro Conference on Software Engineering and Advanced Applications (SEAA)*, IEEE.
- To address the challenge of bias in AI, ML and analytics, the World Economic Forum proposes to reapply the open-source approach to Data Science: https://www.weforum.org/agenda/2022/10/open-source-data-science-bias-more-ethical-ai-technology/.

Chapter 4

- If you want to learn more about how LLMs work, you should engage with the interactive article by the FT Visual Storytelling Team and Madhumita Murgia, available at ig.ft.com/generative-ai/.
- The fascinating story of the reinforcement learning algorithm AlphaZero who managed to learn chess and outperform best in class chess-engines in under four hours, is in: Silver, D., Hubert, T., Schrittwieser, J.

and Hassabis, D. 'AlphaZero: Shedding new light on chess, shogi, and Go', DeepMind website, available at https://deepmind.google/discover/blog/alphazero-shedding-new-light-on-chess-shogi-and-go/.

- The risk of bias in AI was present well before the arrival of ChatGPT. To learn more about how AI applications may reinforce existing societal inequalities and power dynamics, read: Ram, A. The perils of AI bias, *FT Opinions Magazine*, available at https://www.ft.com/content/37a1ddd2-5a54-11e9-939a-341f5ada9d40.

Chapter 5

- About Moore's law and its sustainability you can check Bradshaw, T. and Gross, A. The big question of how small chips can get, *Financial Times*, https://www.ft.com/content/fbf52ede-e1a9-4797-9e52-3f80a7d855d9. To understand more about the technology behind chips, another fascinating article is Rodgers, L., Clark, D., Joiner, S., Haslett, B., de la Torre Arenas, I. and Learner, S. Inside the miracle of modern chip manufacturing, https://ig.ft.com/microchips/.
- A good overview about the computation and storage demand outlook is in Mikkonen, K. and Wilson, A. The looming data centre crunch, https://www.ft.com/content/e597a8b5-f71a-4099-9add-d0e3c1613348.
- An entertaining investigation on the origin of the term big data can be found in Lohr, S. The origins of 'big data': an etymological detective story, *New York Times*, https://archive.nytimes.com/bits.blogs.nytimes.com/2013/02/01/the-origins-of-big-data-an-etymological-detective-story/.
- For a formal definition of the term you can read De Mauro, A., Greco, M. and Grimaldi, M. "A formal definition of Big Data based on its essential features." Library review 65.3 (2016): 122–135, https://doi.org/10.1108/LR-06-2015-0061.
- The idea of managing information as a product was first documented in 1998 by R.Y. Wang, Y.W. Lee, L.L. Pipino and D.M. Strong in the article 'Manage your information as a product', subsequently included in the book *Journey to data quality*, MIT Press, 2006. More recently, this has become a key topic in data and analytics management. McKinsey's V. Desai, T. Fountaine and K. Rowshankish published in 2022 the seminal articles 'How to unlock the full value of data? Manage it like a product', https://www.mckinsey.com/capabilities/quantumblack/our-insights/how-to-unlock-the-full-value-

of-data-manage-it-like-a-product, and 'A better way to put your data to work, https://hbr.org/2022/07/a-better-way-to-put-your-data-to-work.

- The most renowned architecture standards include: the Zachman Framework for Enterprise Architecture, created by J. Zachman at IBM during the 1980s; The Open Group Architecture Framework (TOGAF, whitepaper available here: https://publications.opengroup.org/w182); DAMA International's Data Management Body of Knowledge (DAMA-DMBOK 2, Technics Publications, 2017).
- Gartner offers a view of the data architecture evolution over the past decades, outlining the most important recent developments in the digital resource: Future of Data Architecture, https://www.gartner.com/en/data-analytics/topics/data-architecture.

Chapter 6

- To learn more about the survey with managers, read: Malacaria, S., De Mauro, A., Greco, M. and Grimaldi, M. (2023) An application of the analytic hierarchy process to the evaluation of companies' data maturity. *Springer Nature Computer Science* 4, 696, https://doi.org/10.1007/s42979-023-02065-9.
- The famous Harvard paper asserting that being a data scientist was the sexiest job of the 21st century is: Patil, D.J. and Davenport, T. (2012) Data scientist: The sexiest job of the 21st century. *Harvard Business Review* 90 (10), 70–6.
- Interestingly, the authors of the paper above wrote another article on the same topic after exactly 10 years, highlighting the evolution of the role of data scientist: Davenport, T.H. and DPatil, D.J. (2022) Is data scientist still the sexiest job of the 21st century? *Harvard Business Review* 15, available at https://hbr.org/2022/07/is-data-scientist-still-the-sexiest-job-of-the-21st-century.
- On the data professional roles and the required skill sets, you can read: De Mauro, A., Greco, M., Grimaldi, M. and Ritala, P. (2018) Human resources for big data professions: A systematic classification of job roles and required skill sets. *Information Processing & Management* 54 (5), 807–17.
- For a more in-depth description of the hub and spoke model for data analytics, we recommend: Fountaine, T., McCarthy, B. and Saleh, T. (2019) Building the AI-powered organization. *Harvard Business Review*, 97 (4), 62–73.
- Thomas Davenport describes how the assessment process of analytical competencies was used by a large North American bank, highlighting the need to

create organisation-specific definitions of roles and competencies. For more, see: Davenport, T. (2020) Beyond unicorns: educating, classifying, and certifying business data scientists. *Harvard Data Science Review*, https://doi.org/10.1162/99608f92.55546b4a.

- The growth mindset theory is well addressed in the main work of its creator: Carole Dweck, 'Mindset – updated edition: changing the way you think to fulfil your potential', Robinson, 2017. For further consideration of how companies can encourage a growth mindset in the organisation: How companies can profit from a 'growth mindset', *Harvard Business Review*, 2014.
- John Thompson vividly describes the decision to not have the chief data officer (CDO) report directly to the CEO as the 'original sin'. For more on the advantages and disadvantages of each reporting structure, see: Thompson, J.K. (2020) *Building analytics teams: Harnessing analytics and artificial intelligence for business improvement*, Packt Publishing.

Chapter 7

- For an in-depth exploration of how Excel's limitations can significantly impact data governance and beyond, refer to: Harford, T. (2021) The tyranny of spreadsheets, *FT Magazine*, available at https://www.ft.com/content/18db20d8-7726-43e2-87f1-c5861ad3dff5.
- For a thorough introduction to data governance organisations, clarifying the important roles of data stewards and the other actors, you can read: Plotkin, D. (2021) *Data stewardship*, Elsevier Academic Press.

Chapter 8

- The maturity model was developed by systematically analysing and identifying the essential traits encapsulated in the 21 most established big Data Analytics Maturity models published between the years 2013 and 2020. To learn more, you can read: Malacaria, S., De Mauro, A., Greco, M. and Grimaldi, M. (2023) An application of the analytic hierarchy process to the evaluation of companies' data maturity, *Springer Nature Computer Science.*
- For a comprehensive analysis of how data valorisation can be approached, we recommend: Schmarzo, B. (2020) *The economics of data, analytics, and digital transformation*, Packt Publishing.

- Bernard Marr offers an overview of the data monetisation key aspects in Marr, B. (2017) Monetizing your data, In *Data strategy: how to profit from a world of big data, analytics, and the internet of things*, Kogan Page.
- The Agile manifesto and its twelve principles of Agile software development can be found here: https://agilemanifesto.org.
- Figure 8.3 has been inspired by the Flow Theory, ideated by Mihaly Csikszentmihalyi in his 1975 book *Beyond boredom and anxiety: experiencing flow in work and play*, Jossey-Bass Publishers. This foundational work was further developed in his book, *Flow: the psychology of optimal experience*, Harper USA, 2011.

GLOSSARY

An extended version of this glossary is available on the book website, *data-transformation.net*.

Agile customer-centric project management methodology focused on delivering value through flexibility and collaboration in the shortest time possible.

Algorithm a set of steps, described in a formal way, for the systematic solution of a problem.

Application programming interfaces (APIs) pre-established programming procedures that allow an application to interact systematically with other applications.

Artificial intelligence (AI) the simulation of some aspects of human intelligence, such as problem solving, learning and pattern recognition by machines.

Big data an information asset with such a high volume, velocity and variety that requires specific technology and analytical methods to transform into value.

Business glossary a business definition of data assets, promoting a uniform understanding across an organisation by clarifying data's semantic context.

Business intelligence a technology-driven process for analysing data and presenting actionable information to decision makers.

CDO (chief data officer) a senior leadership role focused on data governance and infrastructure, skilled in blending technical expertise, business acumen and interpersonal skills to elevate data as a strategic business asset.

Classification in machine learning, it refers to the prediction of a categorical value, i.e. the association of an element with its class of belonging through supervised learning algorithms.

Cloud a paradigm for remote and distributed delivery of computing services.

Clustering creation of homogeneous groups of elements through unsupervised learning aimed at recognising structural similarities between the elements of a dataset.

Data Activation Canvas in this book, the tool that supports the structured definition of each data capability.

Data activation the process of using data to trigger specific actions or decisions, thereby unlocking its value for strategic business outcomes.

Data analyst a data analytics professional who uses data analysis, storytelling and ML solutions to solve business problems and uncover insights.

Data analytics a collective term indicating methods, processes and tools used to extract value from data.

Data and analytics strategy a long-term focused game plan that outlines how an organisation will collect, manage, analyse and use data to achieve its business goals and improve decision making.

Data asset a business valuable piece of information or data held by an organisation in any form or format.

Data capability in this book, a data analytics solution that can be used to activate data in a specific business scenario to create value.

Data catalogue A centralised inventory of data assets, described through metadata crucial for effective data governance, composed of data dictionaries and business glossaries.

Data centre a facility containing the technological infrastructure necessary for data storage and processing.

Data custodian a technical professional responsible for data management, including security, scalability and implementation of quality rules, complementing the role of data stewards.

Data dictionary a technical description of data assets within tables, including types, sizes and constraints, clarifying the data's structure and properties.

Data engineer a professional specialising in the technical infrastructure supporting data analytics, focusing on robust, scalable data systems, skilled in constructing and maintaining complex data pipelines for data quality and accessibility.

Data fabric a flexible, reusable and augmented data management and integration design, leveraging logical models and metadata to support data access across the business.

Data governance a collection of practices, policies, standards and metrics that ensure the effective and efficient use and management of data within an organisation, aiming to improve data quality, protect sensitive data and support strategic business objectives.

Data hub a platform that integrates and manages data from various sources to support applications and analytics within an organisation.

Data lake (DL) a storage repository that holds vast amounts of raw data in its native format, supporting flexible data analysis, processing and discovery of structured, semi-structured and unstructured data.

Data lakehouse (DLH) a data architecture that combines the scalable storage of a data lake with the management and performance features of a data warehouse, enabling both detailed big data analysis and high-performance queries on structured data.

Data lineage the tracking of data from its origin through its lifecycle, highlighting transformations and movements across systems.

Data Maturity Model a framework to assess the level of Data Analytics Maturity of an organisation around the levers of people, business and technology.

Data mesh a decentralised approach to data architecture and organisational design that emphasises domain-oriented ownership, self-serve data infrastructure and product thinking for data to improve data accessibility and quality across large-scale environments.

Data model a theoretical representation that outlines how data is organised, structured and related within a system, serving as a reference for database design and data management practices.

Data monetisation the process of turning data into monetary value.

Data platform an integrated technology solution that provides the infrastructure, tools and services for collecting, storing, managing and analysing data at scale, supporting a wide range of data-driven applications and use cases.

Data quality the measure of data's condition, focusing on aspects like completeness, accuracy, uniqueness, consistency and timeliness.

Data science a multidisciplinary scientific field that integrates knowledge of computer science, mathematics and statistics to extract knowledge from data.

Data scientist a professional focused on developing and using data analytics methods to transform data into value. The term is broadly used to indicate those working in the field of data science.

Data steward a business representative accountable for data assets within their domain, defining business aspects of data, documenting it in the glossary and setting quality rules.

Data Transformation the process of systematically integrating data analytics capabilities into a business operating model.

Data warehouse (DWH) a centralised repository designed to store, manage and analyse large volumes of structured data from multiple sources, optimised for query and analysis, serving as a foundational component for business intelligence and data analytics.

Dataset a collection of data organised in tabular form.

Descriptive analytics a type of data analytics focusing on summarising past or present data to understand what has happened or is happening, using data tables and charts to highlight trends and patterns.

Data quality management (DQM) tool software that systematically measures and reports data quality across data domains.

Enablers in this book, the transversal areas that support data-driven transformation and data strategy.

ETL (extraction, transformation, loading) a data integration process that extracts data from various sources, transforms it into a structured format, and loads it into a target database or data warehouse for analysis.

Explainability in the context of machine learning, the level of comprehensibility of a model's decisions or predictions to humans.

Feature in machine learning, an individual measurable property or characteristic of a phenomenon being observed. In supervised learning training, features are input variables that serve as the basis for models to learn patterns and make predictions.

Generative artificial intelligence (GenAI) a subset of AI technologies that use machine learning algorithms to create new, multimodal content, such as text, images, or audio, often in response to natural language prompts.

GPT (generative pre-trained transformer) a popular type of large language model for generating human-like text, based on the transformer architecture and pre-trained on a diverse range of internet text.

GPUs (graphics processing units) the key hardware components specialised in parallel processing to accelerate complex calculations, especially in graphics and visual data, also leveraged in ML and AI.

Label in the context of machine learning, it is the specific outcome or category that a data point is assigned to in supervised learning. Labels are used in the training phase to teach models to predict data correctly, serving as the answer key for the algorithm to learn from.

Large language models (LLMs) machine learning models that use deep learning to understand and generate human language.

Machine learning (ML) a computing paradigm that implements AI by enabling autonomous learning from data inputs without following explicit instructions.

Metadata data that provides information about other data. In a database context, it could refer to data about data types, structures, authorship, etc.

Minimum viable product (MVP) a development strategy that focuses on creating a product with the minimum set of features needed to satisfy early adopters, facilitating rapid feedback and iterative development.

Modern Data Stack in this book, a layered approach to the technological components of our data strategy, made of infrastructure, platforms and applications.

MoSCoW a requirement prioritisation methodology largely used in project management.

Neural network machine learning models inspired by biological neural networks. They consist of computational units called artificial neurons, which make predictions that activate subsequent neurons in a hierarchical structure.

Overfitting a modelling error in machine learning that occurs when a prediction is too closely fit to a limited set of previous, known data points, affecting its performance on unknown, future data.

PII (personally identifiable information) privacy-sensitive data that is identifying or capable of identifying an individual.

Predictive analytics a type of data analytics that employs statistical modelling to forecast future events and unveil the drivers of what has happened in the past.

Prescriptive analytics a type of data analytics employing algorithms to suggest optimal actions based on data analysis and constraints.

Prompts in the context of generative AI, user-defined inputs, often in the form of natural language text, that trigger and guide the AI in generating specific, contextual content such as text, images, or other media types, aligning with the input's intent or theme.

Proof of concept (PoC) a small-scale experimental project or demonstration run in a controlled, low-risk environment to evaluate an idea's practicality and effectiveness.

Proof of value (PoV) a small-scale project that aims to prove the actual value or tangible benefits that the solution can deliver to the business.

RAG (retrieval-augmented generation) a generative AI technique that enhances text generation by dynamically retrieving relevant information from a dataset or document collection during the generation process.

Reinforcement learning a machine learning technique where an agent learns to make decisions by trial and error, using rewards.

Relational database a digital database based on the relational model of data, as proposed by E.F. Codd in 1970.

Scoring in the context of machine learning, it refers to assigning scores to instances, like customers, based on certain models to predict behaviour or properties.

SQL (structured query language) a domain-specific language used in programming and designed for managing data held in a relational database management system.

Supervised learning machine learning that learns from labelled training data to predict outcomes for new, unseen data.

Test set a subset of a dataset used to provide an unbiased evaluation of a model fit on the training dataset and assess its ability to generalise to unseen samples.

Token the smallest unit of processing in LLMs, often a word or part of a word.

Training set the subset of data used to train a model in machine learning algorithms.

Unsupervised learning learning from data without labels to find structure or patterns.

Variable any characteristic, number or quantity that can be measured or quantified. In machine learning, variables can be features, labels, or both, depending on their role in the model features or labels depending on their role in the model.

Visualisation the process of representing data graphically and interacting with these representations to gain insight into the data.

Waterfall a project management methodology characterised by a highly structured approach, linear and sequential in nature.

INDEX

A/B/n testing approach 87
accuracy
  data 13, 175
  Data Activation Canvas model 58–9
  of ML algorithms 103–5
affinity diagram 44
agile 203–4
algorithm
  regression 93
  selection 36
  trust in 6
  see also machine learning algorithms
alternating current (AC) induction motors 19, 20
Alteryx 133
Amazon 17, 18, 24, 113
Amazon Web Services (AWS)
  Amazon Redshift 130
  Amazon S3 130
  AWS Lake Formation 130
analytical data 60
analytical skills 195
anomaly detection 3
Apache Hadoop 130
Apache Hive 133
Apache Spark 130
Apache Superset 132
application programming interfaces (APIs) 28, 61, 62, 129
Apriori 101
artificial intelligence (AI) 82–4
  amplification factor 14–15
  convergence of biology and 91
  defined 82–3
  essential tools for 124–34
  golden checklist on 107–8
artificial neural networks (ANNs) 91
Asimov, Isaac 109
asparov, Garry 97
association rules 95
auditing 68
augmented analysis 120
authentication 68
authorisation 68, 69
authority bias 158

Babylon Health 17
Bezos, Jeff 24
big bets 35–6, 43–7, 53
big data 66, 85, 95, 115, 124, 129, 148
Birmingham Small Arms factory shop 20
bits 110
black box models 58, 102
Brynjolfsson, Erik 21
business glossary 169
business intelligence (BI) 131
business model 12–13
Business Model Canvas 54
business responsibility of data 168
business strategy, definition 29
business understanding 140
business users 125–6, 140, 141, 144

California Consumer Privacy Act (CCPA) 184
capital expense (CapEx) 155
catalogue population 170
central analytics team 147
centralised model 147–8
centres of excellence (CoEs) 149
Chandler, Alfred: *Strategy and Structure* 29
chatbots 2, 4, 87–8
ChatGPT 99, 100
chess 97

chief analytics officer (CAO) 156
chief artificial intelligence officer (CAIO) 156
chief data and analytics officer (CDAO) 156, 158
chief data officer (CDO) 155–7, 162
  business acumen 157
  interpersonal and communication skills 157
  technical expertise 156
chief executive officer (CEO) 156
chief financial officer (CFO) 156
chief information officer (CIO) 156, 158, 162
chief technology officer (CTO) 156
churn 7–10, 91
churn propensity score 8
classification algorithms 93
cloud 110–15, 211
  advantages 114
cloud computing 112
cloud technologies 112
Cloudera CDP 130
Cloudera Impala 133
clustering algorithms 93–4, 127
  bargain hunters 95
  gift givers 95
  hierarchical 101
  trendsetters 95
co-creation with business partners 162, 205–6
coding 140
common data model 22
communication plan 208
communities of practices (CoPs) 149, 161
completeness of data 173, 175
computing technology in businesses 21
Conan Doyle, Sir Arthur 165
consistency of data 174, 175
contextual data 60–1, 62
copyright issues 101
costs
  Data Activation Canvas 71–4
  of data ownership 202
  labour 73, 74
  of LLMs 100
  of machine learning 102
  ongoing 71
  recurring 73
  reduction of 70
  setup 71, 73
CPUs 111, 112
culture, company 66, 67, 157–62
  data cultural inhibitors 158–9
  data-friendly culture 157
  developing 159–62
  openness 6
curiosity for data 6
customer loyalty 71
customer loyalty card 85
customer relationship management 60 (CRM) 60, 129
customer sales booster 43
CX KPI 87

Data Activation Canvas 36, 54–79, 211
  activation scenarios 55–7
  analytical methods 57–9
  business integration 64–7
  cost structure 71–4
  data requirements 59–62
  headings 76–7
    Name 76–7
    Owner 77
    Sponsor 77
    Version 77
  law, biases and ethics 74–6
  revenue streams 69–71
  scalability strategies 62–4
  technology requirements 67–9
  turning big bets into enablers 77–8
  using 78
data activation scenarios 39, 43
data analyst 125, 140, 141, 144
data analytics 211
  for customer churn 7–10
  definition+ 2
  essential tools for 124–34

learning programme for top management 160–1
for retail optimisation 10–12
types of 2–7
data analytics champions 161
Data Analytics Flywheel Effect 24–5
data analytics maturity model 212
data analytics team 25
data and analytics strategy 31
data architects 125
data architecture 36, 117, 140
data as product 123–4
data asset 21–2, 24, 110, 117, 120, 123–5, 129
data attributes 60
data blueprint
designing 67
golden checklist 78–9
data capability 31, 35
accuracy of 58–9
activation scenarios 55–6
analytical methods 57–9
capability features 202
capability performance 201
components 53, 54
costs 73, 202
data governance 202
data quality 202
footprint and coverage 202
organisations affected by 65
ownership of 77, 202
richness and depth 202
scalability strategies 62
user experience 202
value equation and ROI 202
value proposition elements 55
see also Dada Activation Canvas
data catalogue 22, 169–71, 184, 212
ongoing usage and maintenance 170–1
data centre 114, *147*
data communities 161
data culture 22
data custodians 179, 180
data dictionary 120, 169
data discovery 21, 170
data domains 178–9
data-driven value creation, opportunities for 40–1
data engineer *125*, 141, 144–5
data evangelist 157
data experts 33
data fabric 119–20
data fluency 160, 212
data-friendly culture 196–9
data governance 22, 37, 165–87, 212
compliance and standards 184
crawl phase 185
data as an asset 166–8
enabling 168
policy 182–5, 212
principles 183
privacy compliance 184
purpose and scope 183
roles 183, 212
run phase 186–7
setting up 182–4
walk phase 186
data governance board 177, 180
data governance core team 176, 180
data governor *see* data steward
data hub 118–19
data human drivers 138–9
data integrity 184
data job roles 140–2
data kingdoms 118
data lake (DL) 128, 129, 211
data lakehouse (DLH) 130
data lineage 171–2
Data Maturity Model 35, 38, 190–210
evaluation card 197–9
data mesh 119–20
data mining 2
data model, designing 120–3
data monetisation 200
data organisation 116–24
data owner *see* data steward
data-person interface 194–5
data platform 61, 109, 125, 128–30

data-process integration 192–3
data products 120
data protection 114
data quality 128, 173–6, 184, 212
  checks 175
  monitoring and reporting 175
data quality management (DQM) tool 174–6
data-rich 154
data roles 37
  frustrations in 143–5
  vs skill set mapping 142
data science 109, 132
data scientist 67, 85, 87, 125, 139, 141, 144, 147, 152, 196
data silos 23, 117–20
data skills 22, 151, 160
data slicing 131
data steward 159, 177–8, 180, 202
data stewardship 140, 159, 168
data strategy 190–2, 211
  winning 27–31
data team 23, 162
data transfer protocol 61
Data Transformation process 21, 35–50
  board 207
  defined 27
  focused on deliverables 35
  golden checklist on 50–1
  iterative 35
  journey 199–206
  progressive 35
  who and how 206–9
data valorisation 200
data value 26, 200–2
data value enablers 201
data value generators 201
data volume (size) 68
data warehouse (DWH) 128–9, 211
Databricks 130, 133
Data-Driven Transformation *see* Data Transformation process
Dataiku 133
decision tree 91, 92, 93, 101, 102
  for churning customers 8
deep diving 131
deep learning 93
deepfakes 100
DeepMind's AlphaZero 97
descriptive analytics 3, 6, 57
  decision maker's role 5–6
  summarisation 5
  visualisation 5
design thinking 39
developers 126
diagnostics 3
Diffusion Models 101
digital, defined 110
digital operating models 15, 16, 17
digital technologies 110–15
DIKW pyramid 32
dimensionality deduction 95
diseconomies of scale 13–14
distributed architectures 113
distributed model 146–7
drilling down 131
Dweck, Carol 153
Dycam Model 1 111

Edward Dean Adams Power Plant, Niagara Falls 19
electric motors 19, 20
electrification of factories 19
Eliot, T.S.: 'Choruses' 32
embedding 98
enablers 22, 23, 36, 55, 192, 211
enterprise data warehouse (EDW) 119
enterprise resource planning (ERP) 60, 129
entity–relationship diagram 122
ethical framework 192
explainability 102
explanatory model 58
external data, availability of 61, 62
external resources 153–5
extraction, transformation and loading (ETL) 129

Facebook Ads 15
FAIR principles 173
false negatives 105

false positives 104
False Starts 31–4, 211
Ferraris, Galileo 19
Flywheel Effect 21–5, 211
forecasts of metrics 3
foresight 5
FP-Growth 101
fractional CDO 157
fragmented analysis 119
Franklin, Benjamin: *Art of Virtue, The* 189

General Data Protection Regulation (GDPR) (EU) 184
general-purpose technologies (GPTs) 18
Generative Adversarial Networks (GANs) 101
generative agents 4
Generative artificial intelligence (GenAI) 84, 89, 97, 98–101
  limitations and risks of 100
generative pre-trained transformer (GPT) 19, 98, 101
global system for mobile communications (GSM) 111
Golding, William: *Lord of the Flies* 53
Google 113
Google Cloud Platform (GCP)
  Google Cloud Storage 130
  BigQuery 130
Google G Suite 126
graphics processing units (GPUs) 93, 112
growth mindset versus fixed mindset 153

Hadoop 113
Hadoop Distributed File System (HDFS) 130
handover 88
hierarchical clustering 101
high-risk data 170
high-value data 170
hindsight 4, 5
HiPPOs 158
historical sales 61
Hitt, Lorin M. 21
horizontal scaling 64
hub-and-spoke model 148–9
human journey, golden checklist on 163–4
hybrid cloud 115

Iansiti, Marco 17
IBM Cloud Pak for Data 130
IBM Db2 130
IBM Deep Blue 97
IBM Z systems 127
idea
  contests 161
  ease of implementation 44–5
  impact 44
Ideation Workshop 36, 38, 39, 77, 211
indirect economic benefits 70
inference 100
information protectionism 159
infrastructure as a service (IaaS) 126
integrated architecture 193–4
integrated development environment (IDE) 132
integrated organisation 195–6
Intel 110
iterations 203
interactive dashboards 3
interface 69
internal data 60, 62
internal resources 152–3

join 122
Jupyter Notebook for Python 133

K K-means 94, 101
Kempelen, Wolfgang von 82
key evaluation metrics 211
key performance indicators (KPIs) 3, 22
Knime 133
knowledge discovery 92

label 91
labour cost 73, 74
Lakhani, Karim R. 17
large language models (LLMs) 98, 99
  stateless 100
Latent Dirichlet Allocation (LDA) 101

law of diminishing returns 14
leadership roles 155–7
legal framework 192
linear regression 101
logistic regression 101
low hanging fruits 49

machine learning *see* ML
mainframe computers 112, 127
Malthus, Thomas 14
manager of the (near) future 162
market basket analysis 95
master data 119, 121
mean absolute percentage error (MAPE) 104, 105
Mechanical Turk 82
Metabase 132
Metadata 120
Microsoft 113
Microsoft 365 126
Microsoft Azure
  Azure Data Lake Storage 130
  Azure Synapse Analytics 130
Microsoft PowerBI 132
Microsoft SQL Server 130
minimum requirement 63
minimum viable product (MVP) 63, 64, 205
ML 84, 140
  defined 83
ML algorithms 8, 83
  accuracy 102, 103–5
    for generative AI 103
    reinforcement learning 103
    in supervised learning 103
    with unsupervised learning, 103
  complexity and cost 102
  evaluation 102–7
  explainability 102
ML catalogue 100–1, 211
ML Model 90
ML-Way of doing business 84–8, 211
  customer churn 85
  customer segmentation 86
  customer's experience (CX) with chatbot 87–8
  media spending in real time 86–7
  vs Traditional Way 88–9
mobile app 45, 46
Modern Data Stack 109, 124–7, 211
  application layer 125, 131–4
  data platform 125, 128–30
  physical infrastructure 125, 127
Monzo 17
Moore, Gordon 110
Moore's law 110, 111
MoSCoW methodology 116–17, 170

NASA Voyager 2 111
net promoter score (NPS) 87
neural network 93, 101, 102

off-shore workers 155
on-premise computing 115
ongoing costs 71
ongoing support 73
open-minded approach 6
operating expense (OpEx) 155
operating model 13
optimisation 4, 5
Oracle Exadata 130
organisational design model 212
organisational maturity evolution 149–51
organisational models 37, 146–51
  centralised model 147–8
  distributed model 146–7
  external resources 153–5
  hub-and-spoke model 148–9
  internal resources 152–3
  leadership roles 155–7
  organisational maturity evolution 149–51
  talent acquisition 151–2
organisational operating model 192
Osterwalder, Alexander 54
outsourcing data projects 155
overfitting 106–7

parallel computing 111, 113
people counter 45, 46
performance level 67
performance requirements 68–9
personally identifiable information (PII) 114, 170
platform as a service (PaaS) 126
point of sales (POS) systems 10
polynomial regression 107
Porter, Michael E.: *Competitive Strategy: Techniques for Analysing Industries and Competitors* 29
Post-it notes 39, 40, 43
predictive analytics 3, 5, 6, 57
 in Data Activation Canvas model *59*
prescriptive analytics 3–4, 5, 6, 58
 in Data Activation Canvas model *59*
pre-training 98
primary keys 122
Principal Component Analysis (PCA) 101
prioritisation 47–50
private cloud 115
Procter & Gamble (P&G) business strategy framework 30
prompts 84, 98
proof of concept (PoC) 129, 204–5
proof of value (PoV) 205
propensity score 85, 92
prototypes 129
Proximal Policy Optimisation (PPO) 101
public cloud 115
Python 132, 140, 143
 Jupyter Notebook 133

Q Learning 101
Qlik 132
quantum bits (qubitsI) 112
quantum computing 111, 112
quantum processing unit (QPU) 112

R 132, 133, 140
R2 (coefficient of determination) 103–4
RACI matrix 181–2
racks 127
random forest 92, 93, 101
RapidMiner 133
Recurrent neural networks (RNNs) 101
recurring costs 73
Redash 132
reference data (master data) 59
regression algorithms 93
regression model 104
reinforcement learning 89, 95–7
reinforcement learning from human feedback (RLHF) 98
relational database 122
retrieval-augmented generation (RAG) 99
return on ad spend (ROAS) 87, 97
return on investment (ROI) management 23
Ricardo, David 14
root mean squared error (RMSE) 104
role and skillset mapping 212
Rstudio for R 133

SalesForce application 126
Salesforce.com 113
schema-on-read 128
schema-on-write 128
scoring models 4
security level 68
segmentation 3
Selection Matrix 36, 46–7, 77, 211
 ideas on 48
 low-hanging fruit 46, 47
 moonshot 46, 47
 piece of cake 46, 47
 trap 46, 47
sensitivity 105
server farm 127
servers 127
setup costs 71, 73
shadow analytics organisations 23, 25, 151
share-and-reapply sessions 161
simple linear regression 93
simulations 3
Singular Value Decomposition (SVD) 101
smart customer logistics 43
smartphone photo resolution 111
Snowflake 130

software as a service (SaaS) 126
Spark 113
sponsors, primary 162
sponsorship, business on data projects by design 162
sprints 203
staff augmentation 154–5
stakeholders 65, 66
static reports 3
statistical modelling 5
steam engine 18
steering meetings 208
storage architectures 111
store turnover 71
storytelling 140
structured data 128
structured query language (SQL) 133, 140
success measures 192
supervised learning 89,90–3
sustainable competitive advantage 29
systems integration 22

Tableau 132
talent 65–6, 138, 139–45
talent acquisition 151–2
talent assessment 66–7
target variable 91
technicality trap 158–9
technological nephology 114–15
technology 109–35
  infrastructure 193
technology stack 22
Teradata 130
Tesco 17
Tesla, Nikola 19
test set 107
theory versus reality 143–5
Tibco Spotfire 132
time series 3
timeliness of data 174
time-series model, 8
token 118
trade-offs 36
traditional operating model 15, 17
Traditional Way of doing business 84–8
  customer churn 85
  customer segmentation 86
  customer's experience (CX) with chatbot 87–8
  media spending in real time 86–7
  vs ML-Way 88–9
training set 107
transactional data 59
transactional systems 60
transactional tables 121
Transformers-based (GPT, BART) 101
true positives 105
trust in data and algorithms 6
Turgot, Anne Robert Jacques 14
Turing, Alan 82
turnover increase 69

Uber 17, 18
underfitted model 107
unified analysis 119
uniqueness of data 173
unit drive 19–20
unstructured data 128
unsupervised learning 89, 93–5
upskilling programme 160
user interface requirements 67–8

validity of data 173
value amplification with digital operating model 12–18
value capture model 13
value-driven initiatives 191
value proposition 13, 55
Variational AutoEncoders (VAEs) 101
vertical scaling strategy 64
vision 191
visualisation 5
volume of data 67

Walmart 17
waterfall 203–4
Watt, James 18
web scraping 61